To Tina

"Strength and dignity are her clothing,
And she smiles at the future.
She opens her mouth in wisdom,
And the teaching of kindness is on her tongue."

Proverbs 31:25-26 (NASB)

CONTENTS

FOREWORD
PREFACE
ACKNOWLEDGEMENTS

1. INTRODUCTION: MCGRATH'S LIFE, INFLUENCE, SIGNIFICANCE
   AND WRITINGS 1

2. MCGRATH'S EVANGELICAL THEOLOGY AND ITS RELATIONSHIP
   TO HIS EVANGELICAL SPIRITUALITY—PART ONE 29

3. MCGRATH'S EVANGELICAL THEOLOGY AND ITS RELATIONSHIP
   TO HIS EVANGELICAL SPIRITUALITY—PART TWO 55

4. MCGRATH'S EXAMPLE COMPARED TO CONTEMPORARY
   SPIRITUALITY—PART ONE 83

5. MCGRATH'S EXAMPLE COMPARED TO CONTEMPORARY
   SPIRITUALITY—PART TWO 103

6. THE CHALLENGE 123

APPENDIX—McGRATH'S CURRICULUM VITAE 131

BIBLIOGRAPHY 135

INDEX 163

ABOUT THE AUTHOR 167

Foreword

Spirituality, spiritual experiences, and spiritual searches permeate our culture today. From the newspapers to music and the arts, interest in spiritual matters is everywhere. In such a milieu, Evangelical writers no longer have the luxury of writing about spiritual experiences unless they first clarify the theological underpinnings of these experiences. It no longer can be taken for granted that a mutual understanding exists as to who God is and how he relates to individuals. On the same token, if evangelicals are to capture the hearts of a lost and dying world, a dry, cognitive pursuit and proliferation of theological truth is not enough.

Many books have been separately written concerning theology or spirituality. But few have attempted to bridge these two disciplines. This book seeks to bridge that gap. Larry McDonald addresses the merging of theology and spirituality by examining the work of Alister McGrath. McGrath, a leading evangelical theologian, not only seeks to address matters of the head but also of the heart. McDonald overviews how McGrath builds his spirituality upon a theological foundation before comparing McGrath's example to other writers of evangelical spirituality.

McDonald believes that now more than ever before our culture needs theologians who can fully relate theology to life, and practitioners who can articulate a credible theology to complement their practical ministry focus. McGrath's vision to build a spirituality which retains a sound theological basis is a clarion call to evangelicals. It is a call that must be heeded.

Alvin L. Reid, Ph.D.
Southeastern Baptist Theological Seminary
Wake Forest, North Carolina
January 2006

Preface

Almost thirty years ago I began reading classical works as well as contemporary ones in the field of spirituality. I found myself drawn to these intimate portrayals of the daily walk one could have with God. Yet frustration permeated my own attempt to achieve this illusive spirituality. A wise mentor warned me that one could not base their Christian life on experience alone but that experience had to have a foundation. He gently guided me to develop a theological framework which would give a solid basis for who God is and how one relates to Him. My first attempt in reading a book on theology was Paul Little's, *Know What You Believe*. I was astounded at how a systematic presentation of the Christian faith impacted my daily walk with God. Every since then I have found myself with a book on spiritual living in one hand and a book on theology in the other.

As I approached the final research project in my Ph.D. program it seemed only natural that I would continue to pursue studying the relationship between spirituality and theology. I found myself drawn to the writings of Alister McGrath as he wrote in both fields. McGrath certainly has distinguished himself as a prolific writer in theological matters yet he saw a blind spot among evangelicals. He began addressing the shallowness and barrenness of our understanding of spirituality, seeking to correct this deficiency McGrath took up his pen to challenge evangelicals to develop a spirituality that addressed the deepest needs of Christians, but was biblically and theologically based. Instead of a spirituality that moved from one fad to another, he called for evangelicals to understand their historical roots, found in the Reformers, Puritans, and Pietists.

Although one might disagree with elements of McGrath's theology or spirituality, the model he provides in building spirituality upon the solid foundation of theology is one that evangelicals should seek to follow. May there be a new generation of evangelical theologians who can fully relate theology to life, and practitioners who can articulate a credible theology to complement their practical ministry focus.

Larry S. McDonald
Truett-McConnell College
Cleveland, Georgia
January 2006

Acknowledgments

Upon completion of a writing project such as this one there are many people who deserve to be acknowledged. I am grateful for Truett-McConnell College and its president, Dr. Jerry Pounds, who give me the opportunity to teach the next generation of Christian leaders how to build their Christian walk on a solid theological foundation. My colleagues at Truett-McConnell College, Alan Coker, Dr. Michael Justus, and Dr. Sam Pelletier, provide strength in their friendships. Sandy Harris, of the Information Services Department of Truett-McConnell College, provided timely assistance with the formatting of the book. Dr. Alvin Reid served as my mentoring professor in the Ph.D. program at Southeastern Baptist Theological Seminary. His guidance and encouragement have been invaluable.

Most of the writing for this book took place while I served as the Senior Pastor of Olde Mount Vernon Baptist Church in Raleigh, North Carolina. I am grateful for their prayers and especially thankful for Bob Cardon, Steven Criscione, and Mike Hill, deacons at OMV whose unwavering support and friendship brought me great encouragement.

It is difficult to adequately acknowledge and say thank you to my family. My children, Ben, ReBecca, and Jessica, each deserve to have their name attached to this book because they were each a part of seeing its completion. They bring joy and delight to my heart.

Tina, my wife, has been the one person who has walked step-by-step with me in this venture. She not only has excelled at being a delightful companion but also is a superb pastor's wife. Her writing and editing skills have improved this project four-fold as she has saved me from embarrassing mishaps. This book jointly flows from both of our lives as we seek to intimately know God and to faithfully serve Him.

As Tina and I recently completed our twentieth wedding anniversary, the words on our wedding invitation still ring true, "This day I will marry my Friend, the one I laugh with, live for, dream with, Love." Just as the journey of our lives together, and even the dream to teach began on a bluff overlooking the rolling Mississippi River, it continues now to unfold in the mountains of Northeast Georgia. Above all else I am grateful we share the journey and the dream together with our Savior.

CHAPTER 1

INTRODUCTION: MCGRATH'S LIFE, INFLUENCE, SIGNIFICANCE, AND WRITINGS

J. I. Packer addressed theology and spirituality on December 11, 1989, when he was installed as the Sangwoo Yountong Chee Professor of Theology at Regent College in Canada. He entitled his inaugural address, "An Introduction to Systematic Spirituality."[1] In this address he states that he "always conceived theology, ethics, and apologetics as truth for people, and [has] never felt free to leave unapplied any truth [he] taught."[2] In fact, he states that the proper subject-matter of systematic theology is "*God actively relating in and through all created things to human beings.*"[3] Packer emphasizes that theologizing should bring about commitment, discipleship, and worship because one should make "the study of theology a devotional discipline."[4]

In concluding his address, Packer issued a resounding challenge. He said, "I want to arrange a marriage. I want our systematic theology to be practised as an element in our spirituality, and I want our spirituality to be viewed as an implicate and expression of our systematic theology."[5] He characterizes many current writings on spirituality as being egocentric and needing more Biblical and theological control. In contrast, he notes many theological tomes containing no application of Scripture. He desires to see "theological study done as an aspect and means of our relating to God . . . and to see spirituality studies within an evaluative theological frame."[6] Packer calls for an "explicit exchange of vows and mutual commitments, between spirituality and theology, or . . . between systematic and spiritual theology."[7] He sees the results of this marriage as "both our theologizing and our devotional explorations . . . become[ing] systematic spirituality, exercises in . . . knowing God."[8] Over ten years later when Packer was asked who he saw fulfilling the challenge of his inaugural address, without hesitating he stated, "Alister McGrath. He writes systematic and historical theology as well as practical works."[9]

Alister McGrath has accepted the challenge of J. I. Packer to bring theology and spirituality together.[10] According to McGrath, "Spirituality is one of the most developing fields of Christian thought and practice."[11] In fact, McGrath sees "the perceived lack of a credible, coherent and distinctive spirituality [as] one of the greatest weaknesses facing evangelicals today."[12] He laments the massive blind spots found in evangelical institutions due to the neglect and devaluing of evangelical spirituality. McGrath asks, "Where are the journals of evangelical spirituality?"[13] He also believes evangelical weaknesses can be addressed and eliminated, perhaps even becoming tomorrow's strengths. For evangelical spirituality, he especially sees this being resolved within a generation, perhaps even during his lifetime.[14]

While acknowledging the tension in evangelicalism between those who emphasize theological propositions[15] and those who emphasize personal experience,[16] McGrath believes that "spirituality represents the interface between ideas and life, between Christian theology and human existence."[17] He believes the answer is to "return to our evangelical roots in the Reformation and be refreshed, challenged, and nourished by our past."[18] For McGrath, the spirituality of the Reformers was "faithful to the Scripture and deeply rooted in the Christian tradition . . . yet capable of meeting the needs and opportunities of the modern age."[19] In McGrath's view the Reformation birthed classic evangelical spirituality, and the modern period needs to rediscover it. What is there about the spirituality of the Reformation that draws McGrath? He sees the spirituality of the Reformation as organically related to its theology. McGrath states that "spirituality was seen as the concrete and actual expression of Christian theology, flowing from and nourished by deep theological springs."[20]

This combination of theology and spirituality can be found in 1 Timothy 4 as Paul warns the young pastor about the danger of false doctrine (vv. 1-2) and encourages him to follow sound teaching (v. 6). After dealing with the importance of theological soundness, Paul moves to the area of spiritual living as he says, "train yourself to be godly"[21] (v. 7). Paul believed that godliness holds immense value, both now and eternally (v. 8). Then in summarizing his thoughts, Paul says, "watch your life and doctrine closely" (v. 16). For the Apostle Paul there was no separation of one's theological belief and one's spiritual life, or between one's orthodoxy and orthopraxy. He saw the two as coexisting partners rather than as diametric enemies.

McGrath's vision is that an authentic spirituality flow from a solid theological foundation. In over viewing his life and writings, this dual emphasis of theology and spirituality are evident.

This book will explore the centrality of Alister McGrath's theology in the development of his views on spirituality.[22] McGrath has become one of the leading spokesmen for evangelicals in the area of spirituality. Yet he does not address the area of spirituality from a theological void. In fact he allows his theological perspective to lay a foundation and to guide his views of spiritual experiences. The thesis of this book is that McGrath's teaching on spirituality is built upon the foundation of his theology and therefore serves as an example for others to follow. Therefore McGrath's theology and spirituality will be assessed, comparing his works to other evangelical theologians and other writers of evangelical spirituality. McGrath is unique as he not only writes in the field of theology, but he also has made significant contributions to the field of spirituality.

This first chapter will serve as an introduction to McGrath himself. It will overview McGrath's life and influence before comparing him to other evangelical theologians and writers of spirituality. Surveying his works will highlight his significance as one who writes both in theology and spirituality as well as combining the two.

McGrath's Life

Alister Edgar McGrath was born January 23, 1953, in Belfast, Northern Ireland.[23] His father, a physician, was Edgar Parkinson McGrath, and his mother, Annie Jane McGrath was a nurse. McGrath married[24] the former Joanna Ruth Collicutt who is now the principal clinical psychologist at the Rivermead Rehabilitation Unit in Oxford, England. They have two children: Paul Alister and Elizabeth Joanna.

McGrath attended a boarding high school at the Methodist College in Belfast, Northern Ireland. From 1971 to 1978 he attended Wendham College, Linacre College, and Merton College, all of Oxford University where he received his B.A., M.A., and D.Phil. in science with a research specialization in molecular biology as well as a B.A. in theology. He then attended St. John's College of Cambridge University, 1978-1980 where he received the B.D. in theology with a research specialization in medieval theology. He also earned first class honors for his work both in science and theology.[25]

Following his schooling, McGrath served from 1980 to 1983 as Curate at Saint Leonard's Parish Church in Wollaton, Nottingham. He went on to become a Lecturer in Historical and Systematic Theology at Wycliffe Hall, Oxford, the Church of England's leading evangelical seminary. McGrath continued as Lecturer at Wycliffe Hall from 1983 to 1995 when he was promoted to the position of the school's Principal. Since 1983 he also has been a member of the Oxford University Faculty in Theology serving as Research Lecturer (1993-1999) and now is Professor of Historical Theology in the Titular Professorship. From 1993 to 1997 he served as Research Professor of Systematic Theology at Regent College in Vancouver, British Columbia. Since 1990, McGrath has delivered academic lecture series as well as single lectures and speeches in major universities and seminaries in the United States, Canada, Australia, and Europe.

Although McGrath attended a Christian high school, he developed an intense dislike for Christianity.[26] In his early teenage years he focused on the natural sciences, specializing in chemistry, physics, biology, and mathematics. In his later teenage years he focused on pure mathematics, applied mathematics, chemistry, and physics. Influenced by scientific materialism, he felt that God had no useful place or purpose in the universe.

During these high school years McGrath developed an interest in Marxism. He saw God as some religious narcotic which dulled the senses of those who could not cope with life. He did not need a religious crutch that only weak people used. Atheistic views permeated his thought process.

Upon finishing high school, McGrath was awarded a major scholarship to study chemistry at Wadham College, Oxford University. During that first Fall at Oxford, he began to doubt his views and to rethink certain issues, including Christianity. He attended the Oxford Inter-Collegiate Christian Union, the local arm of the Inter-Varsity Fellowship. Michael Green[27] presented a series of talks to this group. Through Green's ministry McGrath saw that Christianity had far more to offer than Marxism. He states that in October, 1971, "I became a Christian, and can honestly say I have never looked back since then. If I had to identify one thing that I got right in life, it was that decision to commit myself to the living and loving God."[28]

Placing great importance upon being a thinking Christian, McGrath decided to study theology at Oxford after completing his doctorate in molecular biology.[29] However, during his study of theology McGrath lost confidence in evangelical thought since his professors regarded it as intellectually challenged. In fact McGrath testified that some of the professors considered their job to be that of clearing students of their evangelical positions. McGrath states that "more than one of the people who taught me made it clear that part of their job was to rid me of my evangelical views."[30] In 1977 two books published raised significant questions for McGrath. James Barr's *Fundamentalism*[31] portrayed British evangelicalism as academically worthless. A collection of essays entitled *The Myth of God Incarnate*[32] dismissed the incarnation as outdated and irrelevant for thinking people. McGrath concluded one could not be a thinking Christian and an evangelical.

In the following years as McGrath attended Cambridge and served as a Curate in a local parish, he continued to wrestle with the issues of his faith. Doubts about liberalism plagued him as he realized it had no hard theological or spiritual core. During his preaching and pastoral work he wondered whether liberalism had anything to say other than endorsing the latest trends. After much wrestling and soul-searching, McGrath decided that evangelical Christianity had far more to offer than other views. He states, "It was not merely Biblically-based; it was pastorally relevant and spiritually exciting. And increasingly, I came to realize its intellectual coherence and strength. I regained my confidence in evangelicalism."[33]

This experience deeply influenced McGrath as he made one of his personal goals to demonstrate the academic credibility of evangelicalism. He states, "My work as a scholar, speaker and writer has centered on the defense of the intellectual foundations of the gospel. It is a great joy to me to know that the enormous attraction of evangelicalism rests on solid foundations. . . . I can now appreciate its intellectual caliber as well, and I intend to pursue and advocate the intellectual, as well as the spiritual attraction of evangelicalism in the remainder of my ministry."[34] McGrath already has developed a considerable reputation as a scholar and popularizer of theology[35] although he considers himself primarily an evangelist or an apologist.[36]

Evident from McGrath's own testimony is his deep desire to build a solid intellectual framework for evangelical theology. Equally clear is his commitment to see an evangelical spirituality built upon this theological framework. This combination of theology and spirituality will also be seen in considering McGrath's writings.

McGrath's Influence and Significance

In the early 1990s a handbook on evangelical theologians was developed.[37] Criteria were developed to determine who to include in the volume. In order to be worthy of inclusion an individual had to be a twentieth-century theologian who not only identified with the evangelical movement but also had significant influence on or in it. The editor also sought to include representatives from various denominations, from both halves of the century, preferring those whose major interest was theological studies rather than biblical.[38] The volume constitutes a virtual who's who of evangelical theologians with names such as B. B. Warfield, J. Gresham Machen, Francis Schaeffer, Carl F. H. Henry, John R. W. Stott, J. I. Packer, and Millard J. Erickson. Included in this distinguished list is Alister E. McGrath, the youngest of the selected theologians by sixteen years, who at that time was not even forty years old. What would warrant his inclusion in such a volume on evangelical theologians? In concluding his chapter on McGrath, Michael Bauman answered by saying, McGrath is an "energetic scholar, effective teacher, committed churchman. . . . [he] has already made his mark on modern evangelical theology."[39] Dennis Okholm and Timothy Phillips concur as they state that McGrath "has established himself as one of the leading young evangelical theologians in the English-speaking world . . . [as his] academic work ranges across theological disciplines."[40] They also add that McGrath writes on "apologetics and spirituality for the layperson in the tradition of C. S. Lewis."[41]

It is apparent that McGrath's impact and influence in evangelicalism flows from his prolific pen, his teaching at Wycliffe Hall of Oxford University and his many lectureships throughout the world. As for his writings, McGrath has written over forty books, almost thirty dictionary and encyclopedia articles, over forty journal articles, over ten chapters in various books, edited several other works, and serves as a Consulting Editor of *Christianity Today*.[42] J. I. Packer quipped that McGrath "writes articles and books the way other people write letters."[43]

McGrath's writings have found enthusiastic readers from many different communities of learners. McGrath has works oriented to the scholarly community, educational community, community of evangelical leaders, and the church community. Rarely does one find an author who can write for such a diversity of groups. Packer states, "Sometimes he [McGrath] addresses his fellow professionals, sometimes a wider public, for as well as being technically accomplished, he has a flair for plain communication and a passion for it that not many scholars share."[44] Packer continues by identifying McGrath's role as one who supplies "God's people with the truth that brings health and straining out the pollution of error."[45] Because of this, Packer says McGrath speaks to both the head and the heart. Packer then calls McGrath an evangelistic theologian who not only presents what Christians believe, but also persuasively invites others into the Christian ranks.[46]

McGrath's influence further stems from his teaching at Wycliffe Hall of Oxford University.[47] Wycliffe Hall was established in 1877 with a vision for training godly Christian leaders for the church with solid Biblical groundings and passionate missionary hearts. Wycliffe's close relationship with Oxford University became official when Wycliffe Hall became a part of the University in 1996, as it was granted the status of a Permanent Private Hall. This status means that Wycliffe benefits from the resources of Oxford University yet retains its own distinctive identity and vision as a Christian community.

Wycliffe finds its core values in a threefold commitment: (1) To Biblical theology in classic Christian orthodoxy based on a conviction of the authority and trustworthiness of the Scriptures; (2) To innovative evangelism and fervor for missions as the outworking of good theology; and (3) To be a prayerful community living out the good news of Jesus Christ. Wycliffe Hall is also an International Center for Evangelical and Anglican Christian Life and Study in the University of Oxford. As a member of the Oxford University community, Wycliffe seeks to exert a transforming influence on the Church and on the wider culture as the Church of England's leading evangelical seminary.

In 1983 McGrath became a Lecturer in Historical and Systematic Theology at Wycliffe Hall and continued there to 1995 when he was promoted to the position of the school's Principal. Since 1983 he also has been a member of the Oxford University Faculty in Theology serving as Research Lecturer (1993-1999) and now is Professor of Historical Theology in the Titular Professorship. As Lecturer and Principal at Wycliffe Hall and Professor at Oxford University, McGrath has influenced and is influencing a generation of Christian and evangelical leaders. Especially within the Church of England, he is following in the footsteps of evangelical leaders, John R. W. Stott and J. I. Packer.

Finally, McGrath's influence comes from his many lectureships and addresses at major universities, seminaries, and centers of learning. In the decade of the 1990s he delivered twelve major academic lecture series on four different continents. These series included the Bampton Lectures at Oxford University, the Inch Lectures at Wheaton College, the Griffith-Thomas Lectures at Dallas Theological Seminary, the Lecture series on Biblical Spirituality at the C. S. Lewis Institute, and the Belote Lectures at the Hong Kong Baptist Theological Seminary.[48] Also, McGrath gave twenty-three single lectures or speeches in the 1990s at diverse places such as Princeton Theological Seminary, University of Melbourne, University of Geneva, University of Cambridge, Harvard Divinity School, and University of Helsinki.[49]

Considering more details of three of these lectures will help further explain how they reflect McGrath's influence. In 1990 McGrath was elected to be the Bampton Lecturer at Oxford University. He was "the youngest to serve in that capacity this century and the only evangelical."[50] In 1998, the inaugural conference of the Alonzo L. McDonald Family Professorship in Evangelical Theological Studies was held at Harvard Divinity School. This Professorship was established to promote the study of evangelicalism with its beginning colloquium theme being "Understanding Evangelicalism."[51] McGrath addressed this conference on the subject, "Trinitarian Theology."[52] In 2000, McGrath and Timothy George co-chaired a three-day international symposium sponsored by Samford University's Beeson Divinity School and Wycliffe Hall, Oxford University. The symposium considered the topic, "For All the Saints: Evangelical Theology and Christian Spirituality" and met at Beeson Divinity School, Birmingham, Alabama. McGrath's major address was entitled, "Loving God with Heart and Mind: The Theological Foundations of Spirituality."[53]

And so it is clear that McGrath's influence is extensive and pervasive. But in addition to his influence, consideration must be given to his significance for this study. This significance is seen in comparing McGrath to two of evangelicals most well-known current writers of basic theology textbooks, Millard J. Erickson and Wayne Grudem.[54] How does McGrath compare to them in his basic theology textbook, and do they combine theology and spirituality in their subsequent writings as McGrath does? Before considering Erickson[55] and Grudem, an overview of McGrath's basic theology textbook will be given to serve as a basis of comparison.

McGrath's most well-know work for the educational community is his textbook introducing Christian theology.[56] He believes many students desiring to study Christian theology are recent converts. Therefore, they possess "little inherited understanding of the nature of Christianity, its technical vocabulary, or the structure of its thought."[57] Because of this, McGrath seeks to introduce and explain Christian theology as simply and clearly as possible in this work.

McGrath uses three major areas to present theology. He begins with landmarks of Christian theology by covering periods, themes, and personalities. He divides church history into the Patristics, the Middle Ages and the Renaissance, the Reformation and Post-Reformation, and the Modern period. As McGrath details each of these periods, he follows the same pattern of clarifying terms, over viewing periods, identifying key theologians and theological developments as well as key names, words, and phrases.

The second major theological area surveys the debates over the sources and methods of Christian theology. Following the discussion of the origins of Christian ideas, McGrath moves into the third major theological area which deals with the doctrinal issues of Christian theology. In this section he covers the major themes of theology which are: God, the Trinity, the Person of Christ, Salvation, Human Nature, Sin and Grace, the Church, the Sacraments, Christianity and World Religions, and Last Things. McGrath also seeks to provide additional readings in theology[58] by making available two hundred and eighty texts drawn from one hundred and sixty-one different sources and arranged in a broadly thematic basis. Each reading follows a common pattern with a concise statement of the author and theme given, a brief introduction to the reading presented, and a background of the passage with its importance highlighted. Finally the source of the text is identified, followed by the text itself in English translation.

McGrath has not written his basic theology book as prescriptive. He seeks "not to tell its readers what to believe, but rather aims to explain to them what has been believed, and to equip them to make up their minds for themselves, by describing the options available to them and their historical origins, and enabling them to understand their strengths and weaknesses."[59] This approach is seen as a virtue by some[60] and a vice by others.[61]

In comparing McGrath's work with Erickson's and Grudem's, the main similarity is the use by all three of the traditional categories of systematic theology in surveying the field. McGrath additionally includes a large section on the history of theology. Immediately apparent are some noticeable differences. The first difference relates to the purpose and focus audience of each book. McGrath's *Christian Theology* is written broadly for beginning students, especially those within a university setting. Erickson states his purpose is to produce an "up-to-date evangelical systematic theology,"[62] and Grudem states, "I write as an evangelical and for evangelicals."[63] Therefore, Erickson and Grudem seek to persuasively argue for their evangelical positions while McGrath surveys differing positions without arguing for any one view. Closely tied to this is Erickson's and Grudem's work being geared for the graduate student while McGrath is primarily oriented for the college student. This is most evident in considering that Erickson's and Grudem's work is over twice the size of McGrath's, therefore covering issues in greater detail.[64] Interestingly, where Erickson and Grudem cover a traditional section on sanctification,[65] McGrath does not. McGrath includes only isolated discussions on the Christian life, pastoral theology, and spiritual theology.[66] Perhaps this absence is due to his purpose and target audience.[67]

Erickson and Grudem have written many works other than their basic theology textbook. Erickson's writings have continued to focus on contemporary issues of theology as well as analyzing contemporary culture.[68] Along with these he has written a few works of a more practical nature.[69] Grudem's other writings have focused primarily upon gender issues, reviewing the roles of men and women. He also examines gender language in Bible translations. Along with writing a commentary on First Peter, Grudem has also written concerning miraculous gifts.[70]

As major writers of evangelical theology, do Erickson and Grudem write works related to spirituality? As of yet they have not. Also, in chapter three writers of evangelical spirituality will be considered. Other than Bruce Demarest, these writers have not written concerning theology. Because of this, McGrath's example of writing books on theology and spirituality, even intertwining the two, stands out as unique.

McGrath's influence and impact have literally been worldwide. His writings have been enthusiastically received, and his lectureships have taken him into many of the most prestigious educational communities. Yet McGrath maintains a commitment to influence his own country and denomination by providing leadership at Wycliffe Hall. His significance for this study is shown in his writing both on evangelical theology and evangelical spirituality.

McGrath's Writings

McGrath writes four types of books, each area intended for a different audience. He writes for the scholarly community, addressing issues relating to scholars.

McGrath also composes textbooks for the educational community meant for use in classroom settings. McGrath addresses leaders of the Evangelical community with persuasive works on various issues. And finally, McGrath writes for the church community at large, seeking to influence the layperson.

Works Written for the Scholarly Community

McGrath's scholarly works focus primarily on Christology and the atonement. He not only traces the history of the doctrine of justification, but he details Luther's theology of the cross and surveys modern German Christology.[71] Also in his scholarly writings he wrestles with the adequacy and reliability of the formation of doctrine as well as scientific theology.

McGrath first writes concerning Luther's theology of the cross.[72] His study concentrates on the development of Luther's doctrine of justification over the years 1509-1519, especially focusing on the medieval theological context. In presenting the dawn of the Reformation at Wittenberg, McGrath cites three elements that were the headwaters of the Reformation: *studia humanitatis*, *via moderna*, and *schola augustiniana moderna*. Luther struggled with his medieval theology. The breakthrough for Luther came as he discovered the righteousness of God and broke with the soteriology of the *via moderna*. With this breakthrough came the emergence of the *theologia crucis*. According to McGrath Luther emphasized that Christian thought "about God comes to an abrupt halt at the foot of the cross. The Christian is forced, by the very existence of the crucified Christ, to make a momentous decision. Either he will seek God elsewhere, or he will make the cross itself the foundation and criterion of his thought about God. The 'crucified God' . . . is not merely the foundation of the nature of God. The Christian can only speak about the glory, the wisdom, the righteousness and the strength of God as they are revealed in the crucified Christ."[73]

McGrath next surveys modern German Christology from the Enlightenment to Pannenberg.[74] He introduces the development of Christology in modern German-speaking Protestantism by looking at themes, problems, and personalities. For McGrath, the significance of Jesus Christ lies at the heart of the Christian faith. However, critical presuppositions and methods have called into question the traditional understandings of Christ's importance. According to McGrath, the Enlightenment marked a decisive and irreversible change in the social, political, and religious outlook of Western Europe as well as the beginning of modern theology.

Thirdly, McGrath focuses on the doctrine of justification,[75] representing the first major study of its history since 1870. After introducing matters of prolegomena, McGrath begins with Augustine before moving to the medieval and Reformation periods. In the Reformation period he covers developments within Catholicism as well as the English Reformation, Anglicanism, and Puritanism. He concludes the book with a section on the modern period, focusing on the Enlightenment critique of orthodox doctrines of justification and surveying the thought of Kant, Schleiermacher, Ritschl, and Barth. He also considers a hermeneutical principle, recent

Pauline scholarship, and ecumenical debates. Although McGrath does not seek to present his own views on this important doctrine, he believes "that the material set out in this work will be of major interest to all concerned with ecumenical discussions, the history of the theology of the Protestant and Catholic Reformations, and the development of Christian doctrine."[76]

Then McGrath focuses upon the beginning foundation of doctrine.[77] The reliability and adequacy of doctrinal formations are the focus of the discipline of doctrinal criticism. This area seeks to identify what these doctrines represent as well as to clarify the pressures and influences which led to their beginning. Additionally, doctrinal criticism develops criteria to evaluate doctrine and to restate it as needed. McGrath's work is partly "a historical analysis, a study of how the phenomenon of doctrine arose, how it has been understood, and how the past has been restructured and reappropriated by Christian theologians, especially in the modern period."[78]

The conclusion of McGrath's study of doctrinal criticism is summed up as he states that "evangelism is of major future importance for the survival and well-being of the Christian church, in that it is only through individuals coming to stand within the Christian tradition that they will fully understand its values, aspirations, and its doctrines."[79] For western culture, McGrath sees evangelism as of strategic importance. In his view, evangelism combines the merits of epistemological rigor, cultural realism, and social pragmatism.

Lastly, McGrath recently published three volumes on scientific theology.[80] In these volumes he seeks to explore the relationship between Christian theology and the natural sciences, especially using the dialogue partners of philosophy and history. McGrath desires for his scientific theology to be "grounded in and faithful to the Christian tradition, yet open to the insights of the sciences."[81] He aspires for more than a mere exploration of a working relationship. He proposes a "synergy, a working together, a mutual cross-fertilization of ideas and approaches."[82]

McGrath identifies a core tenet of evangelical theology as a focus on the person of Jesus Christ, especially his death on the cross.[83] Evident within his scholarly works is a clear focus on the doctrine of Christology and justification as well as doctrinal formation. It is interesting that McGrath concludes his work on doctrinal formation by emphasizing the importance of evangelism. Even in McGrath's scholarly works he incisively lays a theological foundation accompanied by its application.

Works Written for the Educational Community as Textbooks

McGrath has written textbooks intended for the college and seminary community. These entry level works assume no prior knowledge of the subject and therefore contain clearly outlined subject matter and the definition of terms. His works center around three themes. First, McGrath writes about the Reformation with a general introductory book over viewing the period before then writing volumes tracing the intellectual origins of the European Reformation and describing the shaping of western culture through the life of John Calvin. Second, McGrath's textbooks about Christianity contain a general introductory work, progressing to volumes on Christian theology, spirituality and the history of Christian thought. The third area of McGrath's textbooks deal with the relationship of science and religion.

McGrath believes the Reformation period is foundational for evangelicals, therefore he first introduces the period with an overview.[84] He considers the intellectual, social, and political context in which these ideas were set. In the early 1500s a cry for reform sounded forth from individuals in western Europe. This cry was for the administrative, moral, and legal reformation of the church as well as a reformation for the spirituality and theology of the church. The cry of the humanists also became the cry of the reformers: *ad fontes*. For the reformers, the invention of the printing press by Johann Gutenberg allowed considerable access to the Bible and its manuscripts as well as to the Christian theologians of the first five centuries.

Although the term "Reformation" generally is used to refer to the "Magisterial Reformation," McGrath uses the term to speak of four elements: Lutheranism, the Reformed Church, the Radical Reformation, and the Counter-Reformation of the Catholics.

Closely tied into an overview of the Reformation, McGrath also examines the intellectual origins of the European Reformation.[85] He investigates the relationship between the Reformation, scholasticism, and humanism. Scholasticism and humanism were two great intellectual movements of the late medieval period. McGrath seeks to clarify the intellectual origins of the European Reformation by considering the two centuries preceding the Reformation. He examines late medieval religious thought, theology, and hermeneutics and considers their impact upon the origins of both the Reformed Church and the Lutheran Church.

The third focus of McGrath's Reformation emphasis is the life of John Calvin.[86] In surveying Calvin's life, McGrath concludes that Calvin was a key influencer of Western culture. He argues that Calvin was a seminal figure in European history who changed the outlook of individuals and institutions as western civilization began to assume its form. In order to understand the religious, political, social, and economic history of western Europe and North America, McGrath believes one must come to terms with the ideas of Calvin. He thinks that Calvin represents a rare moment when Christianity molded society instead of accommodating it. McGrath argues that even today, Calvin's ideas still influence western culture especially in economic activism, natural sciences, American civil religion, and natural human rights.

Next, McGrath concerns himself with introductory matters of Christianity, theology, and their history. In introducing Christianity,[87] McGrath appropriately deals initially with the person of Jesus, since He is foundational to a proper comprehension of Christianity. McGrath presents an analysis of the Christian understanding of the identity and significance of Jesus which includes discussion of the content and themes of the Bible. Not only is the New Testament portrayal of Jesus presented, but also the significance of Jesus in Christian tradition.

An overview of basic teachings of Christianity comprises McGrath's continued focus on this area. He details the role of creeds and continues with considering the sources and contents of Christian theology. McGrath uses the Apostles' Creed as the means to present Christian beliefs.

Thirdly, McGrath presents the historical development of Christianity by exploring its expansion from Palestine to becoming the world's largest religion. He traces this history by reviewing the early church, the Middle Ages, the Reformation, and the modern church in the West and in the developing world. He believes it is especially important to understand the historical origins of the distinctions between Catholic, Orthodox, and Protestant Christianity.

An introduction to the Christian way of living completes McGrath's work on Christianity for the educational community. Especially focusing on worship, sacraments, the Christian year, and how a Christian relates to culture, McGrath surveys how each of these areas relates to Catholicism, Orthodoxy, and Protestantism. He further defines Protestantism by identifying its various groups as Anglicans, Baptists, Lutherans, Methods, Reformed, Evangelicals, and Charismatics.

After introducing Christianity, McGrath gives a historical introduction to Christian thought and theology.[88] McGrath includes a discussion of the concept of theology, the purpose and place of historical theology, case studies detailing debates, and short readings from original sources.

In spirituality McGrath seeks to equip individuals to engage the riches of the Christian spiritual tradition.[89] He introduces the themes and texts of historical writers including Catholics, Orthodox, Protestants, and Evangelicals. In over viewing Christian spirituality, McGrath desires to show its rich diversity and to identify common themes. This work does not advocate any "one specific form of Christian spirituality, but aims to enable its readers to gain a firm understanding and appreciation of the many traditions represented."[90]

McGrath defines Christian spirituality as "the quest for a fulfilled and authentic Christian existence, involving the bringing together of the fundamental ideas of Christianity and the whole experience of living on the basis of and within the scope of the Christian faith."[91] He presents types of Christian spirituality by looking at theological, historical, and personal variables as well as denominational considerations.

McGrath then considers the theological foundations for spirituality by looking at its relationship to theology as well as case studies considering creation, human nature and destiny, the Trinity, incarnation, redemption, resurrection, and consummation. He examines the Bible as a resource for spirituality and considers Bible images such as the feast, the journey, exile, the struggle, purification, the internalization of faith, the desert, ascent, darkness and light, and silence. After presenting visualization and spatialization in Christian spirituality, McGrath seeks to engage the tradition by presenting excerpts of classic texts.

The third major area of McGrath's textbooks is science and religion.[92] He deals with the way religions and natural sciences converge in many areas as well as the way they differ from each other. McGrath also considers the historical, theological, philosophical, and scientific aspects of the interaction of science and religion.

Predominant themes in McGrath's educational textbooks are the Reformation period, theology and its history, spirituality, and science and religion. Although he writes these works primarily as descriptive, the foundation of McGrath's theology can be seen. McGrath views the heritage of evangelical theology and spirituality as being found in the Reformers' biblical and theological beliefs.

Works Written for Leaders of the Evangelical Community

McGrath strongly identifies himself with the evangelical community.[93] At times he specifically writes with the intention of influencing and shaping evangelicalism and its leaders. He sees a bright future of significant influence for evangelicalism as he attempts to present the intellectual coherence of evangelical theology and spirituality as well as a defense against contemporary rivals. Lastly, McGrath addresses the need to develop a person-centered apologetic.

McGrath presents the intellectual coherence of evangelicalism. In order to move past a defensive posture he adduces a coherent evangelical vision of theology, especially by critically engaging with contemporary rivals.[94] He sees evangelicalism's fundamentalist heritage and pragmatic orientation as well as the secularizing agenda of the professional academy and the potential elitist nature of theology as four major reasons evangelicals have been hostile toward academic theology.

McGrath focuses on the inner intellectual coherence of evangelicalism by considering the emphases of Jesus Christ and Scripture. He then considers the contemporary intellectual and cultural world of evangelicalism's rivals by evaluating their coherence. McGrath seeks to provide a prolegomenon to the formation of an evangelical mind. He "aims to explore the coherence of evangelicalism by bringing out the inner consistency of the evangelical approach and demonstrating the internal contradictions and vulnerabilities of its contemporary rivals."[95]

McGrath believes evangelicalism constitutes more and more of the mainstream of American Protestant Christianity as he sees the Christian vision of the future belonging to evangelicals.[96] Alongside the inspirational nature of evangelicalism is a rigorous theological foundation which has enhanced its intellectual credibility as it produces a growing number of academic theologians. McGrath sees head and heart coming together in a movement that looks to the future with a sense of expectancy and anticipation.

Identifying the Magisterial Reformation, Puritanism, and Pietism as three significant movements of Christian history which prepared the way for evangelicalism, McGrath sees these three as the main fountainheads of evangelical thinking. He further points out that they offer frameworks through which to read and interpret the New Testament. McGrath also draws a distinction between evangelicalism and fundamentalism. He cites that evangelicalism is "distinguished by its stalwart defense of orthodox Christian faith, backed up by solid theological scholarship, and by its commitment to the social application of the gospel message."[97] He sees a cluster of six controlling convictions that define evangelicalism. These convictions are: the supreme authority of Scripture, the majesty of Jesus Christ, the lordship of the Holy

Spirit, the need for personal conversion, the priority of evangelism, and the importance of the Christian community.

McGrath also sees evidences of weakness and complacency in evangelicalism. In particular he identifies the area of evangelical spirituality as one of the greatest weaknesses faced today. Although McGrath sounds a strong warning, he also sees great hope for change. He believes this shortcoming can be reversed in the present generation. He identifies the centrality of Scripture, the transforming character of God, the close connection between spirituality and theology and the rediscovery of spiritual disciplines as four landmarks to guide evangelical spirituality.

McGrath also sees a crisis of spirituality within American evangelicalism as Christians need guidance in regard to prayer, devotion, and personal disciplines. He believes individuals will turn elsewhere for help if evangelicals do not provide it. In this work, McGrath offers an answer to this problem, that is, returning to the evangelical roots of the Reformation. He believes the spirituality of the Reformation lays the foundations of classic evangelical spirituality.[98] Current evangelicals need to know about and benefit from their past which refreshes, challenges and nourishes.

McGrath identifies medieval spirituality as "*virtually totally monastic in its character and origin*"[99] whereas the spirituality of the Reformation shifted from the monasteries to the marketplace. He affirms the importance of this shift because he sees spirituality as the interface between Christian theology and human existence. He believes the spirituality of the Reformation was seen as "the concrete and actual expression of Christian theology, flowing from and nourished by deep theological springs."[100]

McGrath sees four distinguishing themes which underlie the spirituality of the Reformation. The first of these themes emphasizes spirituality as grounded and nourished in the study of Scripture. This central theological method of the Reformers, *sola scriptura*, was equally evident in their spirituality. McGrath argues that experience must be interpreted in light of Scripture and that "no personal word of God to anyone can ever be allowed to have the same authority as Scripture."[101] He believes much of what passes as modern evangelicalism has completely lost sight of this principle.

The second theme McGrath underscores as the quest for human identity, authenticity, and fulfillment. He emphasizes that for the Reformers this quest was always grounded in the doctrine of God. Religious experience as an end in itself was foreign to the Reformation foundation. McGrath argues for the closest connection between spirituality and theology and the utter impossibility of separating the two. He warns against psychology becoming the fundamental resource of Christian spirituality by stating, "Pop psychology makes sloppy theology, which in turn makes for mushy Christianity. A vigorous dose of real theology gives intellectual backbone and stamina to faith."[102]

The Reformation's third theme of spirituality acknowledges the priesthood and vocation of all Christian believers. According to McGrath, spirituality is intended for the entire church, not just for selected leadership. He sees the Reformation rediscovering the laity as the people of God.

McGrath identifies the fourth theme of Reformation spirituality as being grounded in and oriented toward life in the everyday world. He believes this allows Christians to be involved firmly and fully in secular life, bringing a new meaning and depth to both spirituality and life in this world. McGrath believes that Christians are meant to live and work in the world as salt and light.

McGrath summarizes this work by addressing the balance between the subjective experiences of faith and objective character of Christian doctrine. He concludes that "doctrine interprets experience; experience can never be allowed to be an authoritative source of truth itself."[103]

McGrath also sees a need for a broadening of perspective in the area of apologetics.[104] He believes the debate has shifted to the marketplace of ideas and away from academic approaches. The truth claims of Christianity are now tried and tested in the television studio, the national press, the university cafeteria, and the local shopping mall. According to McGrath, "Christianity must commend itself in terms of its relevance to life, not just its inherent rationality."[105]

Although McGrath does not seek to discard or discredit traditional approaches to apologetics, he does believe they need revitalizing and supplementing. While recognizing the strengths of issue-based apologetics, McGrath seeks to articulate a people-based approach. He believes "effective apologetics demands both intellectual rigor and pastoral concern, for when all is said and done, apologetics is not about winning arguments, it is about winning people."[106]

These works written to leaders of evangelicalism clearly identify McGrath's passion for the intellectual consistency in evangelical theology and the roots of evangelical spirituality. The integration of head and heart is evident in McGrath's works as he looks to the future of the evangelical movement. He is especially concerned with the attractiveness of Christianity to the unbelieving world as he seeks to develop bridges to faith through apologetics.

Works Written for the Church Community at Large

McGrath has also written broadly for the church community, especially pointed toward the layperson who seeks to wrestle with issues of personal faith. McGrath's works cover the themes of the cross, basic theology, evangelism and apologetics, and spirituality. In keeping with popular interest, McGrath writes concerning felt needs such as self-esteem, doubt, and suffering. But unlike many modern writers, McGrath's answers come from an intertwining of theology and Christian history.

McGrath seeks to help Christians understand central and basic teachings of theology.[107] Understanding Jesus comprises his first focus, for he identifies Jesus as being the heart of Christianity. McGrath articulates doctrines about Jesus and details the sources of our knowledge of Him. By addressing the doctrine of the incarnation and its significance McGrath overviews the New Testament witness to Christ and then defends the resurrection. Examining the earthly work of Jesus, McGrath presents the New Testament witness of Jesus as the loving God, the victorious God, and the forgiving God.

McGrath then attempts to help believers understand the Trinity, acknowledging that he only begins to "scratch the surface" as he wrestles with why Christians believe in the doctrine of the Trinity. Even with this elementary orientation of purpose, McGrath warns his readers of the difficulty in comprehending the subject matter by quoting Augustine, "If you can understand it, it's not God!"[108] Using the analogy of the tip of an iceberg, he states there is simply far more to God than meets the eye. For the first two centuries, the early church primarily focused on proclaiming the message of God reconciling the world to himself through Christ (the tip of the iceberg). The next two centuries saw the church seek to articulate the doctrine of the Trinity, making sure that every aspect hung together (the part hidden beneath the surface).

Endeavoring to understand doctrine McGrath wrestles with what doctrine is and why it is important. He sees the four major purposes of doctrine as telling the truth about the way things are, responding to the self-revelation of God, addressing, interpreting, and transforming human experience and giving Christians, as individuals and as a community, a sense of identity and purpose.[109] McGrath especially focuses on the relationship between doctrine and the Christian life. He concludes that doctrine addresses and interprets experience.

Justification by faith is another key focus of McGrath's basic writings of theology for the average Christian. He provides the background of this strategic doctrine by tracing the history of its development. He looks at the Biblical foundation, the Augustine and Pelagian Controversy, the Reformation, and denominational differences. McGrath then explains the contemporary significance of the doctrine of justification by considering its existential, personal and ethical dimensions. He concludes by stating that the doctrine of justification concerns the future of Christianity because it underlies all evangelism.[110]

McGrath also explores issues related to the cross.[111] As he exposes the false ideas that have been presented such as the hallucination theory, he concludes that the cross stands at the heart of the Christian faith. McGrath sees the New Testament emphasis of the cross and resurrection as having the power to change individual lives. He presents five Biblical images of the cross: a battlefield, a court of law, a rehabilitation clinic, a prison, and a hospital. McGrath maintains that faith in the message of the cross has a great impact upon how individuals live everyday life.

McGrath also examines the mystery of the cross[112] in unfolding the central message of the Bible. He sees the cross as the heart of the Christian faith. In fact, he believes that the quest for the identity and relevance of Christianity is so intimately linked with the crucified Christ "that *any* version of Christianity which is unable to accommodate the centrality of the crucified Christ must have its claim to be called 'Christian' challenged."[113] McGrath brings this to practical application as he addresses the importance of the cross being preached from the local pulpit, as well as the impact of the cross upon the life of the church and the individual believer.

Finally McGrath relates the cross to the dilemma of self-esteem and Christian confidence.[114] He critiques the best of recent psychological research on self-esteem and then presents a Biblical approach to the subject. He emphasizes the reality of sin, Christ's command to lose oneself, absolute moral standards and salvation by grace, not by human achievement. He believes the objective basis of self-esteem is found in the message of the cross.

McGrath then addresses the issues of suffering and doubt.[115] He acknowledges that often times theology seems isolated from the distress and pain of life. Yet he believes theology is meant to be the servant of the church for "it is intended to offer ordinary Christians a framework within which they may understand and cope with the tragedies and sorrows of their lives."[116] McGrath desires to reflect on suffering, not to give neat answers nor pat solutions. Instead he attempts to examine pain and bewilderment from various angles. McGrath shows how faith can bring help and understanding to even the darkest of situations.

Often with suffering comes doubt. In the first years of faith, many Christians identify with the words, "I believe! Help my unbelief!" (Mark 9:24 KJV). McGrath defines doubt and addresses it as he deals with prevalent misgivings regarding the gospel, self, Jesus, and God. He believes doubt is "an invitation to grow in faith and understanding, rather than something we need [to] panic about or get preoccupied with."[117]

Lastly, McGrath explores issues of apologetics and evangelism.[118] McGrath believes that Christians often explain the gospel so badly that others do not listen. He believes that Christians who understand their faith are better evangelists. He therefore seeks to equip Christians to understand more about the gospel and to deal with questions and problems that arise. McGrath sees apologetics as affirming the truth and the attraction of the gospel. He believes it is the giving of reasons for faith, stressing the reasonableness and attractiveness of Christianity. In contrast, evangelism is described as inviting someone to become a Christian by making the offer.

As McGrath addresses the lay community, he intertwines basic theology, especially that of the cross, along with evangelism and apologetics, wrestling with issues of personal faith. The cross remains a predominant theme as he addresses practical issues such as self-esteem and doubt. In his writings for the lay community McGrath maintains an emphasis on the impact of theology upon the experience of the Christian life.

In surveying McGrath's writings, the Reformation period forms a predominant theme as he covers theologians of the period as well as key theological issues. The formation of doctrine is important to McGrath as he addresses introductory matter of Christianity, theology, and their history. McGrath appears to be strongly convicted that evangelicals are strategic for the future of Christianity. He therefore calls upon evangelicals to clearly identify the intellectual consistency in their theology. Lastly, McGrath addresses the laity with themes of the cross, basic theology, evangelism, apologetics as well as self-esteem, doubt, and suffering.

In addition to McGrath's works in systematic and historical theology are his works on spirituality which highlight the importance he places on this topic. Immediately apparent in his writings on spirituality are the theological themes of the Reformation period, the knowledge of God, the central focus of the cross, and the foundation of Scripture. McGrath therefore distinguishes himself as a central figure in the development of theology and spirituality. Having considered his influence, this next chapter will overview McGrath's Christian theology textbook followed by a comparison to two other evangelical theologians which further confirms McGrath's significance.

Conclusion

In this chapter the necessity of integrating theology and spirituality has been presented. As earlier asserted, this mandate is evident from Scripture with Paul telling Timothy to watch his life and doctrine (1 Tim 4:16). J. I. Packer, the highly respected theologian and well-known writer of spiritual literature, has also brought forth a challenge to wed theology and spirituality. He desires to see theology written that assists Christians in relating to God and spiritual studies written that have a theological framework. Society itself cries out for spiritual experience that is real and spiritual reality that can be experienced.

Also presented in this chapter has been Alister McGrath's acceptance of both Packer's challenge and the outcry of society at-large for the intertwining of theology with spirituality. McGrath's life has uniquely prepared him with the intellectual capabilities as well as the spiritual hunger to see this venture fulfilled. In over viewing his works it becomes even more apparent that McGrath clearly seeks a solid theological foundation from which an authentic spirituality flows. McGrath's evangelical theology and its relationship to his evangelical spirituality will also be detailed.

NOTES

1. See J. I. Packer, "An Introduction to Systematic Spirituality," *Crux* 26:1 (1990): 2-8.

2. Packer, "Systematic Spirituality," 2.

3. Packer, "Systematic Spirituality," 6. Packer's emphasis.

4. Packer, "Systematic Spirituality," 7.

5. Packer, "Systematic Spirituality," 7.

6. Packer, "Systematic Spirituality," 7.

7. Packer, "Systematic Spirituality," 7.

8. Packer, "Systematic Spirituality," 7.

9. J. I. Packer, personal conversation with this writer in Amsterdam at Amsterdam 2000 with the Billy Graham Evangelistic Association, August 1, 2000. This writer served on the Theologian Task Force Group chaired by J. I. Packer which assisted in writing "The Amsterdam Declaration." This declaration is a statement on evangelism which especially addresses related theological issues. For more information on "The Amsterdam Declaration," see www.billygraham.org, accessed August 25, 2000.

10. McGrath comments on Packer's address in *Evangelicalism and the Future of Christianity* (Downer Grove: InterVarsity, 1995), 120-137; *Christian Spirituality: An Introduction* (Malden, MA: Blackwell, 1999), 33; *A Passion for Truth: The Intellectual Coherence of Evangelicalism* (Downers Grove: InterVarsity, 1996), 45-46; and *Spirituality in an Age of Change: Rediscovering the Spirit of the Reformers* (Grand Rapids: Zondervan, 1994), 50-52. Roger Steer connects McGrath with Packer in, *Guarding the Holy Fire: The Evangelicalism of John R.W. Stott, J. I. Packer, and Alister E. McGrath* (Grand Rapids: Baker, 1999). McGrath also has written a biography on Packer entitled, *J. I. Packer: A Biography*, (Grand Rapids: Baker, 1998). This biography centers on Packer's influential professional life especially focusing on British evangelicalism. See John S. Hammett, review of *J. I. Packer: A Biography*, by Alister E. McGrath, *Faith and Mission* 15 (Spring 1998): 104-106.

11. McGrath, *Evangelicalism and the Future of Christianity*, 119. Recent evangelical works on spirituality include the following: Kenneth Boa, *Conformed to His Image: Biblical and Practical Approaches to Spiritual Formation* (Grand Rapids: Zondervan, 2001); Simon Chan, *Spiritual Theology: A Systematic Study of the Christian Life* (Downers Grove: InterVarsity, 1998); Marva Dawn, *Unfettered Hope: A Call to Faithful Living in an Affluent Society* (Louisville: Westminster/Knox, 2003); Bruce A. Demarest, *Satisfy Your Soul: Restoring the Heart of Christian Spirituality* (Colorado Springs: NavPress, 1999); Richard J. Foster, *Streams of Living Water: Celebrating the Great Traditions of Christian Faith* (San Francisco: HarperSanFrancisco, 1998); Klaus Issler, *Wasting Time with God: A Christian Spirituality of Friendship with God* (Downers Grove: InterVarsity, 2001); Gary L. Thomas, *Sacred Marriage: What if God Designed Marriage to Make Us Holy More Than to Make Us Happy?* (Grand Rapids: Zondervan, 2000); and Dallas Willard, *The Divine Conspiracy: Rediscovering Our Hidden Life in God* (San Francisco: HarperSanFrancisco, 1998). Two generic works on spirituality are Elizabeth Lesser, *The New American Spirituality: A Seeker's Guide* (New York: Random House, 1999) and Robert Wuthnow, *After Heaven: Spirituality in America since the 1950s* (Berkley: University of California Press, 1998).

12. McGrath, *Evangelicalism and the Future of Christianity*, 122.

13. McGrath, *Evangelicalism and the Future of Christianity*, 132-133.

14. See McGrath, *Evangelicalism and the Future of Christianity*, 14.

15. For example, see Michael Horton, *In the Face of God: The Dangers and Delights of Spiritual Intimacy* (Dallas: Word, 1996). Horton correctly identifies the danger of allowing experience to determine one's theology. Yet he swings to the other end of the spectrum

by failing to propose a healthy perspective of spirituality for the evangelical.

16. For example, see Henry Blackaby and Claude V. King, *Experiencing God* (Nashville: Broadman & Holman, 1994). Blackaby and King correctly emphasize the need for a believer to personally experience God. Yet they fail to clearly identify the need for the subjective experience to be encased within proper theology.

17. McGrath, *Spirituality in an Age of Change*, 31-32.

18. McGrath, *Spirituality in an Age of Change*, 14.

19. McGrath, *Spirituality in an Age of Change*, 22.

20. McGrath, *Spirituality in an Age of Change*, 32.

21. Unless otherwise noted, all Scripture quotations will be from the *Holy Bible,* New International Version (Grand Rapids: Zondervan, 1978).

22. McGrath defines Christian spirituality as concerning "the quest for a fulfilled and authentic Christian existence, involving the bringing together of the fundamental ideas of Christianity and the whole experience of living on the basis of and within the scope of the Christian faith." McGrath, *Christian Spirituality*, 2. The definition of spirituality and its themes will be further explored in chapter two. Although this book focuses on evangelicals, the problem of the relationship between theology and spirituality is being wrestled with in other traditions. For example, see Mark A. McIntosh, *Mystical Theology: The Integrity of Spirituality and Theology* (Malden, MA: Blackwell, 1998) and Roch Kereszty, "Theology and Spirituality: The Task of Synthesis," *Communio* 10 (Winter 1983): 316-320.

23. For basic biographical information see Susan M. Trosky, ed., *Contemporary Authors*, vol. 134 (Detroit: Gale Research, 1992), 343-344; Miranda H. Ferrara, Editor, *The Writers Directory 1998-2000*, 13d ed. (Detroit: St. James, 1997), 999; and Michael Bauman, "Alister E. McGrath," in *Handbook of Evangelical Theologians*, ed. Walter A. Elwell (Grand Rapids: Baker, 1993), 445-447. Also see Appendix A for McGrath's Curriculum Vitae.

24. McGrath's wife has co-authored one book with him. See Joanna McGrath and Alister McGrath, *Self-Esteem: The Cross and Christian Confidence*, rev. ed. (Wheaton: Crossway, 2002).

25. McGrath writes in great detail concerning his schooling in *The Foundation of Dialogue in Science & Religion* (Malden, MA: Blackwell, 1998), 4-7.

26. McGrath's testimony of coming to Christ is found in *Evangelicalism and the Future of Christianity*, 98-100; Bauman, "Alister E. McGrath," 445-447; and Mark Hutchinson, "Interview with Alister McGrath," *Lucas: An Evangelical History Review* 16 (December 1993): 72-82.

27. For many years Green directed evangelism for the Church of England and now teaches at Wycliffe Hall. His book, *Evangelism in the Early Church* (Grand Rapids: Eerdmans, 1970), is considered a definitive work. He also co-authored with McGrath, *How Shall We Reach Them? Defending and Communicating the Christian Faith to Nonbelievers* (Nashville: Thomas Nelson, 1995). Other works by Green include *Evangelism Through the Local Church* (Nashville: Nelson, 1992); *I Believe in the Holy Spirit*, rev. ed. (Grand Rapids: Eerdmans, 1989); *The Second Epistle General of Peter and the General Epistle of Jude: An Introduction and Commentary*, rev. ed., The Tyndale New Testament Commentary Series, vol. 18 (Grand Rapids: Eerdmans, 1988); and *But Don't All Religions Lead to God* (Grand Rapids: Baker, 2002).

28. Bauman, "Alister E. McGrath," 446. A portion of Bauman's chapter is an autobiographical sketch specifically written by McGrath for the handbook.

29. McGrath wrote articles related to his doctoral work. See Alister E. McGrath, C. G. Morgan, and G. K. Radda, "Positron Lifetimes in Phospholipid Dispersions," *Biochimica at Biophysica Acta* 466 (1976): 367-372 and Alister E. McGrath, C. G. Morgan, and G. K. Radda, "Photobleaching: A Novel Fluorescence Methbod for Diffusion Studies in Lipid Systems," *Biochimica at Biophysica Acta* 426 (1976):173-185.

30. McGrath, *Evangelicalism and the Future of Christianity*, 99.

31. See James Barr, *Fundamentalism* (Philadelphia: Westminster Press, 1977).

32. See John Hick, ed., *The Myth of God Incarnate* (Philadelphia: Westminster, 1977).

33. Bauman, "Alister McGrath," 446.

34. McGrath, *Evangelicals and the Future of Christianity*, 100.

35. See Bauman, "Alister McGrath," 464-465.

36. See Hutchinson, "Interview with Alister McGrath," 75.

37. Walter A. Elwell, ed., *Handbook of Evangelical Theologians* (Grand Rapids: Baker, 1993).

38. See Walter A. Elwell, preface to *Handbook of Evangelical Theologians*, viii.

39. Bauman, "Alister E. McGrath," 464-465.

40. Dennis L. Okholm and Timothy R. Phillips, introduction to *Four Views on Salvation in a Pluralistic World*, ed. Dennis L. Okholm and Timothy R. Phillips, The Counterpoint Series, ed. Stanley N. Gundry (Grand Rapids: Zondervan, 1996), 13.

41. Okholm and Phillips, *Four Views on Salvation*, 13.

42. For a detailed list of McGrath's writings see the section "Works by Alister E. McGrath" at the conclusion of this book. For more information about *Christianity Today* see www.christianitytoday.com.

43. J. I. Packer, foreword to *Studies in Doctrine*, Alister E. McGrath (Grand Rapids: Zondervan, 1997), 7.

44. Packer, *Studies in Doctrine*, 7.

45. Packer, *Studies in Doctrine*, 7.

46. Packer, *Studies in Doctrine*, 8.

47. The following information on Wycliffe Hall is summarized from their website, www.wycliffe.ox.ac.uk, accessed February 12, 2003.

48. For a complete list of McGrath's major academic lecture series see his curriculum vitae in Appendix A.

49. For a complete list of McGrath's single lectures and speeches see his curriculum vitae in Appendix A.

50. Bauman, "Alister McGrath," 447.

51. See Ronald F. Thiemann, preface to *Where Shall My Wond'ring Soul Begin? The Landscape of Evangelical Piety and Thought*, ed. Mark A. Noll and Ronald F. Thieman (Grand Rapids: Eerdmans, 2000), vii-viii.

52. See Alister E. McGrath, "Trinitarian Theology," in *Where Shall My Wond'ring Soul Begin? The Landscape of Evangelical Piety and Thought*, ed. Mark A. Noll and Ronald F. Thieman (Grand Rapids: Eerdmans, 2000), 51-60.

53. Alister E. McGrath, *Loving God with Heart and Mind: The Theological Foundations of Spirituality*, Paper presented as part of the symposium, "For All the Saints: Evangelical Theology and Christian Spirituality," Beeson Divinity School, Birmingham, AL., 2 October 2000.

54. See Millard J. Erickson, *Christian Theology*, 2d ed. (Grand Rapids: Baker, 1998) and Wayne A. Grudem, *Systematic Theology: An Introduction to Biblical Doctrine* (Grand Rapids: Zondervan, 1994).

55. For more information on Erickson's life and background see L. Arnold Hustad, "Millard J. Erickson," in *Handbook of Evangelical Theologians*, ed. Walter A. Elwell (Grand Rapids: Baker, 1993), 412-426; David S. Dockery, "Millard J. Erickson," in *Baptist Theologians*, ed. Timothy George and David S. Dockery (Nashville: Broadman, 1990), 640-644; and Leslie R. Keylock, "Evangelical Leaders You Should Know: Meet Millard J. Erick-

son," *Moody Monthly* 87:10 (1987): 71-73.

56. See Alister E. McGrath, *Christian Theology: An Introduction*, 2d ed. (Malden, MA: Blackwell, 1997).

57. McGrath, *Christian Theology*, xvi.

58. See Alister E. McGrath, ed., *The Christian Theology Reader* (Cambridge, MA: Blackwell, 1995).

59. McGrath, *Christian Theology*, xvi.

60. See Richard J. Plantiga, review of *Christian Theology: An Introduction*, by Alister E. McGrath, *Calvin Theological Journal* 31 (April 1996): 262-264.

61. See Michael Williams, review of *Christian Theology: An Introduction*, by Alister E. McGrath, *Journal of the Evangelical Theological Society* 39 (June 1996): 311-314.

62. Erickson, *Christian Theology*, 11.

63. Grudem, *Systematic Theology*, 17.

64. Both Erickson's and Grudem's work have been condensed for college entry level textbooks. These condensed versions are similar in size to McGrath's work. See Milllard J. Erickson, *Introducing Christian Doctrine*, ed. L. Arnold Hustad, 2d ed. (Grand Rapids: Baker, 2001) and Wayne A. Grudem, *Bible Doctrine: Essential Teachings of the Christian Faith*, ed. Jeff Purswell (Grand Rapids: Zondervan, 1999).

65. See Erickson, *Christian Theology*, 979-995 and Grudem, *Systematic Theology*, 746-762.

66. See McGrath, *Christian Theology*, 145-147, 315.

67. In another venue McGrath has written specifically on the doctrine of sanctification. See Alister E. McGrath, "Sanctification," *The Oxford Encyclopedia of the Reformation*, 1995.

68. His other writings include *Contemporary Options in Eschatology: A Study of the Millennium*, 2d ed. (Grand Rapids: Bake, 1999); *Concise Dictionary of Christian Theology* (Grand Rapids: Baker, 1986); *The Word Became Flesh: A Contemporary Incarnational Christology* (Grand Rapids: Baker, 1991); *How Shall They Be Saved? The Destiny of Those Who do not Hear of Jesus* (Grand Rapids: Baker, 1996); *God in Three Persons: A Contemporary Interpretation of the Trinity* (Grand Rapids: Baker, 1995); *The Evangelical Left: Encountering Postconservative Evangelical Theology* (Grand Rapids: Baker, 1997); *God the Father Almighty: A Contemporary Exploration of the Divine Attributes* (Grand Rapids: Baker, 1998); *Postmodernizing the Faith: Evangelical Responses to the Challenge of Post-*

modernism (Grand Rapids: Baker, 1998); *Truth or Consequences: The Promises and Perils of Postmodernism* (Downers Grove: InterVarsity, 2002); and *The Postmodern World: Discerning the Times and the Spirit of Our Age* (Wheaton: Crossway, 2002).

69. Millard J. Erickson, *Does It Matter How I Live: Applying Biblical Beliefs to Your Daily Life* (Grand Rapids: Baker, 1994); *The Evangelical Mind and Heart: Perspectives on Theological and Practical Issues* (Grand Rapids: Baker, 1993); and *Responsive Faith* (Arlington Heights, IL: Harvest, 1987).

70. His other writings include *The First Epistle to Peter: An Introduction and Commentary* (Grand Rapids: Eerdmans, 1988); and Wayne Grudem and Vern S. Poythress, *The Gender-Neutral Bible Controversy: Muting the Masculinity of God's Word* (Nashville: Broadman and Holman, 2000). Also, see Wayne Grudem, ed., *Are Miraculous Gifts for Today? Four Views* (Grand Rapids: Zondervan, 1996); and Wayne Grudem and John Piper, eds., *Recovering Biblical Manhood and Womanhood: A Response to Evangelical Feminism* (Wheaton: Crossway, 1991)

71. McGrath testifies that in the late 1970s he committed to study "one major period in Christian theology (the Reformation), one major Christian theologian (Martin Luther), and the development throughout history of one specific Christian doctrine (the doctrine of justification)." See Alister E. McGrath, *A Scientific Theology*, vol. 1, *Nature* (Grand Rapids: Eerdmans, 2001), xvi.

72. See Alister E. McGrath, *Luther's Theology of the Cross: Martin Luther's Theological Breakthrough* (Malden, MA: Blackwell, 1990).

73. McGrath, *Luther's Theology*, 1.

74. See Alister E. McGrath, *The Making of Modern German Christology: From the Enlightenment to Pannenberg* (Oxford: Blackwell, 1986).

75. See Alister E. McGrath, *Iustitia Dei: A History of the Doctrine of Justification*, 2d ed. (Cambridge: Cambridge University Press, 1998).

76. McGrath, *Iustitia Dei*, 395.

77. See Alister E. McGrath, *The Genesis of Doctrine: A Study in the Foundations of Doctrinal Criticism* (Grand Rapids: Eerdmans, 1997). For excellent reviews of this work see Andreas Kostenberger, review of *The Genesis of Doctrine: A Study in the Foundations of Doctrinal Criticism*, by Alister E. McGrath, *Faith and Mission* 16 (Summer 1999): 117-120 and David W. Buschart, review of *The Genesis of Doctrine: A Study in the Foundations of Doctrinal Criticism*, by Alister E. McGrath, *Journal of the Evangelical Theological Society* 36 (September 1993): 380-382.

78. McGrath, *The Genesis of Doctrine*, viii.

79. McGrath, *The Genesis of Doctrine*, 198.

80. See Alister E. McGrath, *A Scientific Theology*, vol. 1, *Nature* (Grand Rapids: Eerdmans, 2001), *A Scientific Theology*, vol. 2, *Reality* (Grand Rapids: Eerdmans, 2002), and *A Scientific Theology*, vol. 3, *Theory* (Grand Rapids: Eerdmans, 2004). An earlier work by McGrath has been enfolded into these volumes. See McGrath, *The Foundation of Dialogue in Science & Religion*.

81. McGrath, *A Scientific Theology*, vol. 1, *Nature*, xi.

82. McGrath, *A Scientific Theology*, vol. 1, *Nature*, xi. McGrath identifies T. F. Torrance as the most significant proponent of scientific theology in the twentieth century. See McGrath, *A Scientific Theology*, vol. 1, *Nature*, 76. He has also written a biography on the life of Torrance. See Alister E. McGrath, *Thomas F. Torrance: An Intellectual Biography* (Edinburgh: T & T Clark, 1999).

83. See McGrath, *Beyond the Quiet Time*, x.

84. See Alister E. McGrath, *Reformation Thought: An Introduction*, 3d ed. (Malden, MA: Blackwell, 1999).

85. See Alister E. McGrath, *The Intellectual Origins of the European Reformation* (New York: Blackwell, 1987).

86. See Alister E. McGrath, *A Life of John Calvin: A Study in the Shaping of Western Culture* (Malden, MA: Blackwell, 1990).

87. See Alister E. McGrath, *An Introduction to Christianity* (Malden, MA: Blackwell, 1997).

88. See Alister E. McGrath, *Historical Theology: An Introduction to the History of Christian Thought* (Malden, MA: Blackwell, 1998).

89. See McGrath, *Christian Spirituality*.

90. McGrath, *Christian Spirituality*, xi.

91. McGrath, *Christian Spirituality*, 2.

92. See Alister E. McGrath, *Science and Religion: An Introduction* (Malden, MA: Blackwell, 1999).

93. McGrath defines evangelicalism as "the movement, especially in English-language theology, which places emphasis upon the supreme authority of Scripture and the atoning death of Christ." McGrath, *Historical Theology*, 348. For further study on evangelicalism see George M. Marsden, *Fundamentalism and American Culture: The Shaping of Twentieth*

Century Evangelicalism, 1870-1925 (New York: Oxford, 1980); George M. Marsden, *Understanding Fundamentalism and Evangelicalism* (Grand Rapids: Eerdmans, 1991); George M. Marsden, ed. *Evangelicalism and Modern America* (Grand Rapids: Eerdmans, 1984); and Edith L. Blumhofer and Joel A. Carpenter, *Twentieth Century Evangelicalism: A Guide to the Sources* (New York: Garland, 1990). The central themes of evangelicalism will be further explored in chapter two.

94. See McGrath, *A Passion for Truth*.

95. McGrath, *A Passion for Truth*, 23-24.

96. See McGrath, *Evangelicalism and the Future of Christianity*.

97. McGrath, *Evangelicalism and the Future of Christianity*, 39.

98. See McGrath, *Spirituality in an Age of Change*.

99. McGrath, *Spirituality in an Age of Change*, 26.

100. McGrath, *Spirituality in an Age of Change*, 32.

101. McGrath, *Spirituality in an Age of Change*, 47.

102. McGrath, *Spirituality in an Age of Change*, 52.

103. McGrath, *Spirituality in an Age of Change*, 192.

104. See Alister E. McGrath, *Intellectuals Don't Need God and Other Modern Myths: Building Bridges to Faith Through Apologetics* (Grand Rapids: Zondervan, 1993).

105. McGrath, *Intellectuals*, 9.

106. McGrath, *Intellectuals*, 12.

107. See Alister E. McGrath, *Studies in Doctrine: Understanding Doctrine, Understanding the Trinity, Understanding Jesus, Justification by Faith* (Grand Rapids: Zondervan, 1997).

108. McGrath, *Studies in Doctrine*, 124.

109. McGrath, *Studies in Doctrine*, 237.

110. McGrath, *Studies in Doctrine*, 453.

111. See Alister E. McGrath, *What was God Doing on the Cross?* (Grand Rapids:

Zondervan, 1992).

112. See Alister E. McGrath, *The Mystery of the Cross* (Grand Rapids: Zondervan, 1988).

113. McGrath, *The Mystery of the Cross*, 36. McGrath's emphasis.

114. See McGrath and McGrath, *Self-Esteem*.

115. See Alister E. McGrath, *Suffering and God* (Grand Rapids: Zondervan, 1995) and *The Sunnier Side of Doubt* (Grand Rapids: Zondervan, 1990).

116. McGrath, *Suffering and God*, 10.

117. McGrath, *The Sunnier Side of Doubt*, 8.

118. See Alister E. McGrath, *Explaining Your Faith*, rev. ed. (Grand Rapids: Baker 1995) and McGrath and Green, *How Shall We Reach Them?*.

CHAPTER 2

MCGRATH'S EVANGELICAL THEOLOGY AND ITS RELATIONSHIP TO HIS EVANGELICAL SPIRITUALITY—PART ONE

An internet chat room entitled "Contemplative Evangelical Dialogue" was being monitored by Donald Whitney, seminary professor and writer of evangelical spirituality. He relates how one active member recorded her spiritual experience.

> I had the feeling that if I put 'feet to my faith' and traveled intentionally to a sacred place (not unlike a Holy Land trip), then God would honor that and the result might be a deepening of my faith.... I chose to visit two sites in particular, Avila, where Teresa lived and was the head of the Carmelite order for about 30 years, and Mount Montserrat, where there is a Benedictine Monastery dedicated to the Black Madonna.... Miracles happened and I even had several appearances of what can only be described as angels. ... One of the miracles was that I got to stand in the cell that Teresa lived in for 27 years and feel the power of her presence there.
>
> I wanted to bring back some memory of what my soul had experienced on this trip. I could have used photos or drawings of the places I visited but instead I chose to purchase icons (small paintings on wood) of these two influential and courageous women.
>
> When I came home it just seemed reasonable to have them around during my prayer time to remind me of what I had learned from God through them. Do I pray to them? Not really, I pray to God and to Jesus. But sometimes I'll just lean over and say to Teresa and Mary, 'Well, girls, how're we doing?' ... I believe they are Jesus with skin on and they give me hope and courage.[1]

Whitney responds to this story by asking, "Is this sort of talk and practice outside the boundaries of Evangelical spirituality?"[2] The danger of spiritual experiences unguarded by truth is very real for evangelicals.

After considering the definition of spirituality, this chapter will contemplate two of McGrath's core tenets of evangelical theology and their relationship to his evangelical spirituality. In chapter three discussion of McGrath's core theological tenets will be completed along with a more thorough examination of their effect upon his spirituality. For it is evident in seeking to achieve a deeper spiritual experience Evangelicals must embrace a sound theological framework as their guide, along with a clear understanding of the definition of the goal they seek.

Spirituality Defined

The term "spirituality" has a frightening element to D. A. Carson because it has "become such an ill-defined, amorphous entity that it covers all kinds of phenomena that an earlier generation of Christians, more given to robust *thought* than is the present generation, would have dismissed as error, or even as 'paganism' or 'heathenism.'"[3]

McGrath acknowledges that many evangelicals feel uneasy with the term "spirituality" as it is not a biblical term. He believes this concern from evangelicals over use of a non-biblical term deserves respect and understanding.[4] Yet McGrath also wants to remind evangelicals that they use non-biblical terms in other contexts as he states,

> For example, works have appeared with the phrase 'evangelical theology' in their titles. The word 'theology' is non-biblical, yet widely used by evangelicals because it designates a recognized area of importance. Other words which we happily use include 'Christology,' 'apologetics' and 'homiletics.' Yet we use them, believing them to be useful for the tasks we face as an evangelical community of reflection and application. I suspect that much the same thing is happening in relation to spirituality. Older words, such as 'piety,' are gradually being displaced, even within evangelical circles, by the term 'spirituality.'[5]

Carson identifies spirituality as a theological construct much like the doctrine of the Trinity except that spirituality has a person-variable which makes for difficulty.[6] Even with misgivings over the word McGrath states, "My impression is that evangelicals have adopted the word 'spirituality,' and that it is here to stay. If this is so, our task is to ensure that we understand this term in a biblical manner, by insisting that any attempts to deepen the quality of the Christian experience of God are faithful to Scripture, and rest upon an orthodox theology."[7]

One finds a diversity of themes in surveying definitions of spirituality.[8] Some writers equate spirituality with being filled with the Spirit. For example, Lewis Sperry Chafer defines true spirituality as "the unhindered manifestations of the indwelling Spirit."[9] Bradley Holt concurs as he states, "Christian spirituality is a style of walking in the Holy Spirit."[10] Even Jurgen Moltman brings this emphasis by stating, "Literally, spirituality means life in God's Spirit, and a living relationship with God's spirit.... In a strictly Christian sense, the word has to mean what Paul calls the new life *en pneumati* [in the spirit]."[11]

Other writers combine the Spirit-filled life with thoughts concerning sanctification such as Bernard McGinn when he states, "Christian spirituality is the lived experience of Christian belief in both its general and more specialized forms. . . . It is possible to distinguish spirituality from doctrine in that it concentrates not on faith itself, but on the reaction that faith arouses in religious consciousness and practice. It can likewise be distinguished from Christian ethics in that it treats not all human actions in their relation to God, but those acts in which the relation to God is immediate and explicit."[12] Stanley Grenz and James Houston not only emphasize sanctification but also include each person of the Trinity in their definitions. Grenz defines spirituality as "the quest, under the direction of the Holy Spirit but with the cooperation of the believer, for holiness. It is the pursuit of life lived to the glory of God, in union with Christ and out of obedience to the Holy Spirit."[13] Houston defines Christian spirituality as "the outworking, then, of the grace of God in the soul of man, beginning with conversion to conclusion in death or Christ's Second Advent. It is marked by growth and maturity and fellowship . . . a life of prayer . . . a sense of the eternal dimension in all one's existence . . . and an intense awareness of life lived in the present before God. . . . The Spirit-filled life is one that manifests practically the Spirit of Jesus, with the fruit of love that is joyful, peaceful, patient, kind, good, faithful, gentle, and self-controlled. . . . This is true spirituality."[14]

Klaus Issler emphasizes the relational aspect of spirituality as well as identifies each member of the Trinity as he states, "Christian spirituality involves a deepening trust and friendship with God for those who are in Christ Jesus. More specifically, it is an ever growing, experientially dynamic relationship with our trinitarian God—Father, Son, and Holy Spirit—through the agency of the indwelling Spirit of God."[15] Bruce Demarest also combines the relational with an identification of each member of the Trinity, yet he adds the dimension of sanctification when he states, "The core of Christian spirituality is a loving, deepening relationship with the living God. . . . Christian spirituality concerns the shaping of our inner beings after the likeness of Jesus Christ by the indwelling Spirit and the living out of Jesus' values in service to others."[16] McGrath's emphasis upon the term again combines the relational aspect with sanctification as he states, "Christian Spirituality is reflection on the whole Christian enterprise of achieving and sustaining a relationship with God, which includes both public worship and private devotion, and the results of these in actual Christian life. . . . Christian spirituality concerns the quest for a fulfilled and authentic Christian existence, involving the bringing together of the fundamental ideas of Christianity and the whole experience of living on the basis of and within the scope of the Christian faith."[17]

Even though writers are quick to acknowledge the difficulty with defining spirituality, very few interact in critiquing other definitions. Issler attempts this critique when he affirms Demarest's *Satisfy Your Soul* and McGrath's *Christian Spirituality*, yet differs with the authors in their definitions of spirituality. Both Demarest and McGrath focus on the process of sanctification alongside of the relational element of spirituality. Issler believes this leads to confusion as he sees the relational aspect as preeminent.[18]

Issler emphasizes that "God loves us and yearns for a closer relationship with us."[19] Then, using D. A. Carson, he identifies how the love of God involves at least five differing expressions. These expressions of God's love are: (1) God's intra-trinitarian love, particularly between the Father and the Son; (2) God's providential love for all His creatures as Creator; (3) God's yearning love to save the world through the cross of Jesus; (4) God's wooing love to draw and secure the salvation of His people; and 5) God's relational love experienced with believers.[20] Issler sees the first kind of love as the basis and impetus for the other four loves and believes it sets an ideal pattern for all relationships. Yet he understands the last category of God's relational love experienced with believers as key for spirituality.[21]

Issler is correct in identifying McGrath's emphasis of relational spirituality and spirituality that is lived out in sanctification. In McGrath's view, the two are combined and cannot be separated. Consider the following words of McGrath as he intertwines the two themes.

> Spirituality is all about the way in which we encounter and experience God, and the transformation of our consciousness and our lives as a result of that encounter and experience. Spirituality is about the internalization of our faith. It means allowing our faith to saturate every aspect of our lives, infecting and affecting our thinking, feeling and living. Nobody can doubt how much we need to deepen the quality of our Christian lives and experience, with God's gracious assistance, and live more authentic lives in which we experience to the full the wonder of the love and grace of God. It is about ways in which we can foster and sustain our personal relationship with Christ. Christian spirituality may be thus understood as the way in which Christian individuals or groups aim to deepen their experience of God.[22]

McGrath sees common ideas running through spirituality, such as: "knowing God, not just knowing about God, experiencing God to the full, transformation of existence on the basis of the Christian faith, and attaining Christian authenticity in life and thought."[23] He would affirm Issler's relational approach, yet he would see a danger of becoming too inward focused. For him, spirituality involves not only developing one's inward relationship with God but also living out one's faith in everyday life. McGrath sees this as a distinctive of the Reformation when the centers of spirituality shifted from the monasteries to the marketplace.[24]

It appears to this writer that more work needs to be done clarifying the relationship of spirituality to sanctification. Certainly it seems that the two are intertwined and overlapping. The doctrine of sanctification provides the parameters and guidelines on which to build the dynamics of a personal and intimate relationship with God. With these thoughts in mind, the following definition could be considered. Spirituality is an intimate relationship, individually and corporately, with the Trinitarian God—Father, Son, and Holy Spirit—which transforms the way one lives. However, in wrestling with the definition of spirituality, McGrath summarizes the current interaction of writers by stating, "The term is resistant to precise definition, partly due to the variety of senses in which the term is used, and partly due to controversy within the community of scholars specializing in the field over the manner in which the term ought to be used."[25]

Since the term "spirituality" is so broadly used in society it is especially noteworthy that McGrath has carefully defined his own use of the term. Building upon that definition the next focus of this research will consider McGrath's theology and spirituality in detail.

McGrath's Core Tenets of Evangelical Theology and Their Effect Upon His Views of Evangelical Spirituality

McGrath's works identify central interacting themes which characterize evangelical theology.[26] These topics include a focus on the person of Jesus Christ, the supreme authority of Scripture, the need for personal conversion, and the priority of evangelism.[27] In one work McGrath includes two additional themes: the Lordship of the Holy Spirit and the importance of the Christian community.[28] McGrath's works also identify central themes which characterize evangelical spirituality. These topics include the transforming knowledge of God, Scripture as the center of spirituality, the importance of spiritual disciplines, and the close connection between theology and spirituality.[29] What follows is a presentation of McGrath's views on these areas of evangelical theology and their correlation with his views on evangelical spirituality.

The Person of Jesus Christ and Transforming Character of the Knowledge of God

McGrath sees Christianity as unique among the religions of the world because of the historical figure who stands at its center, Jesus Christ.[30] Because of the uniqueness of Jesus, McGrath says evangelicals are emphatic in affirming both the uniqueness of Christ and His definitiveness. Therefore evangelicals have never felt awkwardness in defending or proclaiming Christ.[31] In fact, McGrath says that "one of the most characteristic features of evangelicalism is that it is radically Christ-centered."[32]

Because of Christ's constitutive and definitive importance for Christianity, evangelicals have held that Jesus possessed "an intrinsic authority which is grounded and focused in his own person and work."[33] McGrath further elaborates by stating, "Evangelicalism argues that authority is inherit in the person of Christ, and insists that it is of paramount importance to remain as faithful as possible to the New Testament portrayal of Christ. . . . Evangelicalism is strongly counter-cultural at this point; in a western cultural context in which the right of individuals to create their own worlds is vigorously asserted, evangelicalism declares that it is a movement under the authority and sovereignty of Christ."[34] He sees "the evangelical emphasis on the authority of Jesus Christ *as he is revealed in Scripture* (rather than as he is constructed by human interest groups or power blocks) [as] profoundly liberating."[35]

Because of the uniqueness and authority of Christ, His significance must be considered. McGrath says the evangelical understanding of this significance is possible only on the basis of the life, death, and resurrection of Jesus Christ. He sees Christ as both constitutive and illustrative of the Christian life.[36] In exploring the significance of Christ, McGrath gives five seminal aspects.[37]

The first of these seminal aspects is the revelational significance of Jesus Christ. McGrath says that God made knowledge of Himself known in the New Testament through the person and work of Christ. For the Christian, Jesus is the embodiment and self-revelation of God. At the heart of the Christian faith is a living person. According to McGrath, for evangelicals this means,

> Underlying the revelational language and conceptualities of the New Testament is an affirmation of the human need to be *told* what God is like. God must be allowed the privilege of naming and disclosing of himself, rather than being forced to suffer the indignity of having human constructs and preconceptions imposed upon him. Evangelicalism is determined to 'let God be God,' and to receive, honour and conceive him as he chooses to be known, rather than as we should have him be. At its heart, evangelicalism represents a relentless and serious attempt to bring all our conceptions of God and ourselves to criticism in the light of how and what God wishes to be known. In this sense, evangelical theology is *responsible*, in the dual sense of being a *response to divine revelation* (rather than a human initiative) and being *answerable* to God for its formulations and conceptions.[38]

McGrath sees the fundamental revelational axiom of the Christian faith as being that only God can reveal God. When this priority of revelation is affirmed, it ultimately affirms that God is the supreme authority on Himself.

The soteriological significance of Jesus Christ provides the second of these seminal aspects as salvation is made possible and available through the death and resurrection of Jesus Christ according to the New Testament. McGrath says the centrality of the cross has long been a leading theme of evangelical theology. He sees the cross as "the *exclusive ground of salvation* . . . the *starting-point of authentically Christian theology* . . . the *centre of all Christian thought*."[39] He says, "There can be no doubt of the New Testament's emphasis on the uniqueness and finality of salvation brought by Jesus Christ."[40]

The third of McGrath's seminal aspects is the mimetic significance of Jesus Christ. The example of Christ is provided for us to imitate and follow. McGrath quickly disassociates this point from the moral example theory which minimizes human sin and presents a deficient view of the person of Christ. McGrath says, "Evangelicalism avoids this minimalist view of sin and inadequate conception of Christ through an emphasis on 'being conformed to Christ.'"[41] He sees the most characteristic thought on the Christian life in Pauline writings to be that of Christomorphic. According to McGrath, "Evangelicalism . . . argues that the life, death and resurrection of Jesus Christ makes possible a new form of existence, which is both instantiated by Jesus Christ, and evoked through a God-worked regeneration within believers as they are conformed to Christ."[42]

The doxological significance of Jesus Christ forms the fourth of the seminal aspects. McGrath sees an intimate connection between theology and the way Christians worship and pray. He believes theology and doxology must not be allowed to separate but be wedded together. The Christological hymns in the New Testament according to McGrath point to the exalted status of Christ in the early Christian communities, indicating that the lordship of Christ was fully incorporated in their worship. For evangelicals, McGrath sees this strongly manifested in the great hymns of evangelicalism. He says, "Worship of Christ as the God who humbled himself to redeem humanity is there mingled with sober reflection on the cost of that redemption and the motivation which it offers for authentic Christian living and evangelism."[43] McGrath summarizes by stating, "The coherence of the evangelical understanding of the significance of Christ extends to the manner in which he is worshipped and adored, as well as that in which is understood theologically."[44]

McGrath's final seminal aspect is the kerygmatic significance of Jesus Christ. An integral part of evangelical understanding is the proclamation of Christ. He is seen as someone who must be proclaimed and to whom a response is expected. McGrath says, "The evangelical insistence on the importance of evangelism is thus an entirely proper and natural outcome of its Christology . . . there is a Christological foundation and motivation to evangelism, which evangelicalism has never seen as an optional extra for a select few, but as integral to the life and witness of the church. The identity of Jesus Christ is such that evangelism is an essential aspect of the response of believers, both individually and corporately, to his person and work."[45]

For McGrath, these five considerations underlie "the decisive Christian affirmation that God has revealed himself in Jesus Christ, who is the foundation and criterion of evangelical theology."[46] He believes it is "clear that Christology plays a decisive role in evangelical theology and spiritual reflection, and gives evangelical theology both its intellectual coherence and evangelistic and spiritual focus. The question 'Who is Jesus Christ?' is thus determinative of the entire evangelical theological enterprise."[47]

Closely tied to the theological study of the person of Christ is the transforming character of the knowledge of God in evangelical spirituality. Jesus Christ came both to redeem mankind and to reveal God to men. McGrath believes that the knowledge of God results in an obedient lifestyle as well as one of adoration of God. For him, this life transformation must be a natural consequence of a devotional study of the Bible.[48] McGrath sees the danger of an exclusive focus on the mind as leading to spiritual impoverishment. From his own experience he states, "I read the Bible as a source of *information*, where others who were wiser than I read it as a source of *formation*— of being shaped and formed by what they read, as they allowed it to impact upon their hearts, minds and emotions. I had yet to discover the ways of reading Scripture in which the mind descends into the heart, as both are drawn into the love and presence of God."⁴⁹

McGrath draws from the Reformation to illustrate this tenet. For him, "*Reformation spirituality insists that the quest for human identity and fulfillment cannot be undertaken in isolation from God.*"⁵⁰ McGrath states, "To find out *who* we are—and *why* we are—is to find out who God is and what he is like."⁵¹ Calvin states this principle in the opening sentence of his *Institutes* where he says,

> Nearly all the wisdom we possess, that is to say, true and sound wisdom, consists of two parts: knowledge of God and of ourselves. But, while joined in many bonds, which one precedes and brings forth the other is not easy to discern.... Knowledge of ourselves not only arouses us to seek God, but also, as it were, leads us by the hand to find him.... It is certain that man never achieves a clear knowledge of himself unless he has first looked upon God's face, and then descends from contemplating him to scrutinize himself.⁵²

McGrath believes that Calvin's emphasis on the experiential knowledge of God "reflects the common Reformation belief that to know God is to experience the power of God. To know God is to be changed by God."⁵³

McGrath also highlights Martin Luther's works as stressing how a believer shares in and is transformed by the promises of God. He believes Luther gives powerful images expressing the "dynamic manner in which knowledge of God changes us—we are united to his promises, we are absorbed into them, and we are saturated and intoxicated by them."⁵⁴ Luther states, "Since these promises of God are holy, true, righteous, free, and peaceful words, full of goodness, the soul which clings to them with a firm faith will be so closely united with them and altogether absorbed by them that it will not only share in all their power, but will be saturated and intoxicated by them. If a touch of Christ healed, how much more will this most tender spiritual touch, this absorbing Word, communicate to the soul all things that belong to the Word."⁵⁵ Thus, McGrath and Luther believe the knowledge of God is "like a vital force, capable of changing those who possess it and are possessed by it. True knowledge of God moves us to worship, obedience, and the hope of eternal life."⁵⁶

McGrath believes this reliance upon the life-changing knowledge of God has important implications for understanding Reformation spirituality and therefore spirituality for evangelicals. He sees it as consolidating the centrality of the Bible for spirituality (as the only source for reliable and authoritative knowledge of God) and the importance of Christology (since in Jesus Christ divinity and humanity are held together in single and indivisible unity). McGrath states, "It is here that the characteristically Christian knowledge of God and knowledge of human nature converge and come to a point of focus.... The manner in which many spiritual writings within the Reformation tradition center upon considering the example of Jesus Christ reflects this basic theological affirmation."⁵⁷

J. I. Packer's *Knowing God*⁵⁸ emphasizes these same themes as Packer deals not only with the apprehension of who God is but also the application to oneself of who God is and what God gives. Adoration of God naturally follows, giving praise to the one who gives these gifts.[59] McGrath believes that Packer's "general strategy is to begin by allowing his readers to apprehend the reality of God; then to move on to allow them to apply these insights to their lives; and finally, to respond to God in adoration."[60] Packer addresses those who assume that a study of the nature and character of God will be unpractical and irrelevant for life. He states that the study of God is the most practical project in which anyone can engage.[61] He explains this further by asking and then answering, "How can we turn our knowledge *about* God into knowledge *of* God? . . . It is that we turn each truth that we learn *about* God into matter for meditation *before* God, leading to prayer and praise *to* God."[62] Packer is the only twentieth-century writer about whom McGrath writes in his section on classic texts of spirituality.[63]

McGrath warns of dangerous trends within the modern emphasis on spirituality. He believes, "Any notion of spirituality as a quest for heightened religious experience as an end in itself is totally alien to the outlook of the Reformation."[64] He also cautions that "psychology alone cannot, and should not be allowed to become the fundamental resource of Christian spirituality."[65] McGrath believes James Houston offers a good model for Christians to follow as "he explores the way meditation and prayer can change our perception of God, our relationship with him and our experience of him."[66] Using illustrations and helpful quotes from great writers of the past, Houston persistently and persuasively affirms how knowing God changes people.[67] Houston states, "When the death and resurrection of Jesus Christ have affected our lives in such a way, our transformed desires will immediately witness to the change within us."[68]

The combining of the person of Christ and the transforming character of the knowledge of God are brought together in McGrath's work, *Knowing Christ*[69] which flows from his personal spiritual pilgrimage of having "amassed information about Christ without knowing him in the warmth and intimacy of a personal relationship."[70] McGrath summarized his condition by stating,

> I gradually came to the realization that my faith was far too academic. Frankly, it was as dry as dust. I was spirituality parched, and the last thing I needed was more of the dry and desiccated material that seemed to be the staple diet of so many at this time. I needed refreshment and a rekindling of my vision of the gospel. I wanted to be excited by my faith, to be set on fire with a new love for Christ. . . . A means had become an end. The text which was meant to lead us to Christ and allow him to convert and renew us had become a goal in its own right. Knowledge of a text had displaced knowledge of Christ. It was a dangerous and deplorable situation which could well lead to a weak and vulnerable faith, inadequately rooted in a personal relationship with the living Christ.[71]

The words of the Apostle Paul, "What is more, I consider everything as loss compared to the surpassing greatness of knowing Christ Jesus my Lord" (Phil 3:8), became the burning desire of McGrath's Christian walk.

McGrath fully endorses the "supreme importance of Scripture in determining and shaping Christian doctrine."[72] Yet he understands doctrine to be the framework that ensures the presence of Christ is understood correctly. Because of his mistakes, McGrath has written *Knowing Jesus* in "an attempt to put into words some of the lessons [he] learned, often painfully, as [he] wrestled with what it meant to know Christ and to see this as the greatest privilege we can hope to be granted."[73]

McGrath emphasizes that Christ can be known in our minds, imaginations, hearts, and memories even during times of loneliness, anxiety, doubt, and suffering. He surveys Biblical incidents of individuals encountering Christ such as the fisherman by the sea, the woman at the well, doubting Thomas, and the life of Peter. Additionally McGrath presents Biblical images of knowing Christ such as the bread of life, the light of the world, the good shepherd, and the true vine. McGrath also considers benefits and barriers to knowing Christ before examining Christ as the fulfillment of prophecy, as God incarnate, as crucified, and as risen and ascended.

McGrath holds a high view of the person of Christ as he embraces the uniqueness of Christ and His definitiveness. Closely tied to this is the knowledge of God which for McGrath is not merely an academic exercise. He believes that knowing God not only transforms one's life but also leads to human identity and fulfillment. Knowledge of God and a transformed life are key elements of evangelical spirituality.

Scripture as the Ultimate Authority and the Center for Spirituality

McGrath sees the sufficiency of Scripture[74] as being of central importance not only to evangelicalism[75] but to the very shaping of evangelical theology. In fact he sees one of the most fundamental distinctives of the evangelical approach to theology as "its insistence that theology be nourished and governed at all points by Holy Scripture and that it seek to offer a faithful and coherent account of what it finds there."[76] Therefore, he sees Scripture as the center of gravity for evangelicalism and as "the central legitimating resource of the Christian faith and theology, the clearest window through which the face of Christ may be seen."[77]

McGrath reasons that full authority was given to Christ, and this leads to a belief in scriptural authority because of the natural connection between the two. He identifies the way Christ himself saw Scripture as God-given. McGrath correctly points out that Jesus did not uncritically accept the view of His contemporaries, but criticized what was unacceptable. McGrath says "Christology and scriptural authority are inextricably linked, in that it is Scripture which brings us to a knowledge of Jesus Christ."[78]

Some seek to set up a dichotomy between Christ and the Bible. For example, McGrath's Oxford colleague, John Barton says, "Christians are not those who believe in the Bible, but those who believe in Christ."[79] McGrath responds by saying,

> While this has some merit as a statement of priorities and emphases, it seems to me that it sets up a misleading false dichotomy. It is not a question

of *either* the Bible *or* Jesus Christ, as if they can be separated. There is an organic and essential connection between them. We honour Christ by receiving both the Scriptures that he received, and those that the church has handed down to us as a divinely inspired witness to Christ.[80]

For McGrath, "the authority of Scripture . . . rests upon both theological and historical considerations; it is through Jesus Christ that the distinctively Christian knowledge of God comes about, and this knowledge is given only in Scripture."[81]

Yet McGrath makes other statements that are puzzling. Although he rightly affirms the close relationship between Christ and the Bible, McGrath states that evangelicalism is not a religion of a book but rather focuses on the person and work of Christ.[82] He continues these thoughts by saying,

> Despite its high view of Scripture, evangelicalism has resisted the temptation to identify the text of Scripture itself with revelation. Scripture is regarded as a channel through which God's self-revelation in Jesus Christ is encountered. Although it is a bearer of that self-revelation in Christ, it is not to be identified directly with that self-revelation. Scripture is not Jesus Christ.[83]

McGrath then challenges Benjamin B. Warfield's understanding of the authority of Scripture[84] as based upon "pressures and influences from the Scottish philosophy of common sense."[85] He states that, "With the waning of the appeal of this philosophy, along with an increasing recognition of the inadequacy of its rationalist foundations, Warfield's distinctive approach to the issue of the authority of Scripture has indeed found itself in 'crisis,' not on account of any waning in evangelical respect for Scripture, but on account of increasing misgivings concerning one particular manner of grounding and expressing that authority."[86]

McGrath identifies rival approaches to authority as culture, experience, reason and tradition.[87] He believes that American evangelicalism has been heavily influenced by rationalism and is susceptible to its dangers. He then identifies Carl F. H. Henry[88] as one who "laid too much emphasis upon the notion of a purely propositional biblical revelation."[89] McGrath sees this as dangerous for evangelicals because it "would set itself on the road that inevitably allows fallen human reason to judge God's revelation, or become its ultimate foundation."[90]

In discussing the Princeton approach of Warfield and the modern American evangelical approach of Henry, McGrath summarizes[91] the thoughts of Donald G. Bloesch[92] to buttress his own arguments. Bloesch sees a strongly rationalist spirit within modern American evangelicals such as Carl F. H. Henry, John Warwick Montgomery, Francis Schaeffer and Norman Geisler. He believes these approaches have a questionably "high confidence in the capacity of reason to judge the truth of revelation."[93] McGrath concurs as he asks, "Whose rationality provides the basis of scriptural authority?"[94]

McGrath believes that as the Enlightenment influence diminishes, "evangelicals are once more free to rediscover and recover the distinctive features of a more biblical approach to theology, which stresses that God's actions in history, recounted and interpreted in Scripture, form a narrative."[95] He sees it as wrong to view God's self-disclosure as merely a transmission of facts about God. According to McGrath, "To reduce revelation to principles or concepts is to suppress the element of mystery, holiness and wonder to God's self-disclosure."[96]

In the past McGrath believes there have been understandable reasons why evangelicals focused on the propositional and cognitive elements of revelation. He believes this allowed evangelicalism to maintain its credibility during a time of rationalistic assault. Yet he sees the understanding of revelation which came from this period as "dangerously deficient, verging on the aridity and sterility which were the hallmarks of the same rationalism which evangelicalism was seeking to oppose."[97]

So what does McGrath propose for evangelicals? He believes that evangelicals need to recover the fullness of biblical revelation by recognizing the narrative quality of Scripture. He does not believe that this "strategy involve[s] the abandoning or weakening of an evangelical commitment to the objective cognitive truth of divine revelation. It is simply to recognize that revelation involves more than this, and to commend the wisdom of avoiding reductionist approaches to the issue."[98] He believes the narrative character and genre of Scripture has been marginalized "in order to facilitate its analysis purely as a repository of propositional statements, capable of withstanding the epistemological criteria of the Enlightenment."[99]

McGrath's view of Scripture is seen by some evangelicals as being closely associated with the views of Karl Barth.[100] Even Clark Pinnock, who calls McGrath the leading intellectual of the evangelical circle, sees McGrath's view of the Bible as being out of step with most evangelicals. Pinnock wonders how long evangelicals will look to McGrath as their spokesman if he continues to make them uncomfortable with his statements.[101] Some of the strongest criticism comes from Carl Trueman as he states,

> McGrath's discussion of revelation, combined with other comments indicate that his own position on scriptural authority is probably not far from that of Barth and neo-orthodoxy. I say 'probably' because McGrath is conscientiously vague concerning the details of his own position, claiming only that he bases biblical authority on the Bible's relationship to Christ. McGrath never defines the precise nature of this relationship, although his use of the language of encounter, his dependence upon Bloesch, his positive approach to Barth on scripture, his hostility to old Princeton, and his failure to engage directly with the thorny questions of inspiration and inerrancy/infallibility clearly indicate a new-orthodox rather than a traditional confessional resolution of the issue.[102]

Perhaps the fullest explanation of McGrath's view of Scripture is found when he identifies the Formula of Concord (1577) and the Westminster Confession of Faith (1647) as summarizing the evangelical consensus on the authority and sufficiency of Scripture. According to McGrath, "Some such position would be widely acknowledged within evangelicalism today."[103] He states, "Although differences of

McGrath's Evangelical Theology and Spirituality – Part One 41

approach and vocabulary may be discerned, attended by the inevitable border disputes relating to these differences, there is nevertheless a shared emphasis on the total reliability and trustworthiness of Scripture as the ultimate foundation and criterion of our saving knowledge of God."[104] McGrath attempts to further clarify by stating, "In general terms, evangelicals agree that Scripture is inspired yet offer different understandings of what this means; most agree that Scripture is 'inerrant,' yet at least nine different understandings of what this means can be identified in recent evangelical writing."[105] When McGrath was asked if he would consider the Bible inerrant as defined by The Chicago Statement of Biblical Inerrancy[106] he stated, "I would not have any difficulty with that, but it wouldn't be my preferred way of speaking. My preferred way of speaking would be to say that the Bible is totally trustworthy. Because that to me links up very, very closely the idea of faith as trust. The Bible is a totally trustworthy guide to a totally trustworthy God. That, to me, is the bottom line."[107]

McGrath seeks to bring a warning to evangelicals concerning an overly rationalistic view of the Bible. He sees this rationalism stemming from the Enlightenment as well as evangelical's defense against attacks. At times McGrath's statements concerning the Bible are puzzling. Yet he always returns to emphasize the trustworthiness of Scripture and to affirm how evangelical theology must be solidly built upon a Biblical foundation.

Flowing from McGrath's emphasis on the authority of Scripture is his position that evangelical spirituality must be Scripture-centered. For him this means more than just saying that Scripture must be the heart of evangelical spirituality. He believes this speaks of the manner in which one approaches and reads the Bible. McGrath emphasizes that "Scripture *ought to be* approached and read in the sure and confident expectation that God will speak to the reader."[108] He believes that by meditating on the text, the reader can deepen his relationship with God. McGrath sees this bringing about a deeper bond of commitment, adoration, fellowship and love with the Bible as the source of spiritual nourishment and refreshment.[109]

McGrath believes the importance of Scripture can be easily stated. What he considers more difficult is to develop methods which enable readers to engage more satisfactorily with the Biblical text. Among contemporary writers, Eugene Peterson offers a model which McGrath sees as one of the best. Peterson encourages readers of the Bible to reflect on the meaning of the text and then relate it to everyday life. As a part of this meditation, Peterson encourages a judicious appeal to use of human imagination.[110] McGrath states, "There is a real need to allow our imaginations to supply such images, always ensuring that they remain controlled by the scriptural text on which we are meditating."[111]

McGrath also traces historically the development of a devotional reading of the Bible[112] beginning with the emphasis of the *Quadriga* or four-fold sense of Scripture used in the Middle Ages. Built upon the patristic distinction between the literal and higher senses of Scripture, this approach began with the literal sense (natural meaning taken at face value) of a passage before considering three spiritual senses - allegorical (symbolic meaning relating to Christian doctrine), tropological (moral meaning relating to conduct of believers), and anagogical (heavenly meaning relating to Christian hope).[113] McGrath believes a potential weakness was avoided in this approach "by insisting that nothing should be believed on the basis of a non-literal sense of Scripture, unless it could be first established on the basis of the literal sense."[114]

McGrath believes one of the most important medieval writers on devotional reading of the Bible was the Carthusian writer Guigo II. According to Guigo II, four stages guided the reading of the Biblical text: reading (*lectio*), mediation (*meditatio*), prayer (*oratio*), and contemplation (*contemplatio*). McGrath elaborates on these four stages by stating,

> Guigo argues that we begin by reading the text of Scripture, in full expectation that we shall encounter something of God in doing so. This leads us on to meditate on what we find—not in the sense of emptying our minds of everything, but rather allowing our minds to focus and concentrate upon the meaning and imagery of the text, with all external thoughts being excluded. This leads to prayer as the only appropriate response to what we encounter. Finally, this leads to a quiet entrance into the presence of God in contemplation.[115]

Guigo II sets forth the relationship between these four with the following statements: "Reading without meditation is sterile, meditation without reading is liable to error, prayer without meditation is lukewarm, meditation without prayer is unfruitful, prayer when it is fervent wins contemplation."[116]

According to McGrath this scheme was widely accepted in the Middle Ages as it offered a framework for unlocking the devotional richness of Scripture. One of the most important early masters of the *devotio moderna*,[117] Geert Zerbolt van Zutphen,[118] adopted the basic themes of Guigo's *scala claustralium* in his major work *de spiritualibus ascensionibus*.[119] McGrath states, "For Zerbolt, the spiritual reading of Scripture prepares the reader for meditation; meditation prepares for prayer; and prayer for contemplation. To meditate without first reading Scripture is to run the risk of being deluded or falling into error, whereas reading Scripture without turning to prayer is arid and barren."[120] Zerbolt defined meditation as "the process whereby thou dost diligently turn over in thine heart whatsoever thou hast read or heard, earnestly ruminating the same and thereby rekindling thine affections in some particular matter, or enlightening thine understanding."[121] McGrath considers this definition a synthesis of the medieval consensus on meditation.[122]

The sixteenth century Protestant Reformation[123] brought a renewed interest in the Bible, especially increasing the laity's accessibility to it. In fact, according to McGrath, one of the central demands of the Reformation was providing Bibles to all people in a language which they could understand. These translations had major impacts upon shaping Western European languages.[124] Martin Luther's translation of the New Testament affected modern German just as the King James Version of the Bible influenced modern English phraseology.[125]

Even as the *sola scriptura* principle was central to the theological method of the Reformers, McGrath believes it was equally evident in their spirituality. He states, "Scripture is the supreme God-authorized and God-given resource for the generation and nourishment of Christian faith. The history of the leading personalities of the Reformation indicated the centrality of the reading of and meditation upon Scripture."[126] The centrality of Scripture for Reformation spirituality is especially seen in the writings of the Reformers. McGrath believes they developed three resources which are of special importance.[127]

The first of these resources was the biblical commentary which helped readers to understand the Bible by explaining difficult phrases, identifying important points and guiding readers to the thrusts and concerns of a passage. McGrath especially identifies John Calvin, Martin Luther, Melanchthon and Huldrych Zwingli as producing commentaries aimed at both academic and lay readers.

The second of the three resources was the expository sermon which sought to bridge the horizons of the scriptural text with its hearers. This style of preaching applied the principles underlying the scripture passage to the situation of the audience. McGrath identifies Calvin's sermons as a model of this as he states, "This Reformer developed the notion of *lectio continua*—the continuous preaching through a book of the Bible, rather than preaching based on passages drawn from a lectionary or chosen by the preacher. For example, during the period between March 20, 1555, and July 15, 1556, Calvin is known to have preached some two hundred sermons on a single biblical book—Deuteronomy."[128]

The third Reformation resource consisted of works on biblical theology such as Calvin's *Institutes of the Christian Religion*.[129] Volumes such as Calvin's assisted individuals in appreciating the theological coherence of Scripture by synthesizing the Bible's statements on theological issues. McGrath believes this "enabled its readers to establish a coherent and consistent worldview that would undergird their everyday lives."[130] He emphasizes that for the Reformers, "Scripture molded doctrine, which in turn shaped the realities of Christian life."[131]

McGrath believes an excellent illustration of the importance of the Bible in spirituality for the Reformers is found when Martin Luther wrote a short book on prayer at the request of his barber, Peter Beskendorf. Luther's approach to prayer was based on the reading of the Lord's Prayer (Matt 6:9-13) and the Ten Commandments (Ex 20:1-17). Luther sets forth a four-fold interaction with the Biblical text as a means of praying. When using the Ten Commandments Luther states,

> I take one part after another and free myself as much as possible from distractions in order to pray. I divide each commandment into four parts, thereby fashioning a garland of four strands. That is, I think of each commandment as, first, instruction, which is really what it is intended to be, and consider what the Lord God demands of me so earnestly. Second, I turn it into a thanksgiving; third, a confession; and fourth, a prayer.[132]

McGrath elaborates on Luther's four basic elements with the following thoughts:

1. *Instruction*. Luther here expects the believer to be reminded of the need to trust God completely in all things, and not to depend on anything else - such as social status and wealth.
2. *Thanksgiving*. At this point, Luther turns his attention to meditation on all that God has done for him, particularly in relation to redemption, but also recalling that God has promised to be his 'comfort, guardian, guide and strength' in times of difficulty.
3. *Confession*. Having reflected on all that God has done, Luther moves on to acknowledge and confess his own failings and weaknesses.
4. *Prayer*. In light of the three previous items, Luther then composes a prayer, weaving together these elements, in which he asks God to renew his faith and trust, and strengthen his resolve to be obedient and faithful.[133]

McGrath indicates "this framework proved popular, and was widely adopted within Lutheran circles and beyond."[134]

From the earliest phases of the Protestant tradition of spirituality, McGrath believes meditating on Biblical passages was of central and vital importance.[135] He sees this principle illustrated in virtually any period of Protestantism, but he highlights the nineteenth century Baptist preacher Charles Haddon Spurgeon. In a message to an assembly of ministers, Spurgeon warned of the overly technical approach to reading the Bible by emphasizing the great need for meditation. He stated,

> How sweetly the Spirit has taught us *in meditation!* Have you not often been surprised and overcome with delight as Holy Scripture has opened us, as if the gates of the golden city has been set back for you to enter? I am sure that you did not then gather your knowledge from men, because it was all fresh to you as you sat alone with no book but the Bible, and yourself receptive, scarely thinking out matters, but drinking them in as the Lord brought them to you. A few minutes silent openness of soul before the Lord has brought us in more treasure of truth than hours of learned research.[136]

The combining of study and meditation are brought together in McGrath's work, *Beyond the Quiet Time: Practical Evangelical Spirituality*[137] where McGrath assists believers by helping them discover the full richness of their faith and developing ways of keeping their faith alive and growing. He sees Christian spirituality as a deepening of the life of faith in relation to Jesus Christ, recognizing in Him the fullness of life that God wishes His people to possess. Therefore, for the Christian, spirituality brings together the emphasis upon Jesus Christ and the Bible.

With this work McGrath attempts to provide Christians with a resource tool for "Quiet Times," while trying to avoid its perils, which he sees as a lack of guidance for understanding the text and its spiritual importance. He provides five lessons as practical guides which include the necessary information and materials. The lesson topics are: being lost, being rescued, being in the world, believing and doubting, and living and hoping.

Each lesson includes Scripture passages, meditation points, sketches of historical Christian leaders, and exercises for practical application. These study guides may be used for individuals or with groups.

McGrath's approach to the devotional reading of the Bible is key for evangelical spirituality. The Bible must be digested in the heart as well as in the mind. Strategic for this is learning to meditate on Scripture as well as incorporating this meditation into one's prayer life. Spirituality apart from the Word of God is subject to error, extremes, and lack of discernment. For evangelicals, the Bible must be central for both theology and spirituality.

NOTES

1. Donald S. Whitney, *Defining the Boundaries of Evangelical Spirituality*, Paper presented as part of the Evangelical Theological Society Annual Meeting, Colorado Springs, CO, 15 November 2001.

2. Whitney, *Defining the Boundaries*. In his paper Whitney states, "The boundaries of Evangelical spirituality are the self-revelation of God. Thus Evangelicals should also recognize that the boundaries of their spirituality specifically include the biblical doctrines of *sola scriptura* and *sola fide*."

3. D. A. Carson, *The Gagging of God: Christianity Confronts Pluralism* (Grand Rapids: Zondervan, 1996), 555. Carson's emphasis. This warning was also issued by Gordon R. Lewis, "The Church and the New Spirituality," *Journal of the Evangelical Theological Society* 36 (1993): 433-444.

4. See McGrath, *Loving God with Heart and Mind*.

5. McGrath, *Loving God with Heart and Mind*, 5-6. A variation of this quote is also found in McGrath, "Evangelical Theological Method: The State of the Art," in *Evangelical Futures: A Conversation on Theological Method*, ed. John G. Stackhouse, Jr. (Downers Grove: InterVarsity, 2000), 21-22.

6. Carson, *The Gagging of God*, 562-563.

7. McGrath, *Loving God with Heart and Mind*.

8. Although Carson does not offer a concise definition of spirituality, he does offer the following priorities for evangelicals. These priorities are: (1) Spirituality must be thought of in connection with the gospel; (2) Christian reflection on spirituality must work outward from the center, i.e., spirituality must be thought about and sought after out of the matrix of core biblical theology; (3) Suspicions should follow forms of theology that place all the emphasis on coherent systems of thought that demand faith, allegiance, and obedience, but do not engage the affections, let alone foster an active sense of the presence of God; (4) What God uses to foster a gospel spirituality must be carefully delineated; and (5) Word-centered

reflection will bring us back to the fact that spirituality is a theological construct. See Carson, *Gagging of God*, 566-569.

9. Lewis Sperry Chafer, *He That Is Spiritual* (Grand Rapids: Zondervan, 1967), 133.

10. Bradley Holt, *Thirsty for God: A Brief History of Christian Spirituality* (Minneapolis: Augsburg, 1993), 123.

11. Jurgen Moltman, *The Spirit of Life: A Universal Affirmation* (Minneapolis: Fortress Press, 1992), 83.

12. Bernard McGinn, introduction to *Christian Spirituality*, vol. 1. *Origins to the Twelfth Century*, ed. Bernard McGinn and John Meyendorff (New York: Crossroad, 1985), xv-xvi.

13. Stanley J. Grenz, *Revisioning Evangelical Theology: A Fresh Agenda for the 21st Century* (Downers Grove: InterVarsity, 1993), 42.

14. James M. Houston, "Spirituality," in *Evangelical Dictionary of Theology*, 1984.

15. Issler, *Wasting Time With God*, 25-26.

16. Demarest, *Satisfy Your Soul*, 74.

17. McGrath, *Christian Spirituality*, 2.

18. Issler, *Wasting Time with God*, 252.

19. Issler, *Wasting Time with God*, 28.

20. Issler, *Wasting Time with God*, 28 and D. A. Carson, "The Difficult Doctrine of the Love of God, part 1," *Bibliotheca Sacra* 156 (Jan-Mar. 1999): 7-9 and "The Difficult Doctrine of the Love of God, part 4," *Bibliotheca Sacra* 156 (Oct-Dec 1999): 397-398.

21. Issler, *Wasting Time with God*, 28.

22. McGrath, *Loving God with Heart and Mind*.

23. McGrath, *Loving God with Heart and Mind*.

24. McGrath, *Spirituality in an Age of Change*, 26.

25. McGrath, *A Brief History of Heaven*, Blackwell Brief History of Religion Series (Malden, MA: Blackwell, 2003), 163.

26. McGrath lists these themes in the following: *Christian Spirituality*, 18-19; *Christian Theology*, 122-122; *Historical Theology*, 249-252; *An Introduction to Christianity*, 413-414; and *A Passion for Truth*, 22. McGrath's theology will be evaluated in a work scheduled for publication in November 2003. See Sung Wook Chung, ed., *Alister E. McGrath and Evangelical Theology: A Vital Engagement* (Grand Rapids: Baker, 2003).

27. McGrath introduces these themes with various descriptions such as: distinctive features of the evangelical ethos, fundamental and controlling convictions and beliefs of evangelicalism, and four assumptions of evangelicalism. See *Christian Spirituality*, 18; *Evangelism and the Future of Christianity*, 55, 59; *Christian Theology*, 121; and *Historical Theology*, 249.

28. See McGrath, *Evangelicalism and the Future of Christianity*, 55-56. In one work, McGrath identifies four distinctive hallmarks of evangelicals attributing them to David Bebbington. These hallmarks: conversionism, activism, Biblicism, and crucicentrism, coincide with McGrath's emphasis. See McGrath, *The Future of Christianity*, 111-112. McGrath also explains the additional two by stating, "The four-point description of evangelicalism reflects a wide consensus within the scholarship of the movement, and is taken from the writings of leading British scholar David Bebbington. The six-point description is my own take on things, based more on writers such as J. I. Packer, which I use when expressing my own perceptions, rather than working within the framework of an existing consensus." See Alister E. McGrath, email to author, June 12, 2002. For further study see David W. Bebbington, "Evangelicalism in its Settings: The British and American Movements since 1940," in *Evangelicalism: Comparative Studies of Popular Protestantism in North America, the British Isles, and Beyond, 1700-1990*, ed., Mark A. Noll, David W. Bebbington, and George A. Rawlyk (New York: Oxford, 1994), 366-367 and David W. Bebbington, *Evangelicalism in Modern Britain: A History from the 1730s to the 1980s* (London: Unwin Hyman, 1989), 2-17.

29. McGrath's writings that focus primarily on spirituality include: *Beyond the Quiet Time*; *Christian Spirituality*; *Spirituality in an Age of Change*; *The Journey: A Pilgrim in the Lands of the Spirit* (New York: Doubleday, 2000); "Theology and Experience: Reflections on Cognitive Approaches to Theology," *European Journal of Theology* 2:1 (1993): 65-74; *The Unknown God: Searching for Spiritual Fulfillment* (Grand Rapids: Eerdmans, 1999); and *Knowing Christ* (New York: Doubleday, 2002).

30. McGrath's writings on Christology include sections in *Christian Theology*, 319-385; "Christology: On Learning from History," in *Who Do You Say That I Am?*, 69-90; *Evangelicalism and the Future of Christianity*, 65-68; *I Believe*, 37-79; *A Passion for the Truth*, 25-52; and *Studies in Doctrine*, 11-80 as well as his complete works of *Luther's Theology of the Cross*, *The Making of Modern German Christology*, *The Mystery of the Cross*, *Suffering and God*, and *What was God Doing on the Cross?*

31. See McGrath, *A Passion for Truth*, 25 and McGrath, *The Making of Modern German Christology*, 1.

32. McGrath, *Evangelicalism and the Future of Christianity*, 65.

33. McGrath, *A Passion for Truth*, 27.

34. McGrath, *A Passion for Truth*, 30. Although emphasizing the authority of Christ, McGrath attempts not to set up a false dichotomy between Christ and Scripture. He states, "Christology and scriptural authority are inextricably linked, in that it is Scripture, and Scripture alone, that brings us to a true and saving knowledge of Jesus Christ." See *Evangelicalism and the Future of Christianity*, 65.

35. McGrath, *A Passion for Truth*, 35. McGrath's emphasis.

36. McGrath, *A Passion for Truth*, 36.

37. The following summary of the five seminal aspects is taken from McGrath, *A Passion for Truth*, 36-50.

38. McGrath, *A Passion for Truth*, 37-38. McGrath's emphases.

39. McGrath, *A Passion for Truth*, 40-41. McGrath's emphases.

40. McGrath, *A Passion for Truth*, 41.

41. McGrath, *A Passion for Truth*, 43.

42. McGrath, *A Passion for Truth*, 45.

43. McGrath, *A Passion for Truth*, 47.

44. McGrath, *A Passion for Truth*, 47.

45. McGrath, *A Passion for Truth*, 48.

46. McGrath, *A Passion for Truth*, 49.

47. McGrath, *A Passion for Truth*, 49.

48. See McGrath, *Evangelicalism and the Future of Christianity*, 135.

49. McGrath, *Knowing Jesus*, 18. McGrath's emphases.

50. McGrath, *Spirituality in an Age of Change*, 48. McGrath's emphases.

51. McGrath, *Spirituality in an Age of Change*, 48. McGrath's emphases.

52. John Calvin, *Institutes of the Christian Religion*, vol.1, ed. John T. McNeill, The Library of Christian Classics, vol. 20 (Philadelphia: Westminster, 1960), 35, 37.

53. McGrath, *Spirituality in an Age of Change*, 49.

54. McGrath, *Spirituality in an Age of Change*, 49.

55. Martin Luther, "The Freedom of a Christian," translated by W. A. Lambert and rev. by Harold J. Grimm, in *Luther's Works*, vol. 31, ed. Harold J. Grimm (Philadelphia: Concordia, 1957), 349.

56. McGrath, *Spirituality in an Age of Change*, 49.

57. McGrath, *Spirituality in an Age of Change*, 50.

58. See J. I. Packer, *Knowing God* (Downers Grove: InterVarsity, 1973).

59. See McGrath, *Christian Spirituality*, 171.

60. McGrath, *Christian Spirituality*, 171.

61. See Packer, *Knowing God*, 14.

62. Packer, *Knowing God*, 18. Packer's emphases.

63. See McGrath, *Christian Spirituality*, 170-173.

64. McGrath, *Spirituality in an Age of Change*, 48.

65. McGrath, *Spirituality in an Age of Change*, 52. For McGrath's assessment of psychology see Joanna McGrath and Alister McGrath, *Self-Esteem: The Cross and Christian Confidence*, rev. ed. (Wheaton: Crossway, 2002).

66. McGrath, *Evangelicalism and the Future of Christianity*, 135.

67. See James A. Houston, *The Transforming Friendship* (Batavia, IL: Lion, 1989) and *The Heart's Desire: A Guide to Personal Fulfillment* (Batavia, IL: Lion, 1992).

68. Houston, *The Heart's Desire*, 156.

69. See McGrath, *Knowing Christ*.

70. McGrath, *Knowing Christ*, 11.

71. McGrath, *Knowing Christ*, 7-8.

72. McGrath, *Knowing Christ*, 7-8.

73. McGrath, *Knowing Christ*, 9.

74. McGrath's writings on Bibliology include sections in *Christian Theology*, 181-235, *Evangelicalism and the Future of Christianity*, 59-64, *An Introduction to Christianity*, 168-187, *A Passion for Truth*, 53-117, "Reclaiming our Roots and Vision: Scripture and Stability of the Christian Church" in *Reclaiming the Bible for the Church*, 63-88, and *Studies in Doctrine*, 31-42.

75. McGrath, *A Passion for Truth*, 53.

76. McGrath, "Engaging the Tradition," in *Evangelical Futures: A Conversation on Theological Method*, ed. John G. Stackhouse (Downers Grove: InterVarsity, 2000), 139.

77. McGrath, *Evangelicalism and the Future of Christianity*, 61.

78. McGrath, *A Passion for Truth*, 56.

79. See John Barton, *People of the Book?* (Louisville, KY: Westminster/Knox, 1988), 83.

80. McGrath, "Reclaiming Our Roots and Vision," 65-66. McGrath's emphasis.

81. McGrath, "Reclaiming Our Roots and Vision," 68.

82. McGrath, *A Passion for Truth*, 53.

83. McGrath, *A Passion for Truth*, 54.

84. For Warfield's view see Benjamin B. Warfield, *The Inspiration and Authority of the Bible*, ed. Samuel G. Craig (Phillipsburg, NJ: Presbyterian & Reformed, 1948).

85. McGrath, *A Passion for Truth*, 58. For a brief overview of Scottish Realism see Douglas F. Kelly, "Scottish Realism," in *Evangelical Dictionary of Theology*, 1984 and Colin Brown, *Christianity & Western Thought*, vol. 1, *A History of Philosophies, Ideas & Movements* (Downers Grove: InterVarsity, 1990), 259-284.

86. McGrath, *A Passion for Truth*, 58.

87. For McGrath's discussion of these rival authorities see *A Passion for Truth*, 66-97.

88. See Carl F. H. Henry, *God, Revelation, and Authority* (6 vols., Waco, TX: Word, 1976-1983).

89. McGrath, *A Passion for Truth*, 106.

90. McGrath, *A Passion for Truth*, 171.

91. For McGrath's summary of Bloesch see *A Passion for Truth*, 170.

93. See Donald G. Bloesch, *Essentials of Evangelical Theology*, vol. 2 (San Francisco: Harper & Row, 1979), 267-268.

93. Bloesch, *Essentials*, 268.

94. McGrath, *A Passion for Truth*, 170.

95. McGrath, *A Passion for Truth*, 107.

96. McGrath, *A Passion for Truth*, 107.

97. McGrath, *A Passion for Truth*, 107.

98. McGrath, *A Passion for Truth*, 107.

99. McGrath, *A Passion for Truth*, 106.

100. For example, see Robert A. Pyne, review of *A Passion for Truth*, by Alister E. McGrath, *Bibliotheca Sacra* 154:614 (1997): 227 and Carl R. Trueman, review of *A Passion for Truth*, by Alister E. McGrath, *Westminster Theological Journal* 59:1 (1997): 137. McGrath acknowledges Barth's influence upon him when he stated, "I found myself impressed by the intellectual coherence of Barth's vision of 'theological science,' and thrilled by the vision Barth offered of a sustained theological engagement with the past. ... While I have misgivings about many aspects of Barth's theology ... it is impossible to understate the positive impact which Barth had upon my estimation of, and enthusiasm for, theology as a serious intellectual discipline." See McGrath, *A Scientific Theology*, vol. 1, *Nature* (Grand Rapids: Eerdmans, 2001), xv-xvi.

101. See Clark Pinnock, review of *A Passion for Truth*, by Alister E. McGrath, *Pro Ecclesia* 8:1 (1999): 115.

102. Carl R. Trueman, review of *A Passion for Truth*, 137.

103. McGrath, "Evangelical Theological Method," 29.

104. McGrath, "Evangelical Theological Method," 29.

105. McGrath, "Evangelical Theological Method," 29. McGrath cites David S. Dockery as the evangelical writer who identifies nine understandings of inerrancy. See David S. Dockery, "Variations in Inerrancy," *SBC Today* (May 1986): 10-11.

106. For more information on "The Chicago Statement of Biblical Inerrancy," see Norman L. Geisler, ed., *Inerrancy* (Grand Rapids: Zondervan, 1980), 493-502.

107. Alister E. McGrath, Principal of Wycliffe Hall, Interview by author, 3 October, 2000, Birmingham, AL, tape recording, Beeson Divinity School, Birmingham, AL.

108. McGrath, *Evangelicalism and the Future of Christianity*, 134. McGrath's emphasis.

109. See McGrath, *Christian Spirituality*, 83.

110. McGrath identifies two of Peterson's works illustrating this principle. See Eugene H. Peterson, *A Long Obedience in the Same Direction: Discipleship in an Instant Society* (Downers Grove: InterVarsity, 1980) and *Reversed Thunder: The Revelation of John and the Praying Imagination* (San Francisco: Harper & Row, 1988).

111. McGrath, *Evangelicalism and the Future of Christianity*, 135. McGrath's caution to control the use of imagination with the Scriptural text is key. Even the well-known writer of spirituality, Richard Foster, erred on this matter and had to offer correction. See Richard Foster, *Celebration of Discipline: The Path to Spiritual Growth* (San Francisco: Harper & Row, 1978), 27 and Richard J. Foster, "Under Fire: Two Christian Leaders Respond to Accusations of New Age Mysticism," *Christianity Today* 31 (September 18, 1987): 17-21. For further study on the use of imagination for Christians see Cheryl Forbes, *Imagination: Embracing a Theology of Wonder* (Portland: Multnomah, 1986).

112. McGrath acknowledges the historical/grammatical approach to interpreting Scripture. But for spiritual nourishment of the individual, he emphasizes the devotional reading of the Bible. Duvall and Hays state, "Devotional reading focuses less on analysis of details and more on a personal, intimate time of listening to the Lord with your heart." See J. Scott Duvall and J. Daniel Hays, *Grasping God's Word: A Hands-On Approach to Reading, Interpreting and Applying the Bible* (Grand Rapids: Zondervan, 2001), 202. For a brief overview of both historical and contemporary views of interpreting the Bible see F. F. Bruce, "Interpretation of the Bible," in *Evangelical Dictionary of Theology*, 1984. For a more thorough study of hermeneutics see Kevin J. Vanhoozer, *Is There a Meaning in This Text? The Bible, The Reader, and the Morality of Literary Knowledge* (Grand Rapids: Zondervan, 1998) and Grant R. Osborne, *The Hermeneutical Spiral: A Comprehensive Introduction to Biblical Interpretation* (Downers Grove: InterVarsity, 1991).

113. See McGrath, *Christian Spirituality*, 83-83 and *Christian Theology*, 206-209.

114. McGrath, *Christian Theology*, 207. McGrath indicates Martin Luther thought the *Quadriga* was a valuable exegetical aid as long as the three spiritual senses of scripture were subordinated to the literal sense, thus not allowing any allegorical, tropological or anagogical view unless it could first be shown to be explicitly stated in the literal sense. See Alister E. McGrath, *Luther's Theology of the Cross*, 76-81.

115. McGrath, *Christian Spirituality*, 85.

116. Guigo II, *The Ladder of Monks and Twelve Meditations*, translated by Edmund Colledge and James Walsh (Kalamazoo, MI: Cistercian, 1978), 82. For further

information on Guigo II see Louis Bouyer, et. al., *A History of Christian Spirituality*, vol 2, *The Spirituality of the Middle Ages*, translated by the Benedictines of Holme Eden Abbey (London: Burns and Oates, 1968), 155-160.

117. For further study of the *devotio moderna* see Louis Bouyer, et al., *A History of Christian Spirituality*, vol 2, 428-439; Otto Grundler, "Devotio Moderna," in Jill Raitt,ed, *Christian Spirituality*, vol. 2, *High Middle Ages and Reformation* (New York: Crossroad, 1987), 176B193; David C. Steinmetz, *"Devotio Moderna,"* in *The Westminster Dictionary of Christian Spirituality*, 1983; and P. H. Davids, *"Devotio Moderna,"* in *Evangelical Dictionary of Theology*, 1984. Davids lists the chief marks of the movement as: (1) A focus on devotion to Christ including meditation on his passion; (2) An emphasis on obeying Christ's commands; (3) A strong involvement in individual piety and spiritual life; (4) A call to repentance and reform; and (5) Elements of nominalism, Christian humanism, and Franciscan asceticism. He identifies the *devotio moderna* movement as similar and perhaps a forerunner to the Anabaptists.

118. For further study of Geert Zerbolt see Louis Bouyer, et al., *A History of Christian Spirituality*, vol 2, 432-433.

119. See Gerard of Zutphen, *The Spiritual Ascent: A Devotional Treatise*. Trans. by J P. Arthur (London: Burns & Oates, 1908) and McGrath, *Christian Spirituality*, 85.

120. McGrath, *Christian Spirituality*, 85.

121. Gerard of Zutphen, *The Spiritual Ascent*, 98.

122. See McGrath, *Christian Spirituality*, 85. The best-known writer of the *devotio moderna* movement was Thomas a` Kempis. See Thomas a` Kempis, *The Imitation of Christ*, ed. and trans. by Joseph N. Tylenda, *Vintage Spiritual Classics* (New York: Random House, 1998).

123. For further study of the Reformation see Alister E. McGrath, *Reformation Thought: An Introduction*, 3d ed. (Malden, MA: Blackwell, 1999). For further study of Reformation spirituality see Louis Bouyer, *A History of Christian Spirituality*, vol. 3, *Orthodox Spirituality and Protestant and Anglican Spirituality*, Trans. by Barbara Wall (London: Burns & Oates, 1969), 63-98.

124. See McGrath, *Christian Spirituality*, 86.

125. See Alister E. McGrath, *In the Beginning: The Story of the King James Bible and How it Changed a Nation, a Language, and a Culture* (New York: Doubleday, 2001).

126. McGrath, *Spirituality in an Age of Change*, 42.

127. McGrath writes about these three resources in two of his works of which this section is a summary. See *Christian Spirituality*, 86-88 and *Spirituality in an Age of Change*,

42-43.

128. McGrath, *Spirituality in an Age of Change*, 43.

129. See John Calvin, *Institutes of the Christian Religion*, 2 vols., ed. John T. McNeill, The Library of Christian Classics, vols. 20-21 (Philadelphia: Westminster, 1960, 1961). For further study on Calvin and spirituality see John Calvin, *The Piety of John Calvin: An Anthology Illustrative of the Spirituality of the Reformer*, trans. and ed. by Ford L. Battles (Grand Rapids: Baker, 1978); John Calvin, *Golden Booklet of the True Christian Life*, trans. by Henry J. Van Andel (Grand Rapids: Baker, 1952); John Calvin, *John Calvin: Writings on Pastoral Piety*, trans. and ed. Elsie A. McKee, The Classics of Western Spirituality: A Library of the Great Spiritual Masters (Mahwah, NJ: Paulist, 2001); William J. Bouwsma, "The Spirituality of John Calvin," in *Christian Spirituality*, vol. 2, 318-333; and Lucien J. Richard, *The Spirituality of John Calvin* (Atlanta: Knox, 1974). For a biography on Calvin, see Alister E. McGrath, *A Life of John Calvin: A Study in the Shaping of Western Culture* (Malden, MA: Blackwell, 1990).

130. McGrath, *Spirituality in an Age of Change*, 43.

131. McGrath, *Spirituality in an Age of Change*, 43.

132. Martin Luther, "A Simple Way to Pray," translated by Carl J. Schindler, *Luther's Works*, vol. 43, ed. Gustav K. Wiencke (Philadelphia: Fortress, 1968), 200. For further study of spirituality and Luther see Jared Wicks, *Luther and His Spiritual Legacy*, Theology and Life Series, vol. 7 (Wilmington, DE: Glazier, 1983) and Marc Lienhard, "Luther and Beginnings of the Reformation," in *Christian Spirituality*, vol. 2, 268-299. For a biography of Luther see Roland H. Bainton, *Here I Stand: A Life of Martin Luther* (Nashville: Abingdon, 1950).

133. McGrath, *Christian Spirituality*, 87. McGrath's emphases.

134. McGrath, *Christian Spirituality*, 87. McGrath believes that although Luther is primarily remembered as a theologian and ecclesiastical activist that he had a deep pastoral concern for the spirituality of Christians. See McGrath, *Christian Spirituality*, 158.

135. For further study on meditation see Peter Toon, *Meditating as a Christian: Waiting Upon God* (London: HarperCollins, 1991) and *The Art of Meditating on Scripture: Understanding Your Faith, Renewing Your Mind, Knowing Your God* (Grand Rapids: Zondervan, 1993).

136. Charles Haddon Spurgeon, "Our Manifesto," *The Metropolitan Tabernacle Pulpit: Sermons Preached and Revised by C. H. Spurgeon during the year 1891*, vol. 37 (Pasadena, TX: Pilgrim, 1975), 37. Spurgeon's emphasis. For an excellent biography on Spurgeon see Lewis A. Drummond, *Charles Spurgeon* (Grand Rapids: Kregel, 1990).

137. McGrath, *Beyond the Quiet Time*.

CHAPTER 3

MCGRATH'S EVANGELICAL THEOLOGY AND ITS RELATIONSHIP TO HIS EVANGELICAL SPIRITUALITY—PART TWO

"A cluttered playing field" is how Eugene Peterson, the respected writer of spiritual theology, describes current day conversations about spirituality. He believes there is an imprecision that pervades most discussions. Peterson sees elements which contribute to this confusion. He sites an attitude of spiritual elitism which looks down on others as unspiritual. Additionally he recognizes as problematic individuals who move away from the Bible to embrace the world of self-help, leading to a diluted gospel message. Finally, Peterson denounces spirituality that becomes theologically amnesic and isolated from God.[1]

What does Peterson propose to clean up this litter? He calls for a "spirituality [that] begins in theology (the revelation and understanding of God) and is guided by it."[2] He then states, "Theology is never truly apart from being expressed in the bodies of men and women to whom God gives life and whom God then intends to live a full salvation life (spirituality)."[3]

As discussed in chapter two, Peterson's call for spirituality to begin in theology is exactly the foundation that Alister McGrath lays. Also discussed in the last chapter was McGrath's view of Jesus Christ and how knowing God transforms a person's life. McGrath sees Christology and soteriology[4] as two sides of the same coin. Older works of theology often drew a sharp distinction between the person of Christ and the works of Christ as if they were independent areas of thought. Although McGrath separates the two for educational presentation purposes, he argues for the close connection of the two. Since the person of Christ has already been considered in chapter two, attention will be given to McGrath's views of the work of Christ in regard to conversion.[5] Following this emphasis, deliberation will be given to the importance of proclaiming this conversion in evangelism and the strategic importance of spiritual disciplines for Christian growth. Finally the ministry of the Holy Spirit will be examined, especially looking at His work in the church.

Conversion, Evangelism, and Spiritual Disciplines

McGrath sees the distinctiveness of the Christian approach to salvation in two ways. First, salvation is understood to be grounded in the life, death, and resurrection of Jesus Christ. For the Christian faith this is constitutive and not just illustrative. McGrath summarizes Colin Gunton by saying, "Christ does not just reveal something of importance to us; he achieves something for us—something without which salvation would not be possible."[6] This describes Christ as being the substitute for mankind and "reflects the fundamental conviction that something new happened in Christ which makes possible and available a new way of life."[7] McGrath says this approach continues to be definitive within modern evangelicalism.

Second, according to McGrath the distinctiveness of Christian salvation is shaped by Jesus Christ. He says that Christ provides a model or paradigm for the redeemed life. He cautions against viewing this as a mere external imitation of Christ which he sees as Pelagian. He states that "the Christian life is a process of 'being conformed to Christ,' in which the outward aspects of the believer's life are brought into line with the inward relationship to Christ, established through faith . . . based upon the idea of God conforming the believer to the likeness of Christ through the process of renewal and regeneration brought about by the Holy Spirit."[8]

McGrath describes the cross of Christ as the foundation of salvation. He avoids use of the phrase "theory of the atonement" because he sees it as cumbersome and unhelpful. Preferring the term "soteriology," McGrath groups four central controlling themes or images when he discusses the meaning of the cross and resurrection of Christ.[9]

The cross as a sacrifice provides the first theme for McGrath's soteriology. Drawing upon Old Testament imagery and expectations, the New Testament presents Christ's death upon the cross as a sacrifice. Especially associated with the Letter to the Hebrews, this approach "presents Christ's sacrificial offering as an effective and perfect sacrifice, which was able to accomplish that which the sacrifices of the Old Testament were only able to imitate, rather than achieve."[10]

The second theme for McGrath's soteriology is the cross as a victory. The New Testament presents considerable emphasis upon "the victory gained by Christ over sin, death, and Satan through his cross and resurrection."[11] According to McGrath, the *Christus victor* theme brings together a series of thoughts, centering on the idea of decisive victory over forces of evil and oppression.

The cross and forgiveness provide the third theme for McGrath's soteriology. This approach centers on "the death of Christ providing the basis by which God is enabled to forgive sin."[12] Why is the idea of forgiveness so important? McGrath answers by stating, "Man needs to know that despite his sin, he may enter into fellowship with God. One of the most remarkable features of the Gospel is the assertion that man is brought to God through God being brought to man."[13]

McGrath identifies three main suggested models that have been used to understand the manner in which forgiveness of sins is related to the death of Christ.[14] The representative model presents Christ as the covenant representative of humanity. McGrath states, "By coming to faith, individuals come to stand within the covenant, and thus share in all its benefits, won by Christ through his cross and resurrection - including the full and free forgiveness of our sins."[15]

The second model of forgiveness of sins is of participation which states that through faith, believers participate in the risen Christ. According to McGrath, "As a result of this, they share in all the benefits won by Christ, through his obedience upon the cross. One of those benefits is the forgiveness of sins."[16]

Substitution is the third model of forgiveness of sins. McGrath states, "Christ is here understood to be a substitute, the one who goes to the cross in our place. Sinners ought to have been crucified, on account of their sins. Christ is crucified in their place. God allows Christ to stand in our place, taking our guilt upon himself, so that his righteousness—won by obedience upon the cross—might become ours."[17] McGrath especially identifies the legal and penal approaches to the death of Christ as of particular importance within evangelical theology citing Leon Morris, John Stott, and J. I. Packer as leaders.[18]

The cross as a moral example provides the fourth theme for McGrath's soteriology. He sees the demonstration of the love of God for humanity as a central aspect of the New Testament meaning of the cross. McGrath states, "In the deepest sense, the love of God for man is that of a God who stoops down from heaven to enter into the world of men, with all its agony and pain, culminating in the grim cross of Calvary."[19]

McGrath does not appear to see any one of these themes as predominate in the Bible. He compares the reaction of theologians to the cross as to individual responses for a great piece of architecture. Some view the building from a distance while others take close photographs of smaller sections. All are parts of the same building but look different and serve different functions. In relating this to the cross McGrath states, "The problem with many approaches to the cross is not so much that they are wrong, as that they are inadequate. Some people seem to think that one formula, sentence or analogy contains everything that needs to be said, or could ever be said, about the meaning of the cross of Christ. . . . But there is always more to the cross than we can imagine. It is inexhaustible."[20] McGrath sees the New Testament using a wide range of images to express the understanding of the work of Christ. He says we may describe these images as analogies, models, or metaphors "but the important point to appreciate is that we are attempting to explain or interpret what was going on between God, man, and Christ in the crucifixion and resurrection in terms of ideas we are already familiar with from everyday life. . . What happened on the cross cannot be reduced to a single statement or image. We have to build up a picture of what was going on by using a wide range of illustrations, each of which casts light on one particular aspect of our subject."[21]

In a similar vein, McGrath believes the terms used to articulate the doctrine of justification were appropriate to a bygone age. But he sees the same language as inadequate for today as Christian teachers of the past recognized the need to apply justification to their specific situation. McGrath then gives examples of how Augustine used neo-Platonist terms, Anselm of Canterbury used feudal terms, Thomas Aquinas used Aristotelian terms, and John Calvin used legal terms. In other words, McGrath believes these men "proclaimed the doctrine in terms that drew upon the experience, hopes, and fears of their own day and age."[22]

McGrath affirms that Protestant denominations have defined justification primarily in forensic terms, that is, an act of God by which a sinner is declared to be righteous. He even makes the distinction between the event of justification (God declares an individual to be righteous) and the process of sanctification (an individual is regenerated and renewed by the Holy Spirit).[23] He further elaborates by stating we are justified through faith on account of Christ; "the objective basis of our justification is the person and work of Jesus Christ, and the means which we appropriate this justification and make it our own is faith."[24]

Even though McGrath affirms these basic teachings of justification, he believes one must "learn to direct his proclamation of the gospel to the felt needs of modern humanity."[25] For McGrath the modern preacher "must become receptor-oriented, sensitive to the needs, fears, and aspirations of his audience, in order to gain a point of contact, a toehold by which his proclamation may be grounded in the existential situation of the hearers."[26] McGrath believes one can do this without compromising or distorting the gospel message, but one must take the "trouble to determine how the gospel, with its richness and multifaceted character, impinges upon modern humanity."[27]

As McGrath assesses contemporary Western society he relates justification to the existential, personal, and ethical dimensions of life.[28] For example, the themes of personal growth, personal development, personal relationships, and personal fulfillment are items on the life agendas of many. He believes the doctrine of justification can be recast in terms of personal relationships. While the traditional language of imputation and forensic are unfamiliar to many, "the idea of personal relationship is familiar to everyone from their own experience."[29] He states,

> The personalist approach to the doctrine of justification by faith thus makes a direct appeal to our experience of personal relationships and shows how these may be transformed. It speaks to us of a God who takes the initiative in addressing us and in offering us the possibility of a renewed and restored personal relationship with us. It remains faithful to the central biblical insights into the personal nature and purposes of God, and to the simple fact, so eloquently witnessed to in scripture and so powerfully confirmed through Christian experience, that God does not encounter us as an idea, concept, or argument—but as a person.[30]

McGrath is not without his critics for his views on justification. David Larsen states that McGrath's views on forensic justification are so broad that it is virtually unrecognizable.[31] Ken Sarles and William Sailer also question the broadness of McGrath's definition as well as his contextualization of the doctrine.[32] Yet, McGrath does not deny forensic justification, he simply sees it as one picture of many that the New Testament presents. He states, "Occasionally the term 'justification' also has a clearly *forensic* dimension in the New Testament, implying the image of a court of law. 'Justification' then assumes the meaning 'declared to be right, or in the right, before God as judge.' The verdict in question is basically about the individual's *status before God*."[33]

Traditionally contextualization has been discussed in missions and church growth literature. With the pluralization of Western civilization, contextualization is now being addressed in most arenas of Christian thought.[34] McGrath believes it is the responsibility of theologians to "know what the doctrine means, [and] to translate its significance into terms their readers and hearers may understand."[35] McGrath sees himself following in the tradition of C. S. Lewis when Lewis states, "We must learn the language of our audience . . . you must translate every bit of your theology into the vernacular. . . . I have come to the conviction that if you cannot translate your own thoughts into uneducated language, then your thoughts were confused. Power to translate is the test of having really understood one's own meaning."[36] McGrath believes if "the doctrine of justification is 'unintelligible,' it is because we have made it so and have failed to *explain* its power and relevance for the human situation."[37]

How does McGrath view salvation in relationship to a pluralistic world with many religions? McGrath defines himself as a particularist who affirms the "distinctiveness of Christian truth and salvation."[38] He sees the New Testament affirming the "*particularity* of the redemptive act of God in Jesus Christ."[39] He states, "The Christian tradition bears witness to a particular understanding of God and cannot be merged into the various concepts of divinity found in other religions. . . . In the Christian understanding, factual or cognitive knowledge of God is not regarded as saving in itself."[40] McGrath sees salvation differing considerably from one religion to another.[41]

In articulating his position, McGrath emphasizes that "Christianity has a particular understanding of the nature, grounds, and means of obtaining salvation."[42] He sees Christianity as "the only religion to offer salvation *in the Christian sense of that term*."[43] This Christian salvation is to be "proclaimed as a real and attractive possibility for those who are presently outside the Christian community."[44]

What about those who have never heard the Christian message? McGrath believes this message is not limited to human preaching. He states, "Where the word is not or cannot be preached by human agents, God is not inhibited from bringing people to faith in him, even if that act of hope and trust may lack the fully orbed character of an informed Christian faith."[45] Although not offering any documentation, McGrath says many Muslims have come to Christ through dreams and visions in which they encounter Christ.[46] McGrath emphasizes that,

"It is God who makes salvation possible through the work of Christ and who uses the preaching of the gospel as a means of actualizing that salvation. But it is not the only means."[47]

As a result of conversion or new birth, Christians should desire to share this life-changing experience with others through evangelism.[48] McGrath believes the evangelical emphasis on evangelism, which once was treated with contempt by mainline Christian denominations, has now been widely recognized as essential for the future of the church. He sees evangelism flowing naturally from four considerations.[49] First, because of the need for personal faith, questions arise concerning that faith and the responsibility of believers toward its development. Second, the evangelical proclamation of Jesus as Lord naturally expresses itself in desiring to extend the kingdom of God. Third, in order to remain faithful to Scripture, the biblical passages to proclaim Christ to the world must be taken with utmost seriousness. Fourth, because of the great joy of knowing Christ, evangelicals desire to share that experience with others.

McGrath's enthusiasm for evangelism shines forth as he states, "A colleague asked me recently if I believed in evangelism. 'Believe in it?' I retorted. 'I *rely* on it!' Evangelism is no longer seen as something undertaken only by cranks or overenthusiastic yet well-meaning college students; it is seen as integral to the life, mission, and well-being of the churches. Evangelism is refreshingly *normal*!"[50] For McGrath, evangelism is as simple as "issuing a personal invitation to come to faith, and become a Christian."[51]

In order for a believer to fully appreciate why the gospel is good news, McGrath encourages Christians to reflect on the biblical understanding of fallen human nature. He emphasizes how sin alienates people from God and prevents them from coming to know Him. The result is a restlessness within mankind because of the God-shaped vacuum within the human heart. McGrath advocates using six images, which he sees as thoroughly grounded in Scripture, as the means of presenting the gospel message. These six images of sinful humanity are: hungry, thirsty, empty, lonely, hopeless, and lost. McGrath sees these six images as especially felt within modern Western culture.[52]

For example, McGrath sees thirst as an indication of human emptiness and need. Individuals attempt to quench this thirst with all kinds of things, including Eastern religions and secular materialism. McGrath believes one can relate the gospel message to this thirst, emphasizing how Jesus gives water which will quench one's thirst forever. He advocates that one must develop the skill of "identifying the aspect of the gospel which is going to be of greatest importance to your friend."[53] McGrath quickly counters that this is not reducing the gospel to one aspect. He states, "All you are doing is working out which of the many facets of the gospel will be of particular relevance to their situation."[54]

McGrath encourages one to prepare a brief summary of the gospel message which can be shared in thirty seconds. He encourages believers to use parables, brief Biblical passages, Paul's theological terms, or personal experience. He believes that it helps to have a thumbnail sketch of the gospel at one's fingertips, so one can give a ready reply even in a brief time.[55]

Yet McGrath also has words of warning to evangelicals in regard to evangelism. He believes the world view and rationalism of the Enlightenment has negatively influenced the movement. He thinks it is a travesty "to equate [Biblical] truth with the Enlightenment notion of conceptual or propositional correspondence, or the derived view of evangelism as the proclamation of the propositional correctness of Christian doctrine."[56] He sees this concept of evangelism as "opening the way to the types of rationalism and formalism which have destroyed the vitality of Christian faith in the past."[57] Faith can become little more than mere intellectual assent to propositions and lose the vital and dynamic connection with the person of Jesus Christ. For McGrath, truth in the New Testament "is not abstract or purely objective; it is personal, and involves the transformation of the entire existence of those who apprehend it and are themselves apprehended by it."[58] Therefore, McGrath defines evangelism as "the proclamation of an objective truth with the expectation that this will give rise to a subjective response—that is to say, a response which involves the heart, mind and total being of those who hear it."[59]

Even though McGrath places evangelism as one of the hallmarks of evangelicalism, most of his writing in this area focuses on apologetics, which McGrath views as pre-evangelism.[60] He makes the distinction between apologetics affirming the truth and attraction of the gospel and evangelism issuing a personal invitation to come to faith. He sees apologetics as "helping people to understand what Christianity is about, and why it is so attractive and meaningful."[61] Therefore apologetics prepares the way for the evangelistic invitation.

Just as McGrath warned of Enlightenment rationalism effecting evangelism, he also sounds the same words of caution for apologetics. He believes the debate has shifted from academic approaches so "Christianity must commend itself in terms of its relevance to life, not just its inherent rationality."[62] He does not desire to discard or discredit traditional approaches to apologetics but only to supplement and complement them. In other words, "the *science* of apologetics needs to be complemented by the *art* of apologetics."[63]

McGrath recognizes the strength of issue-based apologetics, but he sees the great need for a people-based approach. He says, "Responsible apologetics is based on a knowledge of both the gospel and it audience. . . . The effective apologist is one who listens before speaking and who makes every effort to link the resources of the Christian apologetic tradition both to the needs of that person and to the level of that person's ability to handle argumentation and imagery. The art of effective apologetics is hard work."[64] For apologetics to be effective, McGrath says it "demands both intellectual rigor and pastoral concern, for when all is said and done, apologetics is not about winning arguments—it is about winning people."[65]

Once a person responds to the message of Christ, spiritual disciplines are very important for Christian growth and form a core tenet of evangelical spirituality according to McGrath. Many evangelicals easily accommodate themselves to the relaxed attitude of Western culture which McGrath believes seriously erodes Christian effectiveness and maturity. He calls for evangelicals to rediscover their own heritage, in both the New Testament and the older evangelical tradition. He believes this could be a first step toward re-creating a disciplined and effective evangelicalism.[66] Role models for evangelicals in this area, according to McGrath, are Richard Baxter,[67] John Owen,[68] and Matthew Henry,[69] to whom many younger evangelicals have never been exposed. McGrath also identifies Donald Whitney as a contemporary evangelical who makes an excellent contribution to the study of spiritual disciplines.[70]

McGrath addresses the spiritual discipline of a "quiet time" by encouraging evangelicals to "maintain the distinctive evangelical emphasis on Scripture, yet adopt approaches which avoid the weaknesses of the traditional 'Quiet Time.'"[71] Although not articulating his reasons why, McGrath says there is a widespread feeling among younger Christians that the traditional quiet time has become tired and problematic. He desires to develop an approach that affirms the centrality and vitality of the Scripture for the Christian life yet avoids the staleness of older methods.[72]

Illustrating his approach, McGrath develops five Bible studies to be used by individuals or small groups. These topical studies include Scripture reading, brief thoughts from historical Christian leaders, and probing questions and exercises for additional work beyond the study.[73] However, while being well written, they do not appear to move beyond the traditional quiet time in any significant way. It appears that McGrath desires to enhance the traditional quiet time yet in doing so he casts a shadow upon its use.[74]

Although McGrath identifies spiritual disciplines as one of the main tenets of evangelical spirituality, he has written very little in this area. His focus has primarily been upon the balance of discipline and freedom as it relates to the doctrines of justification and sanctification. He sees the doctrine of justification as "lying at the heart of the Reformation struggle for a return to authentic forms of Christian doctrine and spirituality."[75] McGrath considers it one the greatest paradoxes of the sixteenth century that a movement which placed great emphasis upon divine grace would also give enormous weight to human discipline.[76]

Illustrating this point further, McGrath cites Martin Luther's use of the New Testament imagery of a tree. Luther argues that the productivity of the tree is dependent on its roots. In other words, a healthy root structure leads to prolific fruit. For Luther, faith is what provides the sound root which is essential for the life of the tree. Because of the sound root of faith, the Christian is able to produce good fruit naturally.[77] For Luther, "the essence of good works is that they are performed in a spirit of thankfulness and a desire to please God. Faith thus establishes the proper motivation for good works. . . . We are thus liberated from an oppressive achievement-oriented mindset."[78]

McGrath next cites John Calvin's emphasis on the personal presence of Christ within the believer. Calvin indicates that the gospel concerns one's encounter with Christ and the union with Him through faith. A believer receives both the person and the benefits of Christ through faith.[79] For Calvin this means, "Christ . . . does not justify anyone without also sanctifying him or her."[80]

Therefore, both justification and sanctification are direct consequences of the presence of Christ in a believer. McGrath states, "Justification does not cause sanctification; sanctification does not cause justification; rather, both are caused by the transforming presence of Christ, which makes the believer right in the sight of God (justification) and simultaneously begins the process of conforming the believer to the likeness of Christ (sanctification). Sanctification is not understood as a human work; it is the work of God within us, conforming our likeness to that of Christ, who is already present within us."[81]

McGrath believes both Luther and Calvin laid a theological foundation for vital spiritual insights. Both emphasized that justification is not a result of obedience. Rather justification leads to obedience. With this foundation in mind, McGrath then addresses how discipline in the Christian life is a loving response to the love of God. He believes discipline clears one's spiritual life so that God may renew him through the full resources of His grace. McGrath does not believe this emphasis on discipline is inconsistent with the doctrine of justification by faith. He states,

> Justification by faith affirms that the Christian life does not begin through human achievement or merit but as a gracious gift of God on account of all that he has done for us through Jesus Christ. But that life, once started, needs to be continued—and part of that continuation is the process of sanctification, by which we are internally renewed by the work of the Holy Spirit. Discipline is our contribution, aided by God, to that process. We are not justified by discipline; but our sanctification is assisted by our willingness to collaborate with God, giving him breaks in our life in order that we can become like Christ.[82]

McGrath sees discipline as a form of spiritual obedience which leads to new qualities of faith and commitment to God. He believes personal discipline makes a vital difference to one's faith, empowering that faith to survive difficult times since discipline allows one to draw upon the very strength of God Himself.[83]

Along with writing about the balance of discipline and freedom as it relates to the doctrines of justification and sanctification, McGrath has written concerning Biblical images and spirituality. Although these images are not disciplines per se, they do illustrate McGrath's perspective on the Christian life. He sees these Biblical images as having exercised a controlling influence over Christian spirituality through the ages. These images include the feast, the journey, the exile, the struggle, purification, the internalization of faith, the desert, the ascent, darkness and light, and silence.[84] McGrath believes these are only representative of many Biblical images. He sees these images as having potential to stimulate the human imagination as well as deepening the intellectual and existential aspects of one's faith.

McGrath has written on the Christian life using the image of a journey[85] in order to assist those who are tired of superficial ways of approaching the Christian faith. McGrath believes that Christianity's basic ideas are often scrutinized without a connection to an enrichment of faith and a deepening of one's personal spiritual life. He uses the image of the journey to visualize the life of faith, especially referencing the exodus of Israel from Egypt and the journeying of Israel to the Promised Land. He chronicles four stages of the journey through the wilderness, identifying the landmarks as creation, exile, redemption, and consummation. Throughout the work he illustrates each point by giving short synopses of significant Christian leaders. These leaders are Jonathan Edwards, Martin Luther, J. I. Packer, Anselm of Canterbury, Alexander MacLaren, Susanna Wesley, John Bunyan, Dietrich Bonhoeffer, John Stott, Horatius Bonar, and C. S. Lewis.

McGrath believes it can be argued that "evangelicalism's greatest contribution to systematic theology in the second half of the twentieth century relates to the interplay of theology with other spiritual disciplines."[86] He believes that since evangelicals have affirmed the foundational role of theology, they have "gone on to explore the way in which theological foundations lead to the direction and development of various superstructures, particularly in the areas of pastoral care, preaching, spirituality, apologetics, and ethics."[87]

McGrath affirms the great importance of spiritual disciplines for evangelicals and challenges them to develop this element of their lives. He encourages caution against legalism and promotes the balance of discipline with freedom. Even though McGrath emphasizes the strategic nature of the spiritual disciplines, he has written very little detailing them. However as previously noted McGrath points his readers towards the works of Baxter, Owen, Henry, and Whitney in this area.

The work of Christ in salvation forms a core tenet of McGrath's theology. Taking this message of salvation to a lost world is also a hallmark of the same. Flowing from these two areas is McGrath's emphasis upon individual Christian growth, especially related to spiritual disciplines. From here McGrath continues his core tenets with the work of the Holy Spirit both individually and corporately within the body of Christ.

The Lordship of the Holy Spirit and the Christian Community

While McGrath draws no clear connection between his theological views regarding the Lordship of the Holy Spirit[88] and his views regarding spirituality, these theological precepts nevertheless bear noting. For how can spirituality exist apart from the Spirit? It could also be argued that the very nature of the person and role of the Holy Spirit inseparably intertwines these two facets of theology and spirituality.

Similarly McGrath's view of the Holy Spirit as binding together and working through the Christian community[89] closely ties together theology and its practical living out within the body of Christ. Therefore these two subjects of McGrath's core tenets will be considered together.

The Hebrew word, *ruach*, has a range of meanings each of which casts some light on the complex associations of the Christian notion of the Holy Spirit.[90] The English words—wind, breath, and spirit—are used to translate this single Hebrew term. According to McGrath, the Spirit as wind draws a parallel between the power of the wind and of God. The Spirit as breath speaks of life and is often linked with God's work at creation. McGrath then addresses the third use of *ruach* as charism which refers to the filling of an individual with the spirit of God "by which the person in question is enabled to perform tasks which would otherwise be impossible."[91] He sees this especially relating to prophecy.

McGrath defends the deity of the Holy Spirit by stating three important truths.[92] First, almost all the titles of God found in Scripture are applied to the Spirit which includes the designation "holy." Second, the functions given to the Spirit establish who He is. McGrath states, "If the Holy Spirit performed functions which were specific to God, it must follow that the Holy Spirit shares in the divine nature."[93] Third, the early church's baptismal formula included the Spirit which signifies support of the divinity of the Spirit.

What then does the Holy Spirit do? McGrath identifies three broad areas of the work of the Holy Spirit. First, the Spirit has a pivotal role in making God known to humanity in revelation. McGrath states the "task of the Holy Spirit is to lead us into God's truth; without that Spirit, truth remains elusive."[94] The Spirit is of particular importance in relationship to the writing of God's revelation. According to McGrath, the inspiration of Scripture affirms a God-given authority because it is God-breathed (*theopneustos*; 1 Timothy 3:16). McGrath also identifies the Spirit as being involved in the human response to revelation.[95]

The second and third work of the Spirit involves salvation and the Christian life. The Holy Spirit plays a major role in establishing a relationship between Christ and the individual as He convicts of sin and as He is a pledge to their salvation (2 Cor 1:22). The Spirit also has an important encouraging role in human obedience to Christ (Jn 14:25-26).[96] McGrath sees the Spirit as making real the presence of God in personal and corporate worship and devotion. He gives the examples of the Spirit's involvement in prayer, spirituality, and worship. He also emphasizes the Spirit's work in the morality of believers.[97] McGrath believes that many writers, classic and modern, have stressed the important role of the Holy Spirit in prayer, spirituality, and worship.[98]

Within evangelicalism, McGrath sees the Charismatic Movement as the catalyst for bringing the greatest recognition to the person and work of the Spirit[99] and as "one of the most significant developments in Christianity in the twentieth century."[100] C. Peter Wagner distinguishes three waves within the Pentecostal and charismatic movement.[101] The first wave was classic Pentecostalism which arose in the early 1900s in Topeka, Kansas and at the Azusa Street Mission in downtown Los Angeles with Charles Fox Parham and Joseph William Seymour. The second wave was associated with mainline denominations including Roman Catholics and took place in the 1960s and 1970s. The catalyst for this wave began in 1959 with Dennis Bennett, an Episcopal rector, when he announced to his congregation in Van Nuys, California that he had been filled with the spirit and spoke in tongues. Widespread focus on charismatic renewal took place within mainline denominations in Europe, North America, South Africa, and Latin America. The third wave has been called the "signs and wonders" movement. This movement emphasizes power encounters which include divine healing as well as evangelism. A leading figure within this movement, until his recent death, was John Wimber.[102]

Pentecostalism's history has been one of discomfort with theology as well as a pervasive anti-intellectual attitude according to Swiss theologian Walter Hollenweger, a long-time student of Pentecostalism. He believes this is partially due to Pentecostalism's stronghold in oral theology.[103] Hollenweger states oral theology operates "not through book, but through parable, not through thesis, but through testimony, not through dissertations, but through dances, not through concepts, but through banquets, not through a system of thinking, but through stories and songs, not through definitions, but through descriptions, not through arguments, but through transformed lives."[104]

McGrath also identifies this point of conflict by describing the tension among evangelicals between those who center on the Word and those who focus on the Spirit. He says, "Word-centered evangelicals often express a concern that an emphasis on the Holy Spirit might result in Scripture's being by-passed in favor of an immediate personal revelation to an individual."[105] On the other side, "those with a more Spirit-based theology or spirituality argue that a Word-based approach can easily degenerate into a cerebral approach to Christianity that fails to engage with Christian experience. Christianity can easily become understood as intellectual assent to revealed knowledge, rather than as being possessed by the Spirit of the living God."[106] McGrath believes both have important contributions to make and both agree that "a decisive enriching of personal Christian experience is possible through the work of the Spirit."[107]

Closely tied to this discussion of the work of the Spirit is the Christian community among and through which the Spirit works. McGrath sees at the heart of evangelicalism a deep-seated awareness of the importance of the Christian Community. The vitality of the Christian community is strategic to the tasks of evangelism, spiritual nourishment, teaching and discipling. The church as the body of Christ emphasizes the corporate rather than the individualistic notion of the Christian life.[108] Even though evangelicalism is committed to the church it "does not mean that it is committed to any one *denominational* understanding of the church."[109]

In fact, according to McGrath, the evangelical perception of the New Testament allows considerable diversity in relation to theories of the church. Because of this he sees evangelicalism as transdenominational, that is, evangelicalism is not confined to any one denomination. He sees considerable cross-fertilization between leading evangelical institutions. McGrath sees no inconsistencies with speaking of "Baptist evangelicals," "Methodist evangelicals," or "Presbyterian evangelicals." He also believes evangelicalism can be a trend within a mainstream denomination. Because of the affinity among evangelicals, McGrath sees the movement as ecumenical. Rather than being formally linked by denomination, evangelicals exist as a fellowship grounded in and defined by the truth of the gospel.[110]

Drawing from the creeds of Christendom, McGrath affirms the four defining characteristics of the Christian church as unity, holiness, universality, and apostolic.[111] Although McGrath does overview the ordinances of the church, he does not argue for any one position.[112] He strongly emphasizes that, "An evangelical commitment to a corporate conception of the Christian life does not entail the explicit definition of a theology of the church. Precisely because evangelicalism has no defining or limiting ecclesiology, it can accommodate itself to virtually any form of church order."[113] Historically, McGrath believes evangelicals have never been committed to one specific church order or model of the church.[114] For evangelicals, "The visible institution of the church is thus treated as a fundamental resource for the life of faith. Here believers may encounter and support one another and find mutual encouragement through praising God and hearing his Word."[115]

When identifying the core tenets of evangelical theology, McGrath usually lists four. But in his work, *Evangelicalism and the Future of Christianity*, he enumerates six. The list of four McGrath defines as a consensus of evangelical scholars, while the additional two he claims as his own.[116] These additional two tenets form this section on the Holy Spirit and the church. Yet when one studies McGrath's works, one finds very little written about either the Holy Spirit or the church. For example, McGrath acknowledges the tendency to make the Holy Spirit the "Cinderella of the Trinity," yet he covers the subject in only ten pages out of his six hundred and three page book on Christian doctrine.[117] He agrees the doctrine needs an entire chapter devoted entirely to the subject, but still he includes it as only a section of a chapter on the doctrine of God.[118] Although McGrath lists the Holy Spirit and the church as tenets of evangelicalism, in his writings the subject has not been given a high priority.

In chapters two and three McGrath's core tenets of theology have been considered. This consideration included the examination of McGrath's spirituality, as the two are closely related in his writings. That being true, the concluding section of chapter three will give further attention to this close connection of theology and spirituality in McGrath's writings.

The Connection Between McGrath's Theology and His Spirituality

The close connection between spirituality and theology is itself a core tenet of evangelical spirituality according to McGrath.[119] Insisting that spirituality must be built on a solid and reliable foundation in the self-revelation of God, McGrath sees the relationship between spirituality and theology as preventing spirituality from degenerating into a human-centered quest for heightened religiosity as well as preventing theology from becoming an abstract speculation about God. McGrath offers J. I. Packer's *Knowing God* as one of the finest exponents of this point.[120]

In articulating this close connection, McGrath believes that doctrine provides the fundamental framework for Christian living and therefore, spirituality. He sees Christian principles as resting on Christian doctrine. McGrath argues that doctrine is of central importance as "doctrine aims to provide a springboard to propel us into a personal response to the truth and the love of God, revealed in Jesus Christ."[121] Although McGrath believes that the heart of the Christian faith is a person, not a doctrine, he balances this by stating that the person of Christ gives rise to doctrine as soon as questions are asked about the identity of Christ.[122]

Of strategic importance to McGrath is the defining of doctrine because he sees Christian doctrine as the "response of the Christian church to God, as he has revealed himself, especially in the scripture and through Jesus Christ. It is an obedient, responsible, and faithful attempt to make sense of the cluster of astonishing and exciting possibilities opened up by the coming of Jesus Christ."[123] McGrath sees doctrine as serving four major purposes. In overviewing these four purposes McGrath articulates the close connection between theology and spirituality.

The first major purpose of doctrine is to tell the truth about the way things are.[124] Some argue for relevancy to be the *avant garde* of Christianity. But McGrath warns of the danger of people basing their lives upon an illusion or a blatant lie. McGrath states, "To allow 'relevance' to be given greater weight than truth is a mark of intellectual shallowness and moral irresponsibility."[125] He challenges Christians to ask two fundamental questions: Is it true? Is this worthy of belief and trust? McGrath sees doctrine as telling the truth in order that Christians may act upon the reliability of truth as the foundation of the Christian life. He believes a church which despises or neglects doctrine is losing its reason for existence and lapsing into a comfortable conformity with the world. McGrath sees "evangelicalism [as] one of the conspicuously few constituencies within modern Christianity that continues to regard systematic theology as an important discipline, both in terms of its intellectual credentials and its pastoral and spiritual relevance."[126]

Although McGrath sees doctrine as arising within the community of faith to give order and structure to its experience of and encounter with God, he also believes doctrine must become a stimulus to evangelism by attempting to share the experience and knowledge of God in Jesus Christ to those outside the Christian faith. Yet this order and structure as well as this sharing of faith all is based upon doctrine being true. In further elaborating on the truth-claims of Christian doctrine McGrath believes it is an important emphasis that doctrine concerns a historical event that is transmitted in a narrative form. It is occupied with the internal consistency of Christian truth-affirmations, and is oriented toward faith, representing a demand for personal involvement, rather than passive assent.[127]

The second major purpose of doctrine is as a response to the self-revelation of God.[128] God acted through the coming of Jesus Christ. Christian faith and doctrine are a response to God's action. McGrath believes that for Christian theology and spirituality one of the most cherished insights is that Jesus Christ represented God in addressing mankind. But how does one know of God's action? McGrath answers this question by pointing to the centrality of Scripture and buttressing his argument with the words of Martin Luther, "Scripture is the manger in which Christ is laid."[129] McGrath elaborates further as he says, "There is no other witness to the call of God through the life, death, and resurrection of Jesus Christ than this [Scripture]."[130] He sees Scripture as the central resource of doctrine and the common heritage of all Christians. McGrath also quickly subordinates doctrine and tradition to Scripture as he states, "Doctrine is always under scripture, its servant rather than its master. Doctrine stands or falls with the Word of God, revealed in scripture, in that this Word of God precedes, creates, and criticizes all doctrinal statements."[131]

The third major purpose of doctrine is to address, interpret, and transform human experience.[132] McGrath sees two extremes which must be avoided. The first is represented by a purely emotional faith which experiences God but is unable to coherently express that faith. According to McGrath this purely emotional approach is totally subjective. He believes it reduces faith to a muddled bundle of emotions and is completely inadequate. The second extreme is represented by the believer giving mental assent to a list of intellectual propositions. This severely objective approach is also inadequate because faith is more than just adherence to a collection of facts. McGrath believes the balance is found when the Christian faith is "grounded in experience, but its content may still be summarized in propositions."[133] McGrath sees no inconsistency with this view since both the proposition and the experience relate to the same greater reality. He states, "Objective and subjective aspects of faith are like two sides of the same coin—they may be different, but they are both essential aspects of the same thing. They both represent the same thing, viewed from different angles."[134]

With this close connection of the subjective and objective sides of Christian faith, McGrath believes the proper place of doctrine is to address and interpret experiences. He sees experiences as potentially unreliable and misleading; therefore "doctrine interprets our feelings, even to the point of contradicting them when they are misleading."[135] McGrath sees doctrine as stressing "the faithfulness of God to his promises, and the reality of the resurrection hope—even where experiences seem to suggest otherwise."[136] Therefore he concludes by stating, "The cognitive dimension of Christian doctrine is the framework upon which Christian experience is supported, the channel through which it is conveyed. It is a skeleton which gives strength and shape to the flesh of experience."[137]

The fourth major purpose of doctrine is to give Christians a sense of identity and purpose, both individually and as a community.[138] McGrath believes the life, death, and resurrection of Jesus gives the church her identity. He sees the proclamation of Jesus Christ as the reason for the church's existence, this message having the potential to transform the entire world. McGrath believes that as the church focuses on the central message of Jesus Christ, she has adhered to the ideas and values which guide the Christian vision of how mankind should live. He believes that Christians are moved to make doctrinal statements to give substance and expression to their experience with God as well as to transmit these beliefs from one generation to another. McGrath states, "The real lifeblood of the Christian faith is not doctrine as such, but the real and transforming presence of Jesus Christ in the life of individuals and the church. Doctrines are there to defend that presence."[139]

The close connection needed between theology and spirituality is also affirmed by Klaus Issler, but he goes a step further in calling for spirituality to "become a recognized theological component, meriting its own chapter in systematic theology."[140] He argues his case by stating,

> As it stands now, within the theological encyclopedia, principles about a relationship with God are usually treated in discussions of prayer or as an aspect of the work of the Spirit, placed within treatment of the doctrine of sanctification. Yet sanctification primarily refers to the process in which Christians become more righteous and Christlike. Of course, the doctrines of spirituality and sanctification are related, but Scripture always makes our relationship with God the ultimate focus and goal of Christian living (e.g., Jn 17:3). In addition, the process of sanctification is traditionally understood to be finished at the onset of glorification, yet our spirituality—our relationship with God—continues on into eternity. . . . By marking off a distinct subject of Christian spirituality for study and reflection . . . we bring greater clarity to the discussion, and at the same time heighten the importance of pursuing our relationship with God above the matters of sanctification, although they are related in Christian living. The issue is which should be given prominence, both in theory (e.g., theological texts) and in practice (e.g., what best motivates character formation).[141]

Although McGrath does not call for a new section in our systematic theology textbooks as Issler does, he strongly advocates the proper understanding of theology and its relationship to spirituality. For example, McGrath says, "Theology, in this classic sense of the term, is a heartfelt knowledge of divine things, something which affects the heart and the mind. It relates to both *fides quae creditur* and *fides qua creditur*, the objective content of faith, and the subjective act of trusting."[142] For too long theology has been viewed as a purely academic subject with the issues of personal spiritual formation and Christian living being pushed to the side.[143] McGrath believes it is time "to welcome them [spiritual formation and Christian living] back, and to do so by both rediscovering what theology is meant to be all about, and ensuring that the close link between theology and spirituality is preserved."[144] McGrath identifies Athanasius, Augustine of Hippo, Anselm of Canterbury, Thomas Aquinas, and Martin Luther as examples of "theologians who saw no tension between the intellectual exploration of the Christian faith and its practical outworking in spirituality, preaching, ministry, and pastoral care."[145] McGrath states, "Properly understood, theology embraces, informs and sustains spirituality."[146]

In order to illustrate the way theology supports, sustains, and stimulates Christian spirituality, McGrath presents seven areas of Christian theology to show the manner in which theology and spirituality interact.[147] McGrath begins his case studies with the doctrine of creation as he affirms God as Creator. He sees this doctrine as having major implications for spirituality, such as affirming that the material world was created by God and reflects God's goodness. By implication, he affirms that it is not necessary to withdraw from the world in order to secure salvation or to serve God properly. He also sees this doctrine as offering a major stimulus to study nature as a means of learning more about the wisdom and majesty of God.

The second case study McGrath offers concerns human nature and destiny as he affirms that humanity was created in the image of God. For McGrath this means, "If human beings are created with some type of capacity to relate to God, and if it is intended by God that such a relationship should exist and develop, then the question of how a relationship with God can be established and nurtured is of considerable interest."[148] Throughout the centuries Christians have debated this divine/human aspect to a relationship with God. McGrath believes Augustine's famous slogan, "God operates without us, and cooperates with us," communicates the essential truth. McGrath explains Augustine by stating, "This is to be understood that God brings about our conversion without any cooperation on our part; thereafter, however, there is a form of cooperation between God and the believer as the process of Christian living gets under way."[149]

The doctrine of the Trinity provides McGrath with the third case study as he details the way God ordered the salvation of humanity in history (economic Trinity) as well as interprets the relationship of the Godhead in terms of their mutual fellowship (social Trinity). McGrath also details the concept of *perichoresis* which allows for the individuality of the persons of the Godhead to be maintained, while insisting that each person shares in the life of the other two. Closely tied into this is the emphasis on appropriation which insists that the works of the Trinity are unified with every person of the Trinity involved in every outward action of the Godhead.[150] McGrath sees three themes as of particular importance for spirituality in relation to the Trinity. First of all, Christian understandings of worship and prayer are often constructed around the Trinitarian framework. Second, the doctrine of the Trinity gathers together the richness of the complex Christian understanding of God, yielding a vision of God to which the only appropriate response is adoration and devotion. Finally, the doctrine of the Trinity models a perfect community of equals, united by a bond of love.[151]

The doctrine of the incarnation is the fourth case study offered by McGrath. The incarnation focuses on the fact that God chose to enter this world in Jesus Christ. He believes this teaching is particularly important for Christian spirituality in the three areas of the knowledge of God, the suffering of God, and the commitment of God to the created order.

The fifth case study by McGrath involves the redemption of the world through Jesus Christ's death on the cross. He sees four central themes or images which articulate this teaching. The four themes are: (1) The cross as a sacrifice; (2) The cross as a victory; (3) The cross as the basis by which God is enabled to forgive sin; and (4) The cross as a demonstration of the love of God for humanity. According to McGrath, the doctrine of redemption stresses the costliness of human salvation and affirms the reality of human sin and the love of God for sinners.

The resurrection of Jesus Christ from the grave comprises McGrath's sixth case study of doctrine. The resurrection affirms the identity of Jesus as the risen Savior and Lord as well as affirming the Christian hope that Christians will be raised from the dead. Because of this hope Christians do not need to fear death.

McGrath's last case study deals with the doctrine of the final consummation of all things, pointing to the future coming of Jesus Christ as well as eternal life in heaven.[152] McGrath believes a "helpful way of conceiving heaven is to regard it as a consummation of the Christian doctrine of salvation, in which the presence, penalty and power of sin have all been finally eliminated, and the total presence of God in individuals and the community of faith has been achieved."[153]

Mark McMinn states, "Spirituality . . . seems so boundless, so infinitely prone to human distortion. We need theological boundaries in order to maintain orthodox and scripturally sound views of redemption, yet we also need the experiential depth of a personal spiritual journey."[154] Theology and spirituality are interdependent since one without the other is deficient. As McGrath has so aptly emphasized, spirituality alone is a human-centered quest for heightened religiosity. Yet theology by itself becomes an abstract speculation about God. But together these two entities form a dynamic and powerful combination. So how does theology relate to spirituality? McGrath says that for evangelicals, "good theology provides the essential foundation for responsible and authentic Christian spirituality."[155]

In chapter two spirituality was defined as an intimate relationship, individually and corporately, with the Trinitarian God—Father, Son, and Holy Spirit—which transforms the way one lives. Following this discussion on the definition of spirituality, McGrath's core tenets of theology were examined. Consideration was given to the effect his theology has upon his views of evangelical spirituality. It has been clearly seen that McGrath argues strongly for this close connection between theology and spirituality. In the next chapter, McGrath's example of joining theology and spirituality will be compared to spirituality in society and among other selected evangelical writers.

NOTES

1. Eugene Peterson, *Christ Plays in Ten Thousand Places: A Conversation in Spiritual Theology* (Grand Rapids: Eerdmans, 2005), 13.

2. Peterson, *Christ Plays in Ten Thousand Places*, 6.

3. Peterson, *Christ Plays in Ten Thousand Places*, 6.

4. McGrath's writings on the work of Christ for salvation include sections in *Christian Theology*, 386-422; *Evangelicalism and the Future of Christianity*, 72-75; *A Passion for the Truth*, 220-238; "A Particularist View: A Post-Enlightenment Approach," *Four Views of Salvation* and *Studies in Doctrine*, 82-121 and 353-453; *Iustitia Dei*; "Justification by Faith," in *The New Dictionary of Christian Ethics and Pastoral Theology*, 1995; and "Sin and Salvation," in *The New Dictionary of Christian Ethics and Pastoral Theology*, 1995.

5. See McGrath, *Christian Theology*, 2d ed., 317-321.

6. McGrath, *Christian Theology*, 388. Also, see Colin E. Gunton, *The Actuality of Atonement* (Grand Rapids: Eerdmans, 1989), 160-167 for his section on substitution.

7. McGrath, *Christian Theology*, 388.

8. McGrath, *Christian Theology*, 389.

9. This summary of McGrath's four images of the cross is taken from *Christian Theology*, 390-412. Overlapping and interrelated to these four images of the cross are presentations McGrath makes in his other works. In *What was God Doing on the Cross*, 45-85, he uses five images of the cross: a battlefield, a court of law, a rehabilitation clinic, a prison, and a hospital. In *Studies in Doctrine*, 90, McGrath identifies three categories of the cross: transactional, legal, and personal.

10. McGrath, *Christian Theology*, 391.

11. McGrath, *Christian Theology*, 395.

12. McGrath, *Christian Theology*, 399.

13. McGrath, *Studies in Doctrine*, 111.

14. For McGrath's presentation of these models see *Studies in Doctrine*, 111 and *Christian Theology*, 402-403.

15. McGrath, *Christian Theology*, 403.

16. McGrath, *Christian Theology*, 403.

17. McGrath, *Christian Theology*, 403.

18. See Leon Morris, *The Apostolic Preaching of the Cross* (Grand Rapids: Eerdmans, 1955); J. I. Packer, "What did the Cross Achieve? The Logic of Penal Substitution," *Tyndale Bulletin* 25 (1974): 3-45; and John R. W. Stott, *The Cross of Christ* (Downers Grove: InterVarsity, 1986).

19. McGrath, *Studies in Doctrine*, 98.

20. McGrath, *What was God Doing on the Cross?*, 47-48.

21. McGrath, *Studies in Doctrine*, 82-83. Although not specifically identified in his works, McGrath appears to differ with leading evangelicals on this point. British evangelical John Stott states, "the biblical doctrine of atonement is substitutionary from beginning to end." See Stott, *The Cross of Christ*, 10. Also, American evangelical Millard Erickson states the penal substitution theory is the central theme of the atonement. See Erickson, *Christian Theology*, 2d ed., 818-840.

22. McGrath, *Studies in Doctrine*, 358.

23. McGrath, *Studies in Doctrine*, 399.

24. McGrath, *Studies in Doctrine*, 401.

25. McGrath, *Studies in Doctrine*, 408.

26. McGrath, *Studies in Doctrine*, 408.

27. McGrath, *Studies in Doctrine*, 408.

28. For McGrath's discussion of these three dimensions see *Studies in Doctrine*, 408-453.

29. McGrath, *Studies in Doctrine*, 427.

30. McGrath, *Studies in Doctrine*, 436.

31. See David L. Larsen, *Biblical Spirituality: Discovering the Real Connection Between the Bible and Life* (Grand Rapids: Kregel, 2001), 169. Larsen sees evidence of evangelicals hedging on forensic justification. Along with McGrath, he identifies Roger Olson, Gabriel Fackre, N. T. Wright, and James Dunn.

32. See William S. Sailer, review of *Justification by Faith: What It Means for Us Today*, by Alister E. McGrath, *Evangelical Journal* 7:1 (1989): 42-44 and Ken L. Sarles, review of *Justification by Faith: What It Means for Us Today*, by Alister E. McGrath, *Bibliotheca Sacra* 147:586 (1990): 238-239.

33. McGrath, *Studies in Doctrine*, 370-371. McGrath's emphasis.

34. For example, see D. A. Carson, ed., *Telling the Truth: Evangelizing Postmoderns* (Grand Rapids: Zondervan, 2000) and John G. Stackhouse, Jr., ed., *Evangelical Futures: A Conversation on Theological Method* (Grand Rapids: Baker, 2000).

35. McGrath, *Studies in Doctrine*, 357.

36. C. S. Lewis, *God in the Dock: Essays on Theology and Ethics,* Walter Hooper, ed. (Grand Rapids: Eerdmans, 1970), 96, 98.

37. McGrath, *Studies in Doctrine,* 357. McGrath's emphasis.

38. McGrath, *Christian Theology,* 574.

39. McGrath, "A Particularist View: A Post-Enlightenment Approach," in *Four Views on Salvation in a Pluralistic World,* ed. Dennis L. Okholm and Timothy R. Phillips, Counterpoints Series (Grand Rapids: Zondervan, 1996), 163. McGrath's emphasis.

40. McGrath, "A Particularist View," 165.

41. McGrath uses these same thoughts in *A Passion for Truth,* 224-225. There is also considerable overlap with "New Dimensions in Salvation," in *New Dimensions in Evangelical Thought: Essays in Honor of Millard J. Erickson,* ed. David S. Dockery (Downers Grove: InterVarsity, 1998), 317-329.

42. McGrath, "A Particularist View," 174.

43. McGrath, "A Particularist View," 175. McGrath's emphasis.

44. McGrath, "A Particularist View," 175. The thoughts of this paragraph are also found in *A Passion for Truth,* 235-236.

45. McGrath, "A Particularist View," 179.

46. For more study relating to Muslims converting to Christ through dreams see Bill Musk, "Dreams and the Ordinary Muslim," *Missionology: An International Review* 16:2 (1988): 163-172 and Richard K. Kronk, "Non-literary Personal Revelation: The Role of Dreams and Visions in Muslim Conversion" (Th.M. thesis, Dallas Theological Seminary, 1993).

47. McGrath, "A Particularist View," 175. In this work McGrath spends most of his time defending particularism, which he considers a more important issue. Because of this, his section on the plight of the unevangelized raises more questions than it answers. See Terrance L. Tiessen, review of *More Than One Way? Four Views on Salvation in a Pluralistic World,* ed. Dennis L. Okholm and Timothy R. Phillips, *Evangelical Review of Theology* 21:1 (1997): 91-92 and David L. Smith, review of *More Than One Way? Four Views of Salvation in a Pluralistic World,* ed. Dennis L. Okholm and Timothy R. Phillips, *Didaskalia* 7:1 (1996): 65-66.

48. McGrath's writings on Evangelism include sections in *Evangelicalism and the Future of Christianity,* 75-78; *A Passion for Truth,* 175-179 as well as his complete works of *Explaining Your Faith; How Shall We Reach Them* (co-authored with Michael Green); and *Intellectuals Don't Need God.*

49. The four considerations are summarized from McGrath, *Evangelicalism and the Future of Christianity*, 75-76.

50. McGrath, "Starting Where People Are," in *How Shall We Reach Them*, ed. Michael Green and Alister McGrath (Nashville: Nelson, 1995), 4. McGrath's emphases.

51. McGrath, *Explaining Your Faith* (Grand Rapids: Baker, 1995), 15.

52. McGrath, *Explaining Your Faith*, 24-25.

53. McGrath, *Explaining Your Faith*, 25.

54. McGrath, *Explaining Your Faith*, 25.

55. McGrath, *Explaining Your Faith*, 29-32.

56. McGrath, *A Passion for Truth*, 177.

57. McGrath, *A Passion for Truth*, 177.

58. McGrath, *A Passion for Truth*, 178.

59. McGrath, *A Passion for Truth*, 177. For further study in evangelism an excellent resource is Alvin L. Reid, *Introduction to Evangelism* (Nashville: Broadman & Holman, 1998). Two additional resources by Reid relate evangelism in a practical way to today's postmodern teenagers. See Alvin L. Reid, *Light the Fire: Raising Up a Generation to Live Radically for Jesus Christ* (Enumclaw, WA: WinePress, 2001) and *Radically Unchurched: Who are They? How to Reach Them* (Grand Rapids: Kregel, 2002). Also, for his website see www.alvinreid.com.

60. See McGrath, *Explaining Your Faith*, 15.

61. McGrath, *A Passion for Truth*, 15

62. McGrath, *Intellectuals Don't Need God and Other Modern Myths*, 9.

63. McGrath, *Intellectuals*, 11. McGrath's emphases.

64. McGrath, *Intellectuals*, 11.

65. McGrath, *Intellectuals*, 12. McGrath considers himself foremost as an evangelist or apologist. See Hutchinson, "Interview with Alister McGrath," 73-82.

66. See McGrath, *Evangelicalism and the Future of Christianity*, 137.

67. See Richard Baxter, *The Practical Works of Richard Baxter*, 4 vols. (London:

Bohn, 1854), *The Reformed Pastor: A Pattern for Personal Growth and Ministry*, ed. by James M. Houston, Classics of Faith and Devotion Series (Portland: Multnomah, 1982), and *The Saint's Everlasting Rest* (New York: American Tract Society, 1758).

68. See John Owen, *Sin and Temptation: The Challenge of Personal Godliness*, ed. by James M. Houston, Classics of Faith and Devotion Series (Minneapolis: Bethany House, 1996) and *The Works of John Owen*, 16 vols., William H. Goold, ed. (Carlisle, PA: Banner of Truth, 1965-68).

69. See Matthew Henry, *The Complete Works of Matthew Henry: Treatises, Sermons, and Tracts* (Grand Rapids: Baker, 1997), *An Exposition of the Old and New Testament*, 6 vols. (New York: Haven, 1833) and *The Quest for Communion with God* (Grand Rapids: Eerdmans, 1954).

70. See McGrath, *Evangelicalism and the Future of Christianity*, 205. For further resources on Donald S. Whitney see, *Spiritual Discipline for the Christian Life* (Colorado Springs: NavPress, 1991). Additional books by Whitney include *How Can I Be Sure I'm a Christian? What the Bible Says About Assurance of Salvation* (Colorado Springs: NavPress, 1994); *Spiritual Disciplines within the Church: Participating Fully in the Body of Christ* (Chicago: Moody, 1996); and *Ten Questions to Diagnose Your Spiritual Health* (Colorado Springs: NavPress, 2001). For Whitney's website see www.spiritualdisciplines.org, accessed September 12, 2002.

71. McGrath, *Beyond the Quiet Time*, x.

72. McGrath, *Beyond the Quiet Time*, x-xi.

73. The five topics are being lost, being rescued, being in the world, believing and doubting and living and hoping. See McGrath, *Beyond the Quiet Time*, 25-107.

74. Carson chides McGrath on this point. See Carson, *The Gagging of God*, 562.

75. McGrath, *Spirituality in an Age of Change*, 175.

76. McGrath, *Spirituality in an Age of Change*, 175.

77. McGrath, *Spirituality in an Age of Change*, 182.

78. McGrath, *Spirituality in an Age of Change*, 182-183.

79. McGrath, *Spirituality in an Age of Change*, 183.

80. Calvin, *Institutes of the Christian Religion*, vol.1, 798.

81. McGrath, *Spirituality in an Age of Change*, 184.

82. McGrath, *Spirituality in an Age of Change*, 186.

83. McGrath, *Spirituality in an Age of Change*, 187-188.

84. See McGrath, *Christian Spirituality*, 88-109.

85. See McGrath, *The Journey*.

86. Alister E. McGrath, "Evangelical Theological Method: The State of the Art," in *Evangelical Futures: A Conversation on Theological Method*, ed. John G. Stackhouse, Jr. (Grand Rapids: Baker, 2000), 21.

87. McGrath, "Evangelical Theological Method," 21.

88. McGrath's writings on Pnuematology include sections in *Christian Theology*, 279-289; *Evangelicalism and the Future of Christianity*, 68-72; *I Believe*, 79-88; and *An Introduction to Christianity*, 207-213. The use of the term "Lordship of the Holy Spirit" by McGrath is unconventional for evangelicals. His use of this term emphasizes the importance of the role of the Spirit in salvation and sanctification. See *Evangelicalism and the Future of Christianity*, 68.

89. McGrath's writings on ecclesiology include sections in *Christian Theology*, 461-493; *Evangelicalism and the Future of Christianity*, 78-85; *I Believe*, 91-98; and *An Introduction to Christianity*, 213-221.

90. See McGrath, *Christian Theology*, 279.

91. McGrath, *Christian Theology*, 281.

92. McGrath's section on the deity of the Holy Spirit is found in *Christian Theology*, 281-284.

93. McGrath, *Christian Theology*, 283.

94. McGrath, *Christian Theology*, 286.

95. For further study of the role of the Holy Spirit in Biblical interpretation as well as the distinction between revelation and illumination see Duvall and Hays, *Grasping God's Word*, 196-202, R. C. Sproul, "The Internal Testimony of the Holy Spirit," in *Inerrancy*, ed. Norman L. Geisler (Grand Rapids: Zondervan, 1980), 333-354, and Gordon Fee and Douglas Stuart, *How To Read the Bible for All Its Worth: A Guide to Understanding the Bible*, 2d ed. (Grand Rapids: Zondervan, 1993).

96. See Alister E. McGrath, *I Believe: Exploring the Apostle's Creed* (Downers Grove: InterVarsity, 1997), 80-81.

97. See McGrath, *Christian Theology*, 287-288.

98. See McGrath, *Christian Theology*, 288. McGrath cites the following quote from Martin Bucer as an example. "So those who believe are not under the law, because they have the Spirit within them, teaching them everything more perfectly than the law ever could, and motivating them much more powerfully to obey it. In other words, the Holy Spirit moves the heart, so that believers wish to live by those things which the law command, but which the law could not achieve by itself."

99. See McGrath, *Evangelicalism and the Future of Christianity*, 69.

100. McGrath, *Historical Theology*, 252.

101. See C. Peter Wagner, *The Third Wave of the Holy Spirit* (Ann Arbor, MI: Servant, 1988). Also, see McGrath, *Evangelicalism and the Future of Christianity*, 69-70.

102. See McGrath, *Historical Theology*, 252-253 and Tony Lane, *Exploring Christian Thought* (Nashville: Nelson, 1996), 254-255.

103. Walter J. Hollenweger, *Pentecostalism: Origins and Developments Worldwide* (Peabody, MA: Hendrickson, 1997), 194, 196.

104. Hollenweger, *Pentecostalism*, 196.

105. McGrath, *Evangelicalism and the Future of Christianity*, 70.

106. McGrath, *Evangelicalism and the Future of Christianity*, 71.

107. McGrath, *Evangelicalism and the Future of Christianity*, 72.

108. McGrath, *Evangelicalism and the Future of Christianity*, 78.

109. McGrath, *Evangelicalism and the Future of Christianity*, 79. McGrath's emphasis.

110. McGrath, *Evangelicalism and the Future of Christianity*, 82-83 and McGrath, *Christian Theology*, 182.

111. For McGrath's discussion of the four marks see *Christian Theology*, 482-492 and *I Believe*, 91-93.

112. For McGrath's discussion on the doctrine of the sacraments see *Christian Theology*, 494-520.

113. McGrath, *Christian Theology*, 486.

114. See McGrath, *Evangelicalism and the Future of Christianity*, 79, 81.

115. McGrath, *Evangelicalism and the Future of Christianity*, 81.

116. See Alister E. McGrath, email to author, June 12, 2002.

117. See McGrath, *Christian Theology*, 279-289. In McGrath's section on the Trinity he devotes four pages to the *filioque* controversy surrounding the role of the Spirit.

118. McGrath, *Christian Theology*, 279.

119. This writer attended the annual meeting of the Evangelical Theological Society in Toronto, Canada, November 2002, where a sub-group on spiritual formation met for the first time. This sub-group will continue to be a part of the annual meeting of this society. Of interest at this first meeting was a paper delivered on spirituality and theology. See Robert L. Saucy, "Spiritual Formation in Theological Controversy," unpublished paper presented at the Evangelical Theological Society, Toronto, Canada, November 2002. Also, Thom Rainer, Dean of Southern Seminary's Billy Graham School of Missions, Evangelism, and Church Growth, lamented the fact that in theological education classical disciplines (biblical and theological studies) are often being set at odds with the practical (missions, evangelism, and church growth). He called for "the disciplines of classical and practical theology within seminaries . . . to work together for the good of the church and the glory of God." See Jeff Robinson, "Seminary Dean Calls for Unity of 'Odd Couple' Disciplines," *Baptist Press* Release, October 28, 2002.

120. See McGrath, *Evangelicalism and the Future of Christianity*, 136 and Packer, *Knowing God*.

121. McGrath, *Studies in Doctrine*, 235.

122. McGrath, *Studies in Doctrine*, 232-235.

123. McGrath, *Studies in Doctrine*, 237.

124. McGrath, *Studies in Doctrine*, 238-244 and McGrath, *The Genesis of Doctrine*, 72-80.

125. McGrath, *Studies in Doctrine*, 138.

126. McGrath, "Evangelical Theological Method," 20.

127. See McGrath, *The Genesis of Doctrine*, 74-78.

128. See McGrath, *Studies in Doctrine*, 245-255.

129. See McGrath, *Christian Doctrine*, 245. The full quote by Martin Luther states, "Therefore dismiss your own opinions and feelings, and think of the Scriptures as the loftiest and noblest of holy things, as the richest of mines which can never be sufficiently explored, in order that you may find that divine wisdom which God here lays before you

in such simple guise as to quench all pride. Here you will find the swaddling cloths and the manger in which Christ lies." See Martin Luther, "Prefaces to the Old Testament," translated by Charles M. Jacobs, *Luther's Works*, vol. 35, ed. E. Theodore Bachmann (Philadelphia: Fortress, 1960), 236.

130. McGrath, *Studies in Doctrine*, 245. Also see McGrath, *The Genesis of Doctrine*, 55.

131. McGrath, *Studies in Doctrine*, 251.

132. McGrath, *Studies in Doctrine*, 256-264, McGrath, *The Genesis of Doctrine*, 66-72, and Alister E. McGrath, "Theology and Experience: Reflections on Cognitive and Experiential Approaches to Theology," *European Journal of Theology* 2:1 (1993): 67-72.

133. McGrath, *Studies in Doctrine*, 257.

134. McGrath, *Studies in Doctrine*, 257.

135. McGrath, *Studies in Doctrine*, 263.

136. McGrath, *Studies in Doctrine*, 263.

137. McGrath, *The Genesis of Doctrine*, 71. This is in contrast to the view of Stanley Grenz as he states, "The integration of theology and spirituality, or the fostering of the practical intent of the theological enterprise, means that theology must arise out of the life of the believing community. That is, theology must flow from discipleship." See Grenz, *Revisioning Evangelical Theology*, 58. In reviewing a later work by Grenz, John Hammett states, "Grenz sees this experimental piety as the *sine qua non* of evangelicalism." Hammett differs with Grenz by stating, "I know of no other description of evangelicalism that uses the phrase or idea 'convertive piety' as Grenz does, or elevates it to a place of preeminence over doctrine, especially the doctrine of Scripture. . . I think Grenz is off here. Both the Reformation and neo-evangelicalism emphasized doctrine, because without orthodox doctrine, there is not gospel and no convertive piety." See John S. Hammett, review of *Renewing the Center: Evangelical Theology in a Post-Theological Era*, by Stanley J. Grenz, *Faith and Mission* 19:1 (2001): 112-114.

138. See McGrath, *Studies in Doctrine*, 265-276.

139. McGrath, *Studies in Doctrine*, 275.

140. Issler, *Wasting Time With God*, 252.

141. Issler, *Wasting Time With God*, 252.

142. McGrath, *Christian Spirituality*, 28.

143. To study developments in theological education which led to the division of

theology and spirituality see Edward Farley, *Theologia: The Fragmentation and Unity of Theological Education* (Philadelphia: Fortress, 1983).

144. McGrath, *Christian Spirituality*, 28.

145. McGrath, *Christian Spirituality*, 27. Also see McGrath, *The Future of Christianity*, 136-137.

146. McGrath, *Christian Spirituality*, 27 and McGrath, *The Future of Christianity*, 137.

147. This section of seven case studies is summarized from McGrath, *Christian Spirituality*, 35-81.

148. McGrath, *Christian Spirituality*, 42.

149. McGrath, *Christian Spirituality*, 43.

150. Issler also addresses the importance of the doctrine of the Trinity for spirituality. See Issler, *Wasting Time With God*, 40-41, 256.

151. See McGrath, *Christian Spirituality*, 51-52.

152. See McGrath, *A Brief History of Heaven*.

153. McGrath, *Christian Spirituality*, 76.

154. Mark R. McMinn, *Psychology, Theology, and Spirituality in Christian Counseling* (Wheaton: Tyndale, 1996), 258.

155. McGrath, "Evangelical Theological Method," 22.

CHAPTER 4

MCGRATH'S EXAMPLE COMPARED TO CONTEMPORARY SPIRITUALITY—PART ONE

While it has been seen that spirituality is difficult to define, it is also evident that the topic of spirituality has captured the attention of our postmodern generation. The consideration of evangelicalism's leading authors on this subject will doubtlessly prove insightful as to its effect upon evangelicalism.

This chapter will therefore compare McGrath's evangelical theology and evangelical spirituality to spirituality in society as well as to selected current evangelical writers of spirituality. In examining spirituality within Western society attention will be given to surveying the last fifty years of spirituality as well as to postmodernism and pluralism and their effect upon spirituality. Five contemporary evangelical writers of spirituality will be surveyed in the next two chapters, evaluating their theology and spirituality before comparing their works with McGrath's.

Comparison to Spirituality in Society

The last fifty years of American spirituality is analyzed by Robert Wuthnow, Professor of Sociology at Princeton University.[1] He defines American spirituality as "all the beliefs and activities by which individuals attempt to relate their lives to God or to a divine being or some other conception of a transcendent reality."[2] Wuthnow identifies the 1950s as a time when church attendance reached all time highs and consumed the energy of more Americans than in any subsequent decade. Yet he believes the spirituality of the 1950s was superficial and lacked introspection and depth. This shallowness manifested itself as most Americans associated spirituality with church attendance.[3]

The 1960s and early 1970s saw a freewheeling and eclectic style of spirituality. According to Wuthnow, devotional practices included breathing techniques, exercise, and chanting in an effort to make spirituality an activity of the whole person. Spirituality meant paying attention to inner voices of feelings and exposing oneself to alternative experiences. Wuthnow sees the most significant impact on spirituality, during this period, as society's understanding that spirituality and organized religion are different and might run in opposite directions.

The late 1970s and early 1980s brought about an emphasis on spiritual and moral discipline to correct the excesses of the 1960s. In the public arena, Ronald Reagan was President, and William Bennett waged war against drugs. Conservative Evangelical leaders such as Jerry Falwell and Pat Robertson were prominent as they called for stricter standards of morality and activism in the political and public arena. They challenged the country to call upon God for divine guidance. Liberal denominations were declining and conservative ones were growing.[4] The Southern Baptist Convention was embroiled in doctrinal controversy as the denomination made giant strides towards a conservative resurgence.[5] According to Wuthnow, the spirituality of this period focused on individuals applying how-to techniques to their personal lives in areas such as money and sex.[6]

The late 1980s and the 1990s brought about an emphasis on spirituality encountered through mysterious events. Wuthnow says spirit guides, channeling, crystals, encounters with angels, and near-death experiences moved from the tabloids into mainstream culture. New Age groups and books captured America's fascination with miracles and spiritual experiences.[7] Wuthnow believes that one important development of the late 1980s and 1990s was a renewed interest in relating the inner self to the sacred. He believes books of this period "offered a beguiling mixture of therapeutic, recovery, and religious advice that would help create the kind of self needed to seek spirituality despite growing uncertainties about the nature of the sacred."[8]

Each decade was summarized by Wuthnow in identifying the public debates about the self. The 1950s he depicted as being characterized by soft, other-directed suburban bureaucrats who survived by fitting in and conforming. The 1960s found individuals rebelling against the fifties' norms. They searched for themselves, "tuning out" and "turning on," and doing their "own thing." Despite efforts to recover discipline, Wuthnow described the 1970s as the Me Decade, and the 1980s as the Decade of Greed. The 1990s was an era of addictions and self-help groups as America attempted to recover.[9]

America's dry spell of secularism is over according to Wuthnow as spirituality's popularity continues to escalate. He sees a profound change taking place in spiritual practice as spirituality has become a vastly complex quest. For many people, a growing uneasiness about objective knowledge exists. A shift away from objective truth is taking place.[10] Wuthnow predicts that interest in spirituality will not wane in the next century although he believes it will become increasingly difficult to determine precisely what spirituality means.[11]

Just as Wuthnow has chronicled the last fifty years of spirituality, evangelical theologian Millard Erickson has written about the history of shifts in culture and society.[12] He first identifies the premodern time as the period preceding the Enlightenment, including the medieval and ancient periods. Erickson identifies common elements of premodernism as: (1) A belief in the rationality of the universe; (2) A belief that observable nature was not the whole of reality; and (3) A belief in dualism emphasizing an unseen element of reality.[13] He says the premodern era was teleological, viewing the universe as having a purpose. A basic belief in the objective existence of the physical world and a correspondence theory of truth also characterized this period.

The Enlightenment initiated the modern era by abandoning the transcendent conception of reality in focusing on the immanent of human reason. Several characteristics of this time period are identified by Erickson as: (1) A naturalism that restricted reality to the observable system of nature; (2) A humanism that elevated mankind to be the highest reality and value; (3) A scientific method of observation and experimentation as the source of truth; (4) A reductionism of the scientific method as the only means to attain objectivity; (5) A progress in overcoming the problems of humanity; (6) A view of nature as always changing through the process of evolution rather than by a Creator and Designer; (7) A certainty of knowledge because of objectivity; (8) A determinism founded on the belief that fixed causes followed events in the universe; (9) An individualism established on the assumption that individuals can discover truth for themselves without conditioning particularities of time and place; and (10) An anti-authoritarianism which views mankind as the final and most complete measure of truth.[14]

Scholars have disagreed over who originally coined the term "postmodern."[15] Lawrence Cahoone attributes its first use to the German philosopher Rudolf Pannwitz, who in 1917 described the nihilism of twentieth-century Western culture as postmodern.[16] Despite this debate over the origins of the term, a consensus exists that it first widely appeared in the 1930s.[17] Yet postmodernism did not emerge as a cultural phenomenon until between 1960 and 1990.[18] Gene Veith states most writers associate the postmodern shift with the counterculture of the 1960s, 1968 being a pivotal year. He identifies the protests of the Vietnam War, the Civil Rights movement, and the youth idealism of Marxism as key components.[19] Another writer dates the beginning of postmodernism as taking place at 3:32 P.M. on July 15, 1972, when the Pruitt-Igoe housing development in St. Louis was demolished by the government, representing the failure of modernism.[20]

Thomas Oden offers another assessment noting the fall of the Berlin Wall in 1989 as the key event separating modernism and postmodernism.[21] Norman Cantor, evaluating the twentieth century in the United States, aptly states that presence in this time of transition makes evaluation harder since hindsight is often more clear.[22]

Even with disagreement over its beginning, it is still possible to identify characteristics of postmodernism. Erickson identifies these basic motifs as: (1) The objectivity of knowledge is denied; (2) Knowledge is uncertain; (3) All-inclusive systems of explanations are impossible; (4) The inherent goodness of knowledge is questioned; (5) Progress is rejected; (6) The ideal is community-based knowledge because truth is defined by and for the community; and (7) The scientific method is called into question because truth is not known simply through reason but also through intuition.[23]

Stanley Grenz states, "The central hallmark of postmodern cultural expression is pluralism."[24] D. A. Carson further elaborates as he sees philosophical pluralism spawning postmodernism. According to Carson, philosophical pluralism states, "That any notion that a particular ideological or religious claim is intrinsically superior to another is *necessarily* wrong. The only absolute creed is the creed of pluralism. No religion has the right to pronounce itself right or true, and the others false, or even . . . relatively inferior."[25] Carson then identifies eight correlatives of pluralism which show societal trends that are partly causes and effects of pluralism. These eight correlatives are: (1) A secularization which marginalizes religion; (2) A New Age theosophy which focuses on self-awareness, self-fulfillment, and self-actualization in order to be one with the universe/god; (3) A rising Biblical illiteracy; (4) A vague appeal to the cosmic christ often deconstructed from the historical and Biblical Christ; (5) A sheer pragmatism found in baby boomers; (6) A hegemony of pop culture; (7) A rugged individualism veering toward narcissism; and (8) A therapeutic culture developed by a Freudian fraud.[26]

Elizabeth Lesser's work entitled *The New American Spirituality* provides an eye opening example of the effect postmodernism and pluralism have upon spirituality.[27] The Omega Institute, located in Rhinebeck, New York, was co-founded by Lesser in 1977 and has become America's largest adult-education center focusing on wellness and spirituality. She introduces her work with an "aha" moment that she feels compelled to share.

> On this particular day I was eating lunch with Babatund Olatunji, the West African drum master and world-music innovator. Seated next to Baba was the American poet Allen Ginsberg, engaged in conversation with Gelek Rinpiche, a Tibetan Buddhist lama, and Joseph Shabalala, a South African musician and freedom fighter. They were talking about their twin passions, politics and spirituality—and how challenging it is to combine the two. At the other end of the table was the onetime heavyweight champion of the world Floyd Patterson, picking over his plate of tofu salad, and discussing his workshop, 'The Tao of Boxing,' with a Chinese tai chi master, a tiny woman dressed in black pajamas. Next to them sat Huston Smith, the renowned authority on the history of religions, chatting with Ysaye Barnwell of the gospel group Sweet Honey in the Rock, and John Mahawk, a Seneca author and spiritual leader.
>
> Catching bits and pieces of conversations, I turned to Baba Olatunji and asked, 'So, what do you make of this, all these traditions meeting and merging?' Baba leaned back in his chair and surveyed the scene. Then, waving his fork at the extraordinary cast of characters seated around us, he announced, 'This is a new kind of spirituality. It's American, and one day it will be the world.'[28]

In Lesser's work, she encourages her readers to walk a spiritual path with or without religious help because all paths are available and none are exclusively right or wrong or required. She sees the first step of the spiritual path as finding a satisfying definition of spirituality. In searching for this definition, she urges her readers to lay aside their religious beliefs or anything that causes resistance. She believes deconstructing the word 'spiritual' is freeing and enlightening. As one searches for a definition, she instructs her readers to be open to things one has been conditioned to reject, become comfortable with the unknown, and be fearless.[29] Lesser states that 'spirituality is nothing more than a brave search for the truth about existence.'[30] She defines spirituality by stating, "It is a mystery, the mystery behind the 'marvelous structure of the existing world.'"[31]

Alister McGrath has also responded to the extreme rationalism of modernism. He cautions evangelicals against making reason their final authority. Yet even as he issues this warning, McGrath does not swing the pendulum to fully endorse postmodernism, much less pluralism, as Lesser has done. He challenges evangelicals to develop a healthy spirituality arguing that rationalism does not touch or effect the heart. In developing this evangelical spirituality, McGrath wants to ensure that evangelicals do not abandon the truth of their theology. He states, "Evangelicalism provides a significant vantage-point from which to critique aspects of the postmodern worldview, not least its apparent over-reaction to the Enlightenment emphasis on truth. Truth remains a matter which is of passionate importance to evangelicalism, even if there is considerable cultural pressure in western society to conform to its prevailing 'my view is as good as yours' outlook."[32] Therefore, McGrath sees evangelical theology as providing the framework to guide, to evaluate, and to undergird evangelical spirituality.

In dealing with postmodernism's effect on spirituality, it can best be described as lacking a foundation of truth.[33] Lesser illustrates this point well. The relativism of postmodernism combined with the subjectivism of secular spirituality provides a dangerous mixture with no room for objective truth.

Lesser is perhaps at least partially correct in her assessment of spirituality. For "real spirituality," in other words experiencing a life in tune with the One, true living God, truly is the mystery behind the structure of the existing world. However what she, as well as most modern-day secular seekers of spirituality lack is a firm or real plan for at least beginning to unravel and discover this mystery. McGrath's combining the truth of theology with the experience of spirituality becomes even more significant. The presence of truth not only guides one's experience, it also provides a solid foundation upon which personal or societal spirituality can be built. Although McGrath is aware of postmodernism and perhaps adjusts to accommodate new insights from it, he stands in contrast to the overall lucid emphasis of spirituality in Western society.

Comparison to Spirituality in Selected Evangelical Writers

How has the subjectivism of postmodernism affected the emphasis on spirituality among evangelicals? A brief overview of five evangelical writers of spirituality will begin with Henry Blackaby and Richard Foster who heavily emphasize the subjective experience yet negate the importance of completely undergirding these experiences with theological truth. Gary Thomas will be considered next as he clearly seeks to be evangelical in his spirituality yet fails to articulate his evangelical theological views. The last two writers to be considered, Dallas Willard and Bruce Demarest, consciously seek to build an evangelical spirituality upon evangelical theology.[34] Each one of the writers will be compared to McGath's evangelical spirituality based upon the contents of his evangelical theology previously considered in the last chapter.

Henry T. Blackaby, Henry Blackaby Ministries[35]

Henry Thomas Blackaby was born April 15, 1935 in William's Lake, British Columbia, Canada, to Gerald and Jennifer Blackaby. He and his wife, Marilynn, have five children. He is a graduate of Golden Gate Seminary and has served as pastor of churches in California and Canada. In 1988 he became the director of prayer and spiritual awakening with the North American Mission Board (formerly the Home Mission Board) of the Southern Baptist Convention. In 1994, LifeWay Christian Resources, the North American Mission Board, and the International Mission Board, jointly employed him to lead in prayer and spiritual awakening for the three largest agencies of the Southern Baptist Convention. He continued that relationship until recently announcing the beginning of a new ministry, Henry Blackaby Ministries. Blackaby is best known for his discipleship study "Experiencing God,"[36] which has sold 3.5 million copies and has been translated into more than 40 languages. This study has also spawned numerous discipleship products and conferences.

Blackaby's workbook eventually became a full length book[37] in which he warns against merely knowing about God, stating that this never satisfies. He says, "Really knowing God only comes through experience as He reveals Himself to you. . . . We come to know God as we experience Him. God reveals Himself to us through our experience of Him."[38] His aim in this work is to assist Christians in experiencing God in greater and more personal dimensions.

Blackaby sees common experiences that identify the ways God works with a person or group to involve them in His work. He calls these common experiences the seven realities of experiencing God.[39] The bulk of his work centers on explaining these realities.

The first reality states that "God is always at work around you."[40] Blackaby rightly emphasizes that God did not create the world and leave it to function on its own. He believes God is orchestrating history to bring about the redemption of those who are lost. According to Blackaby, God has chosen to bring this about through the work of His people.

God's love relationship with man comprises the second reality. It states that "God pursues a continuing love relationship with you that is real and personal."[41] Blackaby believes God created humanity to have a love relationship with Him. By sending Jesus to die for the world's sin, God was demonstrating his great love. According to Blackaby, this intimate love relationship is the most important element in knowing and doing the will of God.

The third reality states that "God invites you to become involved with Him in His work."[42] Blackaby does not believe that Christians should dream dreams for God and then ask Him to bless their plans. Instead, Blackaby sees God as already working and already having a plan. He desires Christians to discern His plan and to join Him in His work.

Blackaby's fourth reality states that "God speaks by the Holy Spirit through the Bible, prayer, circumstances, and the church to reveal Himself, His purposes, and His ways."[43] Blackaby believes God speaks to His people through the Holy Spirit. He sees the Spirit as using the Bible, prayer, circumstances and the church to communicate to the individual Christian. According to Blackaby, "no one of these methods of God's speaking is, by itself, a clear indicator of God's directions. But when God says the same thing through each of these ways you can have confidence to precede."[44]

"God's invitation for . . . [one] to work with Him always leads . . . to a crisis of belief that requires faith and action" forms the fifth reality.[45] Blackaby believes that God calls Christians to assignments which cannot be accomplished without Him. The God-sized dimensions of these assignments Blackaby sees as bringing about a crisis of belief which requires faith and action. According to Blackaby this crisis of belief hinders many believers from experiencing the power of God because they are unwilling to move forward.

The sixth reality states that one "must make major adjustments in . . . [his] life to join God in what He is doing."[46] Blackaby believes for one to get from where he is to where God is, major adjustments are required. He sees these adjustments relating to one's thinking, circumstances, relationships, commitments, actions and beliefs.

Experiencing God through obedience constitutes the seventh reality. Blackaby states that one comes to "know God by experience as . . . [one] obeys Him and He accomplishes His work through [him]."[47] Obedience, Blackaby maintains, must take place no matter how insensible it may seem. The power and presence of God is experienced in one's life as God accomplishes His purpose, according to Blackaby.[48]

Blackaby has also written concerning an intense cry in America for a fresh encounter with God.[49] He says that frequently the experience of the average Christian is so bad, so dry and so empty that the desire for a fresh touch from God in revival is rampant. He has written this book as "a resource to encounter God through His Word in such a way that God's people may experience true, deep, and lasting revival in their lives. Then they will see God work through their changed lives to touch the rest of the world with His salvation."[50] Blackaby not only illustrates revivals from Scripture accounts, but he also gives historical examples such as the first and second great awakening, the prayer revival of 1857-1858, the Wales revival, and the Shantung revival.

In the Old and New Testament Blackaby sees a cycle of sin and revival in the lives of God's people. When God's people are in this cycle, Blackaby believes God deals with them in a pattern. Blackaby has developed seven phases in God's pattern for revival and spiritual awakening. These seven phases are: (1) God is on mission to redeem a lost world. He calls people into a relationship with Him, and He accomplishes His work through them. (2) God's people tend to depart from Him, turning to substitutes for His presence, His purposes, and His ways. (3) God disciplines His people because of His love. (4) God's people cry out to Him for help. (5) God calls His people to repent and return to Him or perish. (6) God revives His repentant people by restoring them to a right relationship with Him. (7) God exalts His Son, Jesus among His people and draws the lost to saving faith in Him.[51] Blackaby especially believes the spiritual leader's role is strategic both in his public leadership qualities and in his personal life.

Blackaby correctly emphasizes the need for a believer to personally experience God and to have Him transform one's life. His seven realities and seven phases of revival and spiritual awakening strongly articulate this need. In fact, Blackaby's works appear to correspond with McGrath's emphasis upon the transforming character of God.

Yet in comparison to McGrath in other areas Blackaby is either less clear or silent. For example, Blackaby emphasizes the importance of Scripture in guiding a believer to experience God as well as giving direction in life. Yet in contrast to McGrath, Blackaby does not clearly emphasize the priority and authority of the Bible for the Christian life. In most instances he appears to parallel it with other influences. For example, in his section on God speaking through the Bible he states, "In our time, God primarily speaks by the Holy Spirit through the Bible, prayer, circumstances, and the church. These four means are difficult to separate."[52] Nowhere in this section does he make a statement of the clear authority of Scripture in our lives over all other factors. In a later chapter he does offer a corrective balance by stating, "Our experiences alone cannot be our guide. Every experience must be controlled and understood by Scripture."[53] Yet in this present-day era of subjectivism it would seem more appropriate that Blackaby would continually drive home the primary authority of Scripture to guide one's life and experience with God.[54]

Further illustrating this point is when Blackaby states, "The Holy Spirit reveals truth. Truth is not just some concept to be studied. Truth is a Person . . . When the Holy Spirit reveals Truth, He is not teaching you a concept to be thought about. He is leading you to a relationship with a Person."[55] Blackaby appears to force one to decide between truth being a person or a proposition. He creates an "either/or" position when a "both/and" is more appropriate. Truth is found both in a person and in propositions. Jesus Himself modeled this when He said, "I am the way, and the truth, and the life" (Jn 14:6), as well as "Your word is truth" (Jn 17:17).

In addition, McGrath's themes of conversion, evangelism, spiritual disciplines, and the church are only minor themes for Blackaby that he touches upon in passing. His most predominant spiritual discipline emphasized is in the area of prayer. Closely tied into his emphasis on the transforming character of God is the relationship built with God based on prayer. Intertwined with this is the role of the Holy Spirit as Blackaby sees Him as directing a believer in all of these areas.

Although Blackaby does include some of McGrath's themes, his overall emphasis fails to clearly identify the need for the subjective experience to be encased within proper theology. While the success of this book may be attributed to the hunger of Christians to experience God, it also may be credited to its lack of theological emphasis. This deficit of theological clarity perhaps also explains the widespread use of *Experiencing God* across denominational and theological lines.

Richard J. Foster, RENOVARE` Ministries

Richard James Foster[56] was born May 23, 1942 in Albuquerque, New Mexico, to Lee and Marie Foster. He and his wife Alice, a speech therapist, have two sons. Foster is a graduate of George Fox College and holds a Doctorate in Practical Theology from Fuller Theological Seminary. He is an ordained clergyman of the Society of Friends, and in the 1960s and 1970s Foster served in various staff positions in churches in California and Oregon. In 1979 he became Writer in Residence and Associate Professor of Theology at Friends University in Wichita, Kansas. Foster went on to become Professor of Theology at Friends before eventually filling the Jack and Barbara Lee Distinguished Professor of Spiritual Formation position at Azusa Pacific University in Azusa, California. He is also the founder of RENOVARE` Ministries, located in Englewood, Colorado. Bruce Demarest says Richard Foster is "undoubtedly the most popular living spiritual writer in the evangelical world."[57] He feels that Foster has "done more than any other contemporary evangelical to unfold the treasures of Christian spirituality for the church."[58]

Foster is best known for his work *Celebration of Discipline*, which has also been translated into many languages.[59] The desire for instant satisfaction has characterized this present generation, and according to Foster has become a curse of superficiality upon it. He sees the need for Christians to develop greater depth in their spiritual lives. Foster argues that the classical disciplines of the spiritual life are the primary catalysts which move Christians from surface living into the depths of the spiritual realm. According to Foster, God intends for spiritual disciplines to be for ordinary believers and not only for spiritual giants.

Foster presents the purpose of the disciplines as liberation from slavery to self-interest and fear. He believes initial exploration of the disciplines immediately surfaces difficulties of a materialistic philosophical base in society which thwarts the growth of the inward life. Foster argues that the disciplines are a necessity because "they are God's means of grace. The inner righteousness we seek is not something that is poured into our heads. God has ordained the disciplines of the spiritual life as the means by which we are placed where He can bless us."[60]

Foster groups the disciplines under three categories: inward, outward and corporate. The inward disciplines focus on meditating, praying, fasting and studying. The outward disciplines feature simplicity, solitude, submission, and service. Noticeably absent from Foster's outward disciplines is evangelism. The corporate disciplines are clustered around confession, worship, guidance and celebration. Foster has taken chapters from this work and written books further elaborating the themes of prayer, simplicity, meditation and the disciplined life.[61]

Foster's *Celebration of Discipline* has been criticized as emphasizing new age thought and in particular astral projection.[62] The following paragraph has especially been singled out.

> After a while there is a deep yearning within to go into the upper regions beyond the clouds. In your imagination allow your spiritual body, shining with light, to rise out of your physical body. Look back so that you can see yourself lying in the grass and reassure your body that you will return momentarily. Imagine your spiritual self, alive and vibrant, rising up through the clouds and into the stratosphere. Observe your physical body, the knoll, and the forest shrink as you leave the earth. Go deeper and deeper into outer space until there is nothing except the warm presence of the eternal Creator. Rest in His presence. Listen quietly, anticipating the unanticipated. Note carefully any instruction given. With time and experience you will be able to distinguish readily between mere human thought and the True Spirit which inwardly moves upon the heart.[63]

Christian leaders encouraged Foster to rethink his emphasis.[64] In the 1988 revised edition of *Celebration of Discipline,* paragraphs like the above were eliminated.[65]

Andrew Hutchinson, a former student of J. I. Packer, has criticized Foster's works on spiritual disciplines.[66] In evaluating Foster's teachings in comparison to Richard Baxter's, Hutchinson believes Foster lacks a sufficient understanding of the work of grace to support his emphasis on works. In addition, Hutchinson indicates Foster has a "weak notion of the character of the activity of the Holy Spirit in the process of personal godliness."[67] Finally, he see Foster's emphasis as predominantly anthropocentric therefore accommodating itself to the secularizing pressures prevalent in the contemporary Christian church. From his study, Hutchinson concludes there is "sufficient warrant to question the sufficiency of the theological framework within which personal godliness is commonly understood today."[68] Hutchinson's concerns are legitimate although some of them are balanced by Foster's work highlighted in the following paragraphs.

In addition to writing about spiritual disciplines, Foster also surveys the history of spirituality.[69] Foster sees a mighty river of the Spirit bursting forth from the hearts of Christians. He believes it to be a deep river of divine intimacy, of holy living, of jubilation in the Spirit and of unconditional love for all people. He concludes that God is bringing together streams of life that have been isolated from one another for a very long time. According to Foster, when these streams are brought together, they give the Christian community a balanced vision of life and faith. He understands these different traditions as various dimensions of the spiritual life.

Foster is certain that no one models these dimensions more fully than Jesus Christ. He considers the divine paradigm left by Jesus as the challenge, the *imitatio Christi*. Foster then relates six streams of devotion in Jesus' life, articulating how Jesus modeled each of them. Forming the outline of Foster's book, *Streams of Living Water*, these six streams are related to Scripture, to church history, and to contemporary life.

The first of these streams is the contemplative tradition.[70] Foster defines the contemplative life as "the steady gaze of the soul upon the God who loves us."[71] He views this tradition as the prayer-filled life that seeks intimacy with God. The most fundamental characteristics of the contemplative life are love, peace, delight, emptiness, fire, wisdom, and transformation. According to Foster, the Biblical paradigm for this stream is John the Beloved. The historical paradigm is Antonius, the founder of the desert fathers. The contemporary paradigm is Frank Laubach who founded the literacy movement. For Foster, the contemplative tradition emphasizes a life of loving attention to God and therefore should be explored since through it divine rest may be experienced, overcoming human alienation.

The second of these streams is the holiness tradition.[72] Foster delineates this tradition as the inward re-formation of the heart and the development of holy habits. Pictured as a life of virtuous living, this tradition affects appropriate living and brings forth character formation. According to Foster, holiness is the ability to do what needs to be done when it needs to be done. Because misconceptions abound regarding holiness, Foster asserts the equal importance of learning what holiness is not, as well as what holiness is. For him, holiness is not rules and regulations but is the sustained attention to the heart, the source of all action. Holiness is not worldliness but affirms holy living in the world. Holiness is not a consuming asceticism but is bodily spirituality. Holiness is not works righteousness but includes a striving towards righteousness. Holiness is not perfectionism but emphasizes progress in purity and sanctity. Holiness is not absorption into God but loving unity with God. According to Foster, the Biblical paradigm for this stream is James the half-brother of Jesus. The historical paradigm is a Methodist leader of the Second Great Awakening, Phoebe Palmer. The contemporary paradigm is the German martyr, Dietrich Bonhoeffer. For Foster, the holiness tradition brings an emphasis of life functioning as it should, enabling a whole and functional life in a dysfunctional world.

The third of these streams is the charismatic tradition.[73] Foster defines this tradition as focusing upon the empowering gifts of the Spirit as well as the nurturing fruit of the Spirit. He sees this Spirit-empowered way of living as addressing the deep yearning for the immediacy of God's presence among his people. Foster believes there are no non-charismatic Christians. Viewing the Christian life by definition as a life in and through the Spirit, according to Foster, every believer is endowed by the Spirit with one or more spiritual gifts. He is convinced the essential principle guiding the exercise of these gifts is that they build up the church in love rather than destroy. In the charismatic tradition, Foster presents the Apostle Paul as the Biblical paradigm, Saint Francis of Assisi as the historical paradigm, and William Seymour of the Azusa Street Revival as the contemporary paradigm. For Foster, the charismatic tradition is life immersed in, empowered by, and under the direction of the Spirit of God as it divinely empowers the Christian to do God's work and to evidence His life upon the earth.

The fourth of these streams is the social justice tradition.[74] Foster defines this as focusing upon justice and peace in all human relationships and social structures. He views this compassionate way of living as addressing the gospel imperative for equity and magnanimity among all peoples. In this tradition, Foster sees two sweeping movements, the vertical love of God and the horizontal love of neighbors. The three great themes of justice, compassion and peace are lived out in the arenas of personal and social life as well as in the arena of institutional structures. According to Foster, the Biblical paradigm for this stream is the prophet Amos, the historical paradigm is the antislavery Quaker, John Woolman, and the contemporary paradigm is Dorothy Day, who worked to eliminate poverty and unemployment. For Foster, the social justice tradition is a life committed to compassion and justice for all people. Through it Foster believes that God develops compassion to love neighbors freely, thus opening up a place in the world where justice and righteousness prevail.

The fifth of these streams is the evangelical tradition.[75] This tradition is seen by Foster as the proclamation of the good news of the gospel. He believes this stream addresses the crying need of people to see the good news lived and hear the good news proclaimed. Foster presents three major themes in this tradition. The first theme is faithful proclamation of the message rooted in the person of Christ, (His birth, life, death, and resurrection), which provides reconciliation to God. Foster affirms his belief that Christ's death on the cross satisfied the justice of God and opened the way for our reconciliation with God, dependent upon our repentance and acceptance of the free gift of salvation. Yet regrettably, he sees this as only one theory of the atonement.[76] The second theme focuses upon the centrality of Scripture as a faithful repository of the gospel. Thirdly, the evangelical tradition is built upon the confessional witness of the early church as a faithful interpretation of the gospel. According to Foster, the Biblical paradigm for this stream is the Apostle Peter, the historical paradigm is Saint Augustine, and the contemporary paradigm is evangelist Billy Graham.

The strengths of the evangelical tradition are listed by Foster as: (1) The call to conversion; (2) The priority in Christ's missionary mandate to disciple the nations; (3) The commitment to Biblical fidelity; and (4) The witness to sound doctrine. But Foster also points out the potential dangers within this tradition: (1) The tendency to fixate upon peripheral and nonessential matters; (2) The tendency toward a sectarian mentality; (3) The tendency to present too limited a view of salvation; and (4) The tendency toward bibliolatry. Disturbingly, Foster does not consider Biblical inerrancy as an evangelical essential.[77] He does not seem to realize that the evangelistic fervor of the evangelical tradition can only come from a belief in Biblical inerrancy and therefore sound, fixed truth.[78]

For Foster, the call to word-centered living is a life based upon the living Word of God, the written Word of God, and the proclaimed Word of God. He challenges believers to explore this tradition as through it comes the knowledge of God that provides a balance to life and enables the proclamation of a reason for the hope that is within the Christian.

The sixth of Foster's streams is the incarnational tradition.[79] Foster defines this tradition as making present and visible the realm of the invisible spirit. He views this way of living as addressing the need to experience God actively in daily life. He states the "incarnational tradition concerns itself with the relationship between spirit and matter. In short, God is manifest to us through material means."[80] Foster sees two dimensions of the incarnational life: (1) The religious dimension expressed in corporate worship; and (2) The arena of everyday life which comprises family, work, and society. According to Foster, the Biblical paradigm is found in the life of Mary, the mother of Jesus. The historical paradigm is Susanna Wesley, the mother of John and Charles. And the contemporary paradigm is Dag Hammarskjold, the former director of the United Nations.

The translation of the incarnational tradition into the practice of everyday life according to Foster is accomplished by invoking God's presence into this material world. As Christians recover a spirituality of work, marriage, and family life, the incarnational tradition makes present and visible the realm of the invisible Spirit through which God is experienced in daily life.

As already stated, Foster's works have been widely acclaimed, especially his *Celebration of Discipline*. Donald Whitney described it as the most influential book on spirituality in the twentieth century.[81] Certainly through his influence a renewed discovery of spiritual disciplines and devotional classics has taken place. His six streams of spirituality provide a helpful thought process through which to categorize emphases and individuals.

When compared to the consideration of McGrath in chapter two, Foster certainly excels in articulating spiritual disciplines and their importance. He is to be commended for this as well as historically surveying the traditions within spirituality. Intertwined within his disciplines one finds emphasis upon meditating and studying Scripture as well as the discipline of the church with confession, worship, guidance, and celebration. In his historical streams Foster not only emphasizes the word-centered stream of evangelicalism with its focus on conversion, evangelism, and the message of Christ's death, burial, and resurrection but also the Spirit-filled stream with its focus upon the fruit of the Spirit and the empowering gifts of the Spirit.

Although Foster measures up well in some areas of comparison to McGrath's emphases, in others he falls short. Foster appears to lack a theological centeredness to guide him in evaluating the many authors he favorably quotes.[82] These authors fall over a wide theological spectrum with few being of an evangelical persuasion. Whitney, who described *Celebration of Discipline* as the most influential book on spirituality in the twentieth century, also lamented that Foster successfully introduced evangelicals to mystical writers.[83] Because of his lack of theological orientation, Foster not only includes questionable individuals in his streams,[84] but he also isolates evangelicals to one stream instead of looking at church history through the lense of evangelicalism. Even when presenting evangelicalism he chides evangelicals for believing inerrancy is important. He then fails to see the connection between the authority of Scripture and the urgency and passion for evangelism.

In contrast, McGrath calls for evangelicals to return to the spirituality of the Reformation.[85] He sees this period of history as laying the foundation for classic evangelical spirituality.[86] Reformation spirituality represented "the interface between ideas and life, between Christian theology and human existence."[87] McGrath advocates this Reformation spirituality because it was "organically related to its theology."[88] He states, "Time and time again, spirituality was seen as the concrete and actual expression of Christian theology, flowing from and nourished by deep theological springs."[89] McGrath clearly identifies his theology and spirituality as evangelical. He calls evangelicals to their Reformation roots. When asked about Foster's theology McGrath stated, "Foster does not seem to have his own theology. He reaches out and borrows people when he likes them."[90] Foster clearly lacks an evangelical rudder to keep his ship sailing in the right direction.

NOTES

1. See Wuthnow, *After Heaven*, 1998.

2. Wuthnow, *After Heaven*, viii.

3. Wuthnow, *After Heaven*, 40-41.

4. See Dean M. Kelley, *Why Conservative Churches are Growing: A Study in Sociology of Religion*, rev. ed. (Macon, GA: Mercer University Press, 1986).

5. For further study of the Southern Baptist controversy see Jerry Sutton, *The Baptist Reformation: The Conservative Resurgence in the Southern Baptist Convention* (Nashville: Broadman & Holman, 2000); Paul Pressler, *A Hill on which to Die: One Southern Baptist's Journey* (Nashville: Broadman & Holman, 1999); Ralph Elliott, *The "Genesis Controversy" and Continuity in Southern Baptist Chaos: A Eulogy for a Great Tradition* (Macon, GA: Mercer University Press, 1992); and Nancy Ammerman, *Baptist Battles: Social Change and Religious Conflict in the Southern Baptist Convention* (New Brunswick, NJ: Rutgers University Press, 1990).

6. See Wuthnow, *After Heaven*, 89-91.

7. For an overview see Paul Heelas, *The New Age Movement: The Celebration of the Self and the Sacralization of Modernity* (London: Blackwell, 1996).

8. Wuthnow, *After Heaven*, 142. Examples of these books include Deepak Chopra, *The Seven Spiritual Laws of Success: A Practical Guide to the Fulfillment of Your Dreams* (San Rafael, CA: Amber-Allen, 1995) and *How to Know God: The Soul's Journey into the Mystery of Mysteries* (Philadelphia: Running, 2001); John Bradshaw, *Homecoming: Reclaiming and Championing Your Inner Child* (New York: Bantam, 1990); Gerald G. May, *Addiction and Grace: Love and Spirituality in the Healing Addictions* (New York: HarperCollins, 1988); J. Keith Miller, *A Hunger for Healing: The Twelve Steps as a Classic Model for Christian Spiritual Growth* (San Francisco: HarperSanFrancisco: 1991); and M. Scott Peck, *The Road Less Traveled: A New Psychology of Love, Traditional Values and Spiritual Growth* (New York: Simon & Schuster, 1978).

9. Wuthnow, *After Heaven*, 147.

10. Wuthnow, *After Heaven*, 149.

11. Wuthnow, *After Heaven*, 14.

12. See Millard J. Erickson, *Postmodernizing the Faith: Evangelical Responses to the Challenge of Postmodernism* (Grand Rapids: Baker, 1998), 14-20. Another helpful overview of the premodern, modern, and postmodern periods is found in Gene E. Veith, Jr., *Postmodern Times: A Christian Guide to Contemporary Thought and Culture*, Turning Point Christian Worldview Series, ed. Marvin Olasky (Wheaton: Crossway, 1994), 27-46.

13. Erickson, *Postmodernizing the Faith*, 15.

14. Erickson, *Postmodernizing the Faith*, 16-17. For an analysis of modernism in twentieth century America see Norman Cantor, *The American Century: Varieties of Culture in Modern Times* (New York: HarperCollins, 1998).

15. For an overview see Margaret Rose, "Defining the Post-Modern," in *The Post-Modern Reader*, ed. Charles Jencks (New York: St. Martin, 1992), 119-136.

16. Lawrence Cahoone, introduction to *From Modernism to Postmodernism: An Anthology*, ed. Lawrence Cahoone (Malden, MA: Blackwell, 1996), 3.

17. For example, in the 1930s certain developments in the arts used this term. See Craig Van Gelder, "Postmodernism as an Emerging Worldview," *Calvin Theological Journal* 26 (November 1991): 412. Also in 1934 the Spanish literary critic Federico de Onis used this term. See Cahoone, introduction to *From Modernism to Postmodernism*, 3.

18. See Stanley J. Grenz, *A Primer on Postmodernism* (Grand Rapids: Eerdmans, 1996), 17.

19. See Veith, *Postmodern Times*, 40-41.

20. See Charles Jencks, *The Language of Post-Modern Architecture* (London: Acad-

emy Editions, 1984), 9.

21. See Thomas C. Oden, *Two Worlds: Notes on the Death of Modernity* (Louisville, KY: Westminster/Knox, 1989), 2.

22. See Cantor, *The American Century*, 425-502.

23. See Erickson, *Postmodernizing the Faith*, 18-19. Other excellent resources analyzing contemporary culture include Walter T. Anderson, *Reality Isn't What it Used to Be: Theatrical Politics, Ready-to-Wear Religion, Global Myths, Primitive Chic, and Other Wonders of the Postmodern World* (New York: HarperCollins, 1990) and Leonard I. Sweet, *SoulTsunami: Sink or Swim in New Millennium Culture* (Grand Rapids: Zondervan, 1999).

24. Grenz, *A Primer on Postmodernism*, 20.

25. Carson, *Gagging of God*, 19. Carson's emphasis.

26. Carson, *Gagging of God*, 37-52.

27. See Lesser, *The New American Spirituality*.

28. Lesser, *The New American Spirituality*, xi.

29. Lesser, *The New American Spirituality*, 28-30.

30. Lesser, *The New American Spirituality*, 31.

31. Lesser, *The New American Spirituality*, 39.

32. McGrath, *Passion for Truth*, 200.

33. See Veith, *Postmodern Times*, 191-207.

34. Demarest divides spirituality writers into three categories: progressives, moderates, and conservatives. He identifies individuals in progressive spirituality as Henri Nouwen, E. Glenn Hinson, Howard Rice, and Morton Kelsey. Individuals identified in moderate spirituality are Richard Foster, James Houston, Eugene Peterson, J. I. Packer, Dallas Willard, Peter Toon, and Alister McGrath. In the conservative category Demarest only identifies Michael Horton who he describes as an opponent of the spirituality movement. See Demarest, *Satisfy Your Soul*, 74-79. Others have divided spirituality and sanctification views as: Wesleyan, Reformed, Pentecostal, Keswick, Augustinian-Dispensational, Lutheran, and Contemplative. See Donald L. Alexander, ed., *Christian Spirituality: Five Views of Sanctification* (Downers Grove: InterVarsity, 1988); Melvin E. Dieter, ed., *Five Views on Sanctification*, Counterpoint Series (Grand Rapids: Zondervan, 1987); and Lawrence O. Richards, *A Practical Theology of Spirituality* (Grand Rapids: Zondervan, 1987).

35. Personal information on Blackaby may be found in Martin King, "Henry Blackaby 'Transitions" to New Ministry Organization," *Baptist Press* Release, May 11, 2000 and Joel C. Yow, "Interpreting the Spirituality of Henry Thomas Blackaby" (Th.M. thesis, Southeastern Baptist Theological Seminary, 1999), 92-94.

36. For the workbook format see Henry T. Blackaby and Claude V. King, *Experiencing God: How to Live the Full Adventure of Knowing and Doing the Will of God* (Nashville: Sunday School Board of the Southern Baptist Convention, 1990).

37. See Blackaby and King, *Experiencing God*. Michael Horton identifies Blackaby's views as being part of the Keswick Movement. See Michael Horton, *In the Face of God*, 166-170.

38. Blackaby and King, *Experiencing God*, 5-6.

39. Blackaby's chart and diagram of the seven realities are found in *Experiencing God*, 32-33.

40. Blackaby and King, *Experiencing God*, 32.

41. Blackaby and King, *Experiencing God*, 32.

42. Blackaby and King, *Experiencing God*, 32.

43. Blackaby and King, *Experiencing God*, 32.

44. Blackaby and King, *Experiencing God*, 35.

45. Blackaby and King, *Experiencing God*, 32.

46. Blackaby and King, *Experiencing God*, 32.

47. Blackaby and King, *Experiencing God*, 32.

48. Blackaby and King have been criticized for emphasizing an Old Testament extrinsic experience with God that has no awareness of the New Testament intrinsic experience. Although they illustrate many of their principles from Old Testament individuals, this writer does not concur with this characterization of Blackaby's and King's work. For more information on this critique see Gene Ford, review of *Experiencing God: How to Live the Full Adventure of Knowing and Doing the Will of God*, by Henry T. Blackaby and Claude V. King, *Affirmation and Critique* 1:2 (1996): 58-59.

49. See Henry T. Blackaby and Claude V. King, *Fresh Encounter: Experiencing God Through Prayer, Humility and a Heartfelt Desire to Know Him* (Nashville: Broadman & Holman, 1996).

50. Blackaby and King, *Fresh Encounter*, vi.

51. Blackaby and King, *Fresh Encounter*, 60.

52. Blackaby and King, *Experiencing God*, 103.

53. Blackaby and King, *Experiencing God*, 117.

54. Blackaby's lack of clarity at this point has led a reviewer to state, "One gets the impression that our *understanding* of God's specific will for a situation can be (if their steps are followed) just as authoritative as God's revealed will in the Scriptures." See Bob Dalberg, review of *Experiencing God: Knowing and Doing the Will of God*, by Henry Blackaby and Clyde King, *Reformation and Revival Journal* 6 (Winter 1997): 161-166. Dalberg's emphasis.

55. Blackaby and King, *Experiencing God*, 108-109.

56. Personal information on Foster may be in found in Linda Metzger, ed., *Contemporary Authors*, vol.15 (Detroit: Gale Research, 1985), 132 and Siang-Yang Tan, "Practicing the Presence of God: The Work of Richard J. Foster and its Applications to Psychotherapeutic Practice," *Journal of Psychology and Christianity* 15:1 (1996): 17.

57. Demarest, *Satisfy the Soul*, 262.

58. Demarest, *Satisfy the Soul*, 77.

59. Richard J. Foster, *Celebration of Discipline: The Path to Spiritual Growth* (San Francisco: Harper & Row, 1978).

60. Foster, *Celebration of Discipline*, 6.

61. See Richard J. Foster, *Prayer: Finding the Heart's True Home* (San Francisco: HarperSanFrancisco, 1992); *The Challenge of the Disciplined Life: Christian Reflections on Money, Sex & Power* (San Francisco: Harper & Row, 1985); *Freedom of Simplicity* (San Francisco: Harper & Row, 1981); and *Meditative Prayer* (Downers Grove: InterVarsity, 1983).

62. See Beth Pitzl, "Celebration of Discipline - New Age in the Christian Churches," *The Watchman Expositor*, www.watchman.org, accessed July 13, 2000.

63. Foster, *Celebration of Discipline*, 27.

64. Richard J. Foster, et al., "Under Fire: Two Christian Leaders Respond to Accusations of New Age Mysticism," *Christianity Today* 31 (September 18, 1987): 17-21.

65. See Richard J. Foster, *Celebration of Discipline: The Path to Spiritual Growth*, rev.

ed. (San Francisco: HarperSanFrancisco, 1988) and Demarest, *Satisfy Your Soul*, 77.

66. See Andrew T. G. Hutchinson, "Personal Godliness: Puritan and Contemporary, An Evaluation of the Theology of Personal Godliness in the Writings of Richard Foster in Light of the Practical Writings of Richard Baxter" (Master of Christian Studies thesis, Regent College, 1988).

67. Hutchinson, "Personal Godliness," iii.

68. Hutchinson, "Personal Godliness," iii.

69. See Richard J. Foster, *Streams of Living Water: Celebrating the Great Traditions of Christian Faith* (San Francisco: Harper, 1998).

70. Foster, *Streams of Living Water*, 28-58.

71. Foster, *Streams of Living Water*, 49.

72. Foster, *Streams of Living Water*, 59-96.

73. Foster, *Streams of Living Water*, 97-134.

74. Foster, *Streams of Living Water*, 135-184.

75. Foster, *Streams of Living Water*, 185-234.

76. Foster, *Streams of Living Water*, 406. Foster states, "Some may wonder why I do not say more about the vicarious, substitutionary death of Christ on the cross for the forgiveness of sins. The answer is not that I feel these matters are unimportant, but that I do not want people to mistake a theory of the atonement for the experience of saving grace. Personally, I hold that Christ's death on the cross satisfied the justice of God and opened the way for our reconciliation with God, dependent upon our repentance and acceptance of the free gift of salvation. But again, this is one theory of the atonement, and many people have no doubt experienced saving grace and abundant life with Christ as his disciple without believing every jot and tittle of this particular theory." See Foster, *Streams of Living Water*, 406.

77. Foster, *Streams of Living Water*, 228-229.

78. For further study see L. Russ Bush, "Evangelism and Biblical Authority," in *Evangelism in the Twenty-First Century: Twenty-One Contributors in Honor of Lewis A. Drummond*, ed. Thom Rainer (Wheaton, IL: Shaw, 1989), 103-111 and The Amsterdam Declaration.

79. See Foster, *Streams of Living Water*, 235-272.

80. Foster, *Streams of Living Water*, 260.

81. See Donald S. Whitney, "Unity of Doctrine and Devotion," in *The Compromised Church*, ed. John Armstrong (Wheaton: Crossway, 1998), 247.

82. See Alister E. McGrath, Principal of Wycliffe Hall, interview by author, 3 October, 2000, Birmingham, AL, tape recording, Beeson Divinity School, Birmingham, AL.

83. See Whitney, "Unity of Doctrine and Devotion," 248.

84. For example, Desmond Tutu. See Foster, *Streams of Living Water*, 136

85. McGrath also identifies the Pietists and Puritans as key groups for evangelical spirituality. See McGrath, interview by author.

86. McGrath, *Spirituality in an Age of Change*, 15.

87. McGrath, *Spirituality in an Age of Change*, 31-32.

88. McGrath, *Spirituality in an Age of Change*, 32.

89. McGrath, *Spirituality in an Age of Change*, 32.

90. McGrath, interview by author.

CHAPTER 5

MCGRATH'S EXAMPLE COMPARED TO CONTEMPORARY SPIRITUALITY— PART TWO

Gary L. Thomas, Center for Evangelical Spirituality[1]

Gary Thomas, the founder and director of the Center for Evangelical Spirituality located in Bellingham, Washington also serves as an adjunctive faculty member in the Doctor of Ministry program at Western Seminary in Portland, Oregon. He holds a master's degree with a concentration in systematic theology from Regent College in Vancouver, British Columbia, where he studied under J. I. Packer.

The ministry of Thomas and the Center for Evangelical Spirituality is one of writing and speaking which integrates Scripture, church history and the Christian classics. Thomas believes "evangelical Christians can learn a great deal from historic Christian traditions without compromising the essential tenets of what it means to be an evangelical Christian."[2] Accepting Scripture as the final word, Thomas promotes Christian growth and the refinement of authentic evangelical Christian spirituality.

Thomas' book, *Sacred Pathways*[3] was chosen by *World* magazine as one of the top ten books of 1996. He has also served as a collaborative writer for Chuck Colson, Norma McCorvey (a.k.a. Jane Roe of *Roe v. Wade*), Franklin Graham and Senator John Ashcroft. He contributed to the *Spiritual Formation Bible*[4] and has had over 85 articles published by numerous magazines including *Christianity Today*, *Moody*, *Marriage Partnership*, *New Man*, *World* and *Discipleship Journal*.

Although the Evangelical Center for Spirituality has no official doctrinal statement,[5] Thomas affirms the statements of Regent College in Vancouver, British Columbia and the National Association of Evangelicals. Thomas believes "the broader Christian traditions are much closer in their spiritualities than they are in their dogmas."[6] Therefore he shies away from addressing strictly theological issues, except to bring clarification to the area of sanctification.[7]

In seeking to introduce the rich legacy of the classical Christian life, Thomas emphasizes that each generation does not need to reinvent the Christian faith, only the classics need rediscovering.[8] He sees the devotional writings of ancient Roman

Catholics and Eastern Orthodox Christians as very profitable even though he might disagree with some of their theology. Thomas does not desire to "split theological hairs," he wants to examine "the seasons, stages, and characteristics of the soul's pursuit of God, themes on which there is wide agreement across various Christian traditions."[9] He identifies John of the Cross, Francois Fenelon and Jonathan Edwards as his favorite classical spirituality writers.[10]

Thomas draws a distinction between Christian spirituality and much of today's interest in spirituality. He sums up today's spirituality as "good intentions, wrong results."[11] In contrast he defines Christian spirituality as God-centered, not man-centered, and based on objective truth, not subjective experience that is others-focused.[12] After discussing spiritual goals, Thomas turns to identifying four elements of the spiritual life: surrender, simplicity of heart, humility and remembrance of death. Thomas then addresses spiritual difficulties and dryness before finally considering spiritual direction.

Thomas believes the way an individual Christian relates to God and draws near to Him is a sacred pathway or spiritual temperament.[13] Through the study of Scripture and church history, Thomas discovered various ways people found intimacy with God. He thinks this focus on spiritual temperament helps individual believers understand how best to relate to God and develop new ways of drawing near to Him.

Noting that Christians often exhibit various styles of loving God, Thomas sees these spiritual temperaments as an explanation for this phenomenon. He argues that some denominations, and even church splits developed because of differences on how to best relate to God in love and worship. Thomas gives the Reformation as an example. He states, "all four players—Roman Catholics, Lutherans, Calvinists, and Anabaptists—were trying to love God, but with unique expressions of that love. Many differences had theological roots, but some were also related to worship preferences."[14]

Thomas identifies the nine sacred pathways as: (1) Naturalists, loving God out-of-doors; (2) Sensates, loving God with the senses; (3) Traditionalists, loving God through ritual and symbol; (4) Ascetics, loving God in solitude and simplicity; (5) Activists, loving God through confrontation; (6) Caregivers, loving God by loving others; (7) Enthusiasts, loving God with mystery and celebration; (8) Contemplative, loving God through adoration; and (9) Intellectuals, loving God with the mind.[15] Thomas thinks that mature Christians will display more than one of these spiritual temperaments, while maintaining one as predominant. Needless to say, Thomas thinks that Jesus is an example of all the sacred pathways.

In addition, believing that conversion is only the beginning of the Christian life Thomas emphasizes that spiritual formation, rooted in the virtues, must follow.[16] For him, virtue is the "inner orientations and behaviors evidenced in the life of Jesus while He walked on earth."[17] Thomas sees virtue being displayed when a Christian chooses to serve, to respect, to be gentle, to submit to the will of God and to act as Jesus would. In contrast, he defines vices as being ruled by the power of self, prone to chaotic outbursts of anger, selfishness and destruction. Thomas says that "while the virtues bring spiritual health, the vices are a spiritual cancer, destroying us from within."[18]

Thomas addresses fourteen virtues, which he believes are virtues recognized throughout the ages. He sees them readily lived out in the life of Christ. Chief of these virtues is humility which is evidenced by Christ's incarnation. He identifies the other virtues as: surrender to the will and purposes of God, detachment from dependence on worldly securities, love that's clear of self-interest, chastity that springs from purity of heart, generosity with possessions, vigilant watch-care over one's soul, patience for the long haul of growth, discernment to perceive God with the eyes of the soul, thankfulness in all things, gentleness of spirit, fortitude during difficult times, obedience to God's will, and penitence in addressing wrongful acts.

Thomas believes these virtues show Christians how to slowly begin to resemble Christ. He argues that while real change is possible, it is not instant. According to Thomas virtues are something one practices, not something one becomes. For example, Thomas says he will never be completely humble but he can practice humility. He concludes by saying, "The virtues are not a difficult performance we are called to give before a demanding, tyrannical parent, but a life-affirming, soul-refreshing invitation to become persons of integrity—the persons God created us to be."[19]

Josef Solc cautions that Thomas' approach to the virtues separates salvation from spiritual growth as if the two were not interconnected. Solc believes that Thomas can be misleading unless one practices the virtues from a larger frame of reference that connects salvation and spiritual growth.[20]

Thomas has also written to help Christians see how the challenges, joys, struggles and celebrations of marriage draw believers to God and inspire growth in Christian character.[21] He desires for believers to discover in the "challenges of marriage the opportunities to learn more about God, grow in our understanding of Him, and learn to love Him more."[22] He asks the penetrating question, also the subtitle of the book, "What if God designed marriage to make us holy more than to make us happy?" Thomas sees the ultimate purpose of his work on marriage as not necessarily to inspire Christians to love their spouse more, but to equip them to love God more.

Thomas depicts marriage as teaching truths about God as well as love and respect for others. He believes a good marriage can foster prayer and even expose sins. Emphasizing the spiritual discipline of perseverance, Thomas discusses how difficulties build character and teach the art of forgiveness in marriage. After dealing with marital sexuality as a means for gaining spiritual insights and character development, Thomas presents how marriage increases awareness of God's presence, especially assisting in developing a spiritual calling, mission and purpose.

Thomas' emphasis upon developing an authentic evangelical spirituality and accepting Scripture as the final word lays an excellent foundation that coincides with McGrath's example. He parallels McGrath's thoughts by emphasizing evangelical spirituality as God-centered and based on objective truth, not man-centered and based on subjective experience. Thomas excels in bringing forth Christian virtues, different styles of loving God, and how God uses marriage to mature believers.

Even though much of Thomas' works are of a practical nature he attempts to undergird them with a solid theological orientation. His integration of Scripture, church history, and Christian classics is commendable. Yet when one identifies his center for spirituality as "evangelical," it seems natural for that center to define what evangelical beliefs are held. But Thomas has no written doctrinal statement, commends the devotional writings of Roman Catholics and Eastern Orthodox with little caution, and sees no problem with affirming spiritualities of different traditions even though their dogmas are quite different. For an evangelical to even hint that the differences of the Reformation can be explained by preferences of worship style brings concern. McGrath's clarion call for evangelicals to find their spiritual roots in the Reformation stands in stark contrast to Thomas.

Dallas Willard, University of Southern California[23]

Dallas Willard was born September 4, 1935, in Buffalo, Missouri to Albert and Mamie Willard. His father was a politician and his mother, a teacher. Willard attended William Jewell College before receiving a B.A. at both Tennessee Temple and Baylor University. He then received his Ph.D. at the University of Wisconsin at Madison where he taught before launching his long teaching career at the University of Southern California in 1964 which continues to today.

Willard's philosophical publications are mainly in the areas of epistemology, philosophy of the mind and of logic, and on the philosophy of Edmund Husserl. He has translated many of Husserl's early writings from German to English. Contributions were also made by Willard to the *Encyclopedia Britannica*.[24]

Willard's wife, Jane, is a marriage and family counselor with offices in Van Nuys and Canoga Park, California. They have two children.

In considering the spiritual life Willard first looks at the search for God's guidance.[25] He sees this guidance as developed by a conversational relationship with God. Willard is convinced that an inability to discern God's guidance stems from a failure to understand, accept and grow into this conversational relationship with God.[26] He believes that God created man for fellowship with Himself and that He will speak to the individual human when it is appropriate.[27] While embracing this affirmation, Willard recognizes the paradox concerning divine guidance. On the one hand, numerous testimonies claim God's personal guidance by conscious communication from God. Yet, uncertainty pervades regarding how divine guidance works and its place in the church and the Christian life.[28]

Willard identifies three general problem areas to be addressed. First, from the Bible and church history, it is known that God's communications come in many forms. The second problem deals with motivation. By having an extreme preoccupation with knowing the will of God, a Christian may succumb to the pitfall of using it as a manipulative device for securing safety, comfort, and righteousness. Third, misunderstanding the nature of God and His intent for His people presents various extremes that individual Christians embrace.[29]

In light of these issues, Willard distinguishes three general guidelines for discerning God's direction. First, Willard believes that God's guidance for us is intended to develop into an "intelligent, freely cooperative relationship between mature persons who love each other."[30] Second, any attempt to understand divine guidance must be based upon the content of the Bible, and by extension, the lives of Christians who have lived throughout the ages. Third, God does not speak to believers because they are good nor does His speaking to Christians make them good. The fact of God's infallibility does not mean our reception of His message is the same.[31]

Willard thinks it is possible to clearly understand what life with God is like, in particular that a believer is never alone because of the presence of God. He discusses various forms which God's presence may take. Willard describes the first form as the dark night of the soul. This night depicts God's closeness to an individual which remains unevidenced. The second form is the sensing of powerful expression of God's presence. God's acting in extraordinary events encompasses the third form of God's presence. Lastly, a conversational relationship may exist in which God speaks to an individual through His Word or the mind of Christ. Willard sees three common positions taken that are hurtful to the search for guidance: the "message a minute" view, the "it's all in the Bible" view, and the "whatever comes" view.[32]

Willard sets forth six ways in the Biblical record by which God addressed people. These ways include: phenomenon plus voice, supernatural messenger or angel, dreams and visions, audible voice, human voice, and the spirit of man.[33] Willard believes "there is no foundation in Scripture, in reason, or in the nature of things why any or all of these types of experiences might not be used by God today."[34] But Willard quickly affirms the close of the canon and the adequacy of the principles and doctrines that constitute the faith and practice of the Bible. He believes nothing further will be said by God to extend or contradict the Bible.

Willard holds that the single basic truth outlining any relationship with God is the instrumentality of His Word.[35] He then shows how God rules, guides, and redeems through His Word. Man's redemption occurs in being birthed, engrafted, and washed by the Word of God.[36]

How does one know if guidance comes from God or not? According to Willard, one can know "that the word is from God if it is the plain statement and meaning of the Bible or if it can be obtained from biblical teaching as a whole by a sound manner of interpretation."[37] Willard sees the combination of three "lights" as he states, "God's impressions within and His words without are always corroborated by His providence around, and we should quietly wait until those focus into one point."[38] He further elaborates by stating, "Yet all who have much experience in the way of Christ will know that it is somehow right to look for guidance in circumstances, the Bible, and inner impulses. And all will know that these three somehow serve to correct each other. While they provide no formula for making decisions, they must not be simply abandoned."[39]

Willard goes on to acknowledge the possibility that an individual can still be mistaken, given that no person is infallible. He then states that he finds comfort and encouragement in the face of his fallibility by his close association with the Bible. He concludes, "We have repeatedly emphasized the centrality of the written Word in the functioning of divine guidance. More of God's speaking to me, personally, has come in conjunction with study and teaching of the Bible than anything else."[40]

Willard also considers the manner through which God changes one's spiritual life.[41] In Willard's view, Christianity must address the need for human transformation as seriously as do modern revolutionary movements, if it is to succeed in guiding humanity. In addition, he sees a need to clarify and exemplify realistic methods of human transformation. His central claim in this book is that Christ likeness occurs by modeling the overall style of Jesus' life. Willard identifies the practices of Jesus as solitude and silence, prayer, simple and sacrificial living, intense study and meditation upon God's Word and God's ways, and service to others.[42]

Willard seeks to bring about a practical theology that answers questions regarding how one grows spiritually. He sees practical theology's overall task as twofold. The first task is the effective proclamation of the gospel message to all humanity. Secondly, the task is to make disciples of every nation by developing these disciples' character into the character of Christ himself. Willard describes the phrase, "teaching them to do all things whatsoever I have commanded you," as the Great Omission by present day Christians from the Great Commission of Matthew 28:19-20.[43] He sees the revival of the disciplines for the spiritual life over these last twenty-five years as having great significance and potential for eliminating this omission.

Even with this revival, Willard sees a void of understanding in the theological basis of the disciplines. He states, "We need a foundation, a practical, workable theology of them. We must understand why the disciplines are integral to meaningful life in Christ."[44] Thus Willard does not attempt to write on how to practice the disciplines. Instead, he seeks to establish this one thought: "Full participation in the life of God's Kingdom and in the vivid companionship of Christ comes to us only through appropriate exercise in the disciplines for life in the Spirit."[45]

In seeking to develop a psychologically sound theology of the spiritual life and its disciplines, Willard attempts to deal with the most basic points of a person's relationship with God. He identifies four key areas which he develops as the basic thought structure of this work.[46]

First Willard seeks to clarify the nature of spiritual life itself. He believes the primary resource for the spiritual life is the human body. Willard argues that in Romans 6 Paul deals with "how our body and its members are to be transformed into servants of God through the replacement of habits of sin by habits of righteousness."[47] He points to three stages of personal redemption: (1) Being baptized into Christ; (2) Reckoning—the taking on of a new attitude; and, (3) Submitting our members to righteousness.[48] Willard sees the outcome of these three stages expressed in Romans 6:17-18. He believes the practice which prepares us for righteous living includes not only actions directly commanded by Christ, but also those activities which help us carry out these commands. He sees the spiritual disciplines as a "vitally necessary submission of our body and its members to righteousness."[49]

Willard's foundational emphasis is upon the physical body as being primary in following Christ. Yet his discussion of this area leaves many unanswered questions. He is not clear in articulating the meaning of terms such as "old man," "new man," "flesh," "world," "spirit," and "soul." For Willard to place such importance upon the body in following Christ, clarity upon these terms is essential. Closely tied to this point, Ramesh Richard believes Willard's use of some proof texts is questionable.[50]

The second key area of a personal relationship with God Willard addresses is the decline of the disciplines in Western Christianity. In this section Willard traces the extremes in practice and theology of monasticism and asceticism.[51] Because of these extreme lifestyles of withdrawal from society in the pursuit of spirituality, Protestants have negatively viewed the spiritual disciplines. Willard also identifies the modern mindset of searching for the easiest and most convenient lifestyle. Hedonism undergirds much of modern society.[52]

Willard's third key area defines spiritual disciplines and identifies the disciplines relevant for Christians today. According to Willard, spiritual disciplines are "an activity undertaken to bring us into more effective cooperation with Christ and His Kingdom."[53] Willard sees the disciplines as activities that assist growth in grace with the goal of receiving more of Christ's life and power.

Willard groups the disciplines into areas of abstinence and engagement. He identifies the disciplines of abstinence as solitude, silence, fasting, frugality, chastity, secrecy, and sacrifice. He sees solitude as most fundamental in beginning the spiritual life, and Willard also emphasizes the need to return to solitude often. The disciplines of engagement Willard cites as study, worship, celebration, service, prayer, fellowship, confession, and submission.[54] Although he acknowledges that other disciplines can be added, Willard believes these are the foundational disciplines that will guide one to the right course of life.[55]

It is unfortunate that Willard does not include evangelism as a discipline of engagement. He rightly identifies weaknesses in the current day practice of evangelism, yet he does very little to articulate a positive example of how evangelism should be modeled. He fails to give a practical example of how to lead someone to Christ, and then guide them to continue in discipleship. Willard missed a golden opportunity to showcase how evangelism and discipleship are partners which walk hand-in-hand with each other. It is difficult to imagine how could he include Bible study, worship, fellowship, and prayer as disciplines of engagement but exclude evangelism? He appears to view evangelism as an overflow of the Christian walk and negates it as an intentional practice or discipline.

Willard then devotes an entire chapter addressing the issue of poverty and spirituality. He sees the idealization of poverty as one of the most dangerous illusions of Christians in the contemporary world. He concludes by affirming that stewardship is the true spiritual discipline in relation to wealth.[56] Interestingly, throughout this work Willard has argued for the close connection of the internal and external aspects of the Christian life. Yet in this chapter he indicates that freedom from possessions is more internal than external.[57]

The fourth and final key area of a personal relationship with God Willard speaks to is how a widespread transformation of character can transform the world. He sees faith alone as a basis from which the evil in human character can be addressed. Willard maintains one realistic hope for the world's problems as "the person and gospel of Jesus Christ, living here and now, in people who are his by total identification found through the spiritual disciplines."[58]

Finally, Willard presents the spiritual life regarding discipleship to Jesus as the very heart of the gospel.[59] He sees the current condition of Christians as one having little impact in churches and society. Willard wants Christians to move past a "consumer, bumper sticker" mentality in order to experience the reality of following Christ and His teachings in this life. He believes the Sermon on the Mount provides the basis for such an understanding, therefore he develops six basic emphases from this sermon.[60]

Willard's first emphasis of the Sermon on the Mount deals with the background assumption that life in the kingdom relies upon Jesus (Matt 4:17-25). Willard sees the problem with current evangelical teachings as a gospel of sin management. Conservatives focus upon a message of forgiveness of sin and eternal life in heaven. Liberals focus upon social evils and their elimination. Willard believes in either case that transformation of life and character have been removed from the redemptive message.

If only a gospel of sin management is preached, Willard argues the "resources of God's kingdom remain detached from human life."[61] He sees the answer as developing a straightforward presentation, "in word and life, of the reality of life now under God's rule, through reliance upon the word and person of Jesus. In this way we can naturally become his students or apprentices."[62]

Willard's assessment of those who emphasize forgiveness of sin and eternal life has brought him criticism. David Larsen accuses Willard of an assault on forensic justification and a minimization of the cross.[63] Yet Willard appears to attempt asserting a valid point. He wants Christians to know that between forgiveness of sins and eternal life in heaven is a life-long relationship with Christ. However Willard sets himself up for criticism by using inflammatory language in stating that many "presume a Christ with no serious work other than redeeming humankind.... they foster 'vampire Christians,' who only want a little blood for their sins but nothing more to do with Jesus until heaven, when they have to associate with him."[64] Willard certainly could have made his point without casting any doubt upon his view of the atonement.

In his second emphasis of the Sermon on the Mount Willard deals with ordinary people living life in the kingdom as the light and salt of the world (Matt 5:1-20). Willard's view of the Beatitudes is unique in that he does not see them teaching how to be blessed. He does not believe they indicate conditions that please God.

Rather, he thinks they single out cases that provide proof that the rule of God is available in all life circumstances. Willard believes the Beatitudes indicate people who, "from the human point of view, are regarded as most hopeless, most beyond all possibility of God's blessing or even interest, and exhibiting them as enjoying God's touch and abundant provision from the heavens."[65] Willard acknowledges that his teaching on the Beatitudes goes against the traditional interpretation of them yet he offers very little substantiation for his views. Such a major shift from the traditional interpretation would necessitate a more thorough documentation of one's views in the mind of this writer.[66]

Willard's third emphasis of the Sermon on the Mount depicts the kingdom heart of goodness as God's kind of love (Matt 5:21-48). Willard describes six contrasts as Jesus teaches of goodness beyond the Scribes and Pharisees. These contrasts include an intense desire to help without anger, contempt, or murder; sexual attraction without cultivation of lust or sex outside of marriage; a commitment to marriage that excludes divorce; speech without verbal manipulation which only states how things are, or are not; refusal to harm the one who has harmed; and a commitment to love and bless one's enemies.[67]

Continuing to his fourth emphasis of the Sermon on the Mount, Willard sees a warning against false securities (Matt 6). He views one of these false securities as a desire to win the approval of others, especially in bringing relief to the needy, praying in order to be seen by others, and fasting for exhibitionism and respectability. Another false security Willard cites is the desire to secure ourselves by means of material wealth. Willard believes either error will block interaction with God and healthy growth in the kingdom. He believes Christians need to please an "audience of one."[68]

The fifth emphasis of the Sermon on the Mount Willard says warns against condemnation as well as a call to a community of prayerful love (Matt 7:1-12). According to Willard, love is illustrated in three ways: (1) Not condemning or blaming others (Matt 7:1-5); (2) Not forcing wonderful things upon them (Matt 7:6); and (3) Clearly asking for what is wanted from others—and from God (Matt 7:7-11).[69] Willard sees confidence in God as the only thing that makes it possible to treat others as they should be treated.[70]

The sixth and final emphasis of the Sermon on the Mount Willard portrays as concerning warning about failure to follow what the Sermon on the Mount requires and the effects of that disobedience (Matt 7:13-27). Willard sees four pictorial contrasts: (1) The narrow gate and the wide gate (Matt 7:13-14); (2) The good tree and the bad tree (Matt 7:15-20); (3) Final judgment for those who do God's will and for those who substitute good deeds (Matt 7:21-23); and (4) Obedience or negligence by those who hear God's Word (Matt 7:24-27).[71]

Willard suggests the means to become a disciple as repeatedly expressing to Jesus our desire to see Him more fully. By using every opportunity to come to Christ an individual makes a decision to be His disciple.[72] It is implicit that one must first be a disciple before he is able to make disciples. His next intent must be to make disciples, to assist others to the knowledge that Jesus really is the Christ.[73]

Willard sees a threefold dynamic he calls the "Golden Triangle" which brings about spiritual growth: (1) The action of the Holy Spirit; (2) Ordinary events of life; and (3) Planned disciplines to put on a new heart.[74]

Coinciding with McGrath's emphasis on spiritual disciplines, Willard attempts to develop a practical theology of spiritual disciplines as he articulates the place of the body in spiritual life. He also covers historically and practically the disciplines of abstinence and engagement. Willard develops the teaching of a conversational relationship with God, viewing guidance as stemming from this intimate relationship. Along with McGrath, Willard gives preeminence to God's leading and speaking through His written Word, stating that inner impulses by the Spirit and God's providence in the circumstances of life are secondary to dominance of the Scriptures.

Stemming from his strong view of the Scripture, Willard wrestles with understanding the Bible's teaching concerning Christian living. Commonly more writers of spirituality deal with the subject historically and experientially than biblically. Although this writer is not convinced of Willard's view of the body as being primary in following Christ and his interpretation of the Beatitudes, Willard is to be commended for his attempt to articulate spirituality from the Bible.

In the area of evangelism Willard presents a one-sided picture. He identifies evangelism weaknesses in current day practice. Yet, he does very little to articulate a positive example of how evangelism should be modeled. In fact, he seems to drive a further wedge between evangelism and discipleship. A more balanced presentation would have combined the two, showing their partnership with each other. A discussion of the Biblical doctrines of justification, sanctification, and glorification would have laid a solid foundation for that combination.

In contrast McGrath identifies weaknesses in current evangelism practices and does not stop at that point. As previously covered, McGrath seeks to present a credible model for evangelicals to follow, upholding evangelism as one of the hallmarks of evangelicalism.

Finally, along with McGrath, Willard has a strong emphasis upon the person of Christ and the transforming power of knowing God as well as the role of the Holy Spirit. Willard's work has been enthusiastically received as filling a void within evangelicalism. It has challenged the church to move past the superficial, so that Christ can deeply transform individual believers as well as entire churches. Willard is to be commended in that he avoids simplistic formulas for spiritual success.

Bruce A. Demarest, Denver Seminary[75]

Bruce Demarest is a long time professor of theology at Denver Seminary. He obtained degrees from Wheaton College, Trinity Evangelical Divinity School, and the University of Manchester, studying science, New Testament, and Biblical and historical theology. He spent ten years with Serving in Mission International in West Africa and the International Fellowship of Evangelical Students in Europe. He also has taught at numerous seminaries in the United States, Canada, the Middle East, and Asia. Demarest and his wife, Elisie, have three children and live in Littleton, Colorado. Best known for his co-writing of *Integrative Theology*,[76] Demarest now has turned his pen to the subject of spirituality.

Demarest's own pilgrimage with spirituality began with a renewal team from the Archdiocese of Denver being invited to his Presbyterian church to teach an eight-week course. After his wife was greatly impacted by the class he was persuaded to join. Greatly challenged to experience a deeper relationship with God, Demarest learned how to open his heart as well as his head to truth. Demarest described this by stating, "When it came to relating to God with my inner being, trusting Him, letting His Spirit search my heart, allowing Him to clear the path in my spirit so He could change me from the inside out, in all honesty, this was foreign territory."[77]

Over the next several years Demarest met regularly with leaders of Christian renewal groups as he sought for greater spiritual reality. He felt that he was being tutored in the principles and practices of Christian spirituality and formation as he learned new spiritual habits. He sensed a new awareness of God's being and work as he developed a strong and quiet steadiness in the promises of God. During a sabbatical leave from his seminary, Demarest attended a six-week residential program at the Benedictine Abbey—a renewal center in Pecos, New Mexico. Perhaps his own words best articulate his experience as he states,

> Previously I would have felt out of place at a Benedictine abbey. To me, the Protestant Reformers of the sixteenth century separated from the Roman church over critical matters, such as papal authority, justification by faith or by works, the veneration of Mary, and praying to the saints. And like most other evangelicals, I had rejected the idea of receiving *any* spiritual instruction from the ancient church. But having gotten to know many wonderful, vibrant Christians in the Catholic renewal movement, I'd come to realize we had made an error. The Reformers and we their evangelical descendants, acting in reaction to medieval Rome, threw out a great deal of spiritual wisdom, insight, and important practices, along with the doctrinal and ecclesiological bath water.
>
> As I traveled to New Mexico, I took stock of where I stood. God was leading me to honor what was true in my own tradition while welcoming back authentic Christian insights and practices from the older tradition . . .
>
> We were more or less evenly divided between Catholic charismatic Christians, renewal Anglicans, and free-church evangelicals like myself. To my surprise, many of these folks had connections to such evangelical bastions as Wheaton College, Bethel, Dallas, and Fuller seminaries; to stalwart ministries like The Navigators; and to Christian counseling centers across the country. Beyond our connections, we also shared this in common: *We wanted to reconnect with the ancient wisdom of the church.* Each of us—some with decades of ministry experience—were drawn to this place in search of a deeper connectedness with Christ.
>
> Our days at Pecos centered around practicing God's presence, stimulated by three worship times per day: the morning Eucharist, afternoon

prayers, and evening vespers. Again, as each day's lectures plumbed the heart of the spiritual life, I found myself stimulated and moved. Small group sessions encouraged sharing our lives with one another in prayer.

Each of us also received two hours of weekly spiritual direction. This meant we met with a spiritual counselor—someone gifted in touching on the tender, needy, or resistant places where God was at work in our lives—and then agreed to act on his or her directions in prayer, reading, and the first necessary steps toward change in actual life. I became as aware of God as I'd ever been, during quiet walks under pristine blue skies and rugged mountains.

At the end of six weeks, virtually everyone—Catholic, Anglican, charismatic, and evangelical—testified to the many true ways the experience had transformed his or her spirit and life.[78]

From his experience, Demarest began writing about the integration of the head and hands into the disciplines of the heart as an unfinished task for today's children of the Reformation. In his chapter on spirituality and Christian living[79] which is included in a *festschrift* for Millard Erickson, Demarest defines spirituality as "the communion with God in which we, individually and corporately, live in response to the gracious work of the Spirit."[80]

Demarest identifies five areas that form an evangelical consensus on authentic spirituality. These areas include inspired Scripture as the primary guide, personal conversion as the *sine qua non*, private and corporate prayer as central, world evangelism fully embraced, and renewed commitment to social concern. He also identifies three deficiencies of evangelical spirituality as intellectualism, legalism and reactive postures.

As Demarest surveys contemporary trends in evangelical spirituality he is greatly encouraged by the rediscovery of spiritual disciplines. He sees spiritual disciplines as creating an environment of availability to the Lord as well as an openness to His invitation to fellowship. Other trends he observes among evangelicals are a reassessing of the quality of worship, a development of a greater sensitivity to the role of the Holy Spirit, and a hunger for direct experience with God. Demarest then considers areas for future exploration in spirituality. He believes spirituality might be enhanced through symbolism and human senses as well as through a catholicity of spirituality.

Demarest sees spiritual formation as an emphasis whose time has come. He challenges evangelicals to follow the leads of Augustine, Calvin, and the Puritans who related "intimately to the God who engages our minds and lovingly touches our hearts."[81]

Demarest surveys the general field of spirituality by identifying and explaining generic, religious, and Christian views. He sees generic spirituality's focus as human self-fulfillment with little or no regard for God. He identifies the following features as part of this generic spirituality: (1) It is highly eclectic, picking and choosing from a wide range of beliefs and practices; (2) It often focuses on the self, and its driving passion is the satisfaction of felt, personal needs; (3) It is indifferent to religious beliefs; and (4) It often centers on social or environmental issues. Generic spirituality may involve "a crusade to raise literacy levels or to save the spotted owls." According to Demarest, generic spirituality has wide appeal because it makes people feel good about focusing on self and their own goals, desires, and achievements.[82]

Religious spirituality is viewed by Demarest as involving the search for transcendence and purpose by appealing to a higher power, or powers. He believes religious spirituality is a potent force in the non-Christian religions, such as Islam, Hinduism, and Buddhism. It drives such Christian heresies as Gnosticism. And it empowers quasi-religious systems such as yoga, Transcendental Meditation, and the New Age. It is also the sparkplug embedded in self-help movements like Alcoholics Anonymous, which states that its aim is to nourish a religious spirituality by seeking a relationship with a Higher Power.

Demarest sees the many forms of religious spirituality reflecting common characteristics. Each possesses a well-defined form that can include a creed, dogma, prayer, and rituals. They are often relativistic, claiming that there are many ways to achieving the soul's goal. In the quest for salvation, works are elevated above grace, with the promise that we can ascend the ladder to God by our human effort.[83]

On the other hand Demarest believes that Christian spirituality concerns the shaping of our inner beings into the likeness of Jesus Christ. It involves cultivating a healing, renewing, and satisfying relationship with Christ, and a deepening love for Him, giving flesh to the new life through obedient and fruitful living. Christian spirituality describes our growth in godliness and piety.

What distinguishes Christian spirituality from the many non-Christian alternatives in our world? According to Demarest certain characteristics of Christian spirituality will help growing disciples to hate what is evil and cling to what is good. Biblical and Christian spirituality is unashamedly Trinitarian. At the heart of Christian spirituality is a satisfying relationship with the living God who exists as Father, Son, and Holy Spirit. Christian spirituality is also revelational; that is, it is framed and nourished by the Word of God rightly unfolded by sound principles of interpretation. Christian spirituality is Christ-centered. It is grounded in the person of Jesus Christ, the Savior. Christian spirituality is also creational and affirms that the material world created by God is good, not evil. Christian spirituality is salvational. It is the gracious gift of life that flows from God's heart of love. True spirituality begins with conversion to Christ through repentance and faith; it is established by the miracle of the new birth. It enlarges through growth into the likeness of Jesus Christ, and it will finally consummate with the perfecting of body and soul at the Savior's second coming. Christian spirituality is both individual and corporate. It involves nourishing the spiritual life of each believer as well as the Christian social unit. Christlike character develops through the encouragement, challenge, and support of fellow believers in local churches who themselves are growing in Christ. And finally, Christian spirituality is pneumatic, meaning that it is empowered by the Holy Spirit. The Spirit testifies to Christ, heals deeply ingrained wounds, and restores our souls.[84]

Demarest defines Christian spirituality as "the shaping of our inner character and outer conduct in cooperation with the work of the Spirit, so that we are gradually being conformed to the likeness of Jesus Christ."[85] He believes the "litmus test of spiritual reality is a transformed life—one that manifests the fruit and graces of the Spirit in a way that radiates Christ's reality to you."[86] Demarest emphasizes the balance of orthodoxy (right beliefs), orthopathy (right affections), and orthopraxy (right actions). He believes this balanced path of growth guards one from the trap of self-deception.

Not all evangelicals will be happy with areas of Demarest's work. His sections on icons, religious art, dreams, breathing exercises, imagination, and the labyrinth walk are sure to raise eyebrows and even stir the ire of others. His redemptive counseling approach which seeks to integrate psychology with Scripture will certainly be questioned by *nouthetic* counselors.

In comparison to McGrath, Demarest emphasizes similar themes for both evangelical theology and evangelical spirituality. Demarest's five areas that form an evangelical consensus on authentic spirituality include McGrath's emphasis of Scripture, conversion, spiritual disciplines, and evangelism. Demarest additionally cites a renewed commitment to social concern. Demarest also highlights characteristics of Christian spirituality. These characteristics include the following emphases: Trinitarian, revelational, Christ-centered, creational, salvational, individual and corporate, and pneumatic. Each of these coincide with McGrath's intertwining of theology and spirituality. Demarest affirms his commitment to both theology and spirituality as he states, "Isolated from spirituality, theology can become dry and barren. Isolated from theology, spirituality can drift into platitudinous piety. Theology and spirituality must be bound together in mutually nourishing relationships."[87]

Are there any major differences between McGrath's and Demarest's emphases? The most obvious is Demarest's experience with Roman Catholic renewal leaders and his enthusiastic endorsement of it. McGrath does not discount that evangelicals can learn spirituality from ancient Catholic writers. But he is cautious and believes that far too many evangelicals first go to these writers without exploring the roots of evangelical spirituality, especially with the Reformers, and with the Puritans and Pietists. While interviewing McGrath at the International Symposium on Evangelical Theology and Christian Spirituality at the Beeson Divinity School in Birmingham, Alabama in 2001, McGrath was asked about his concerns with evangelical spirituality He stated, "One of the concerns would be that evangelicals simply borrow other people's techniques. For example, this conversation we were having this afternoon you may have noticed some people were saying, 'Oh, we have tried Ignatian spirituality, or we have tried Celtic spirituality.' I am not criticizing that; my feeling is that we really need to make sure we fully try our own spirituality before we start looking around elsewhere."[88]

Yet Demarest has excelled in giving an introductory overview of Christian spirituality. His theological training and background provide an excellent foundation for him to address an admittedly subjective discipline that historically has been given to extremes. McGrath points out that the lack of an evangelical spirituality is a major blind spot in today's Christian culture. Demarest's work is a welcomed addition to the continuing development of this area as it complements McGrath's emphasis of building one's spirituality upon a solid theological foundation.

NOTES

1. Background information obtained from promotional materials of the Center for Evangelical Spirituality and from www.garythomas.com, accessed June 23, 2000.

2. www.garythomas.com, accessed June 23, 2000.

3. See Gary L. Thomas, *Sacred Pathways: Discover Your Soul's Path to God* (Grand Rapids: Zondervan, 2000).

4. See *NIV Spiritual Formation Bible* (Grand Rapids: Zondervan, 1999).

5. In fact, when Thomas was asked for a copy of his doctrinal statement he responded, "I'm somewhat embarrassed to admit that I have not written an official doctrinal statement for the Center for Evangelical Spirituality." See Gary L. Thomas, email to author, June 23, 2000. As of March 3, 2003 no doctrinal statement has been posted on the Center for Evangelical Spirituality's website.

6. Gary L. Thomas, email to author, June 23, 2000.

7. Thomas, email to author.

8. See Gary L. Thomas, *Seeking the Face of God: The Path to a More Intimate Relationship*, (Eugene, OR: Harvest House, 1999).

9. Thomas, *Seeking the Face of God*, 13.

10. Thomas gives a selected bibliography of Christian spiritual classics with a short synopsis of each work. See Thomas, *Seeking the Face of God*, 237-239 and www.garythomas.com. Also, on his website, Thomas includes short biographies of Augustine, Martin Luther, Francis De Sales, Brother Lawrence and Fenelon.

11. Thomas, *Seeking the Face of God*, 15.

12. Thomas, *Seeking the Face of God*, 15-18.

13. See Thomas, *Sacred Pathways*.

14. Thomas, *Sacred Pathways*, 19.

15. For a short overview of each of these pathways see Thomas, *Sacred Pathways*, 22-

29.

16. See Gary L. Thomas, *The Glorious Pursuit: Embracing the Virtues of Christ*, (Colorado Springs: NavPress, 1998).

17. Thomas, *The Glorious Pursuit*, 20.

18. Thomas, *The Glorious Pursuit*, 20.

19. Thomas, *The Glorious Pursuit*, 180.

20. See Josef Solc, review of *The Glorious Pursuit: Embracing the Virtues of Christ*, by Gary L. Thomas, *Faith and Mission* 17:1 (1999): 107-108.

21. See Gary L. Thomas, *Sacred Marriage: What if God Designed Marriage to Make Us Holy more than to Make us Happy?* (Grand Rapids: Zondervan, 2000).

22. Thomas, *Sacred Marriage*, 17.

23. For biographical information see *Contemporary Authors*, vol.116 (Detroit: Gale Research, 1986), 494-495 and the Spiritual Formation Series biographical profile in each volume of the series. For example, see J.P. Moreland, *Love Your God with All Your Mind: The Role of Reason in the Life of the Soul*, Spiritual Formation Series, ed. Dallas Willard (Colorado Springs, CO: NavPress, 1997), 247.

24. For further research on Willard's philosophical writings see "Meaning and Universals in Husserl's *Logische Untersuchungen*" (Ph.D. diss., University of Wisconsin at Madison, 1964); *Logic and the Objectivity of Knowledge: A Study in Husserl's Early Philosophy* (Athens, OH: Ohio University Press, 1984); "Robin D. Rollinger, Husserl's Position in the School of Brentano," *Husserl Studies* 18:1 (2002): 77-81; and "A Realist Analysis of the Relationship Between Logic and Experience," *Topoi* 22:1 (2003): 69-78.

25. See Dallas Willard, *In Search of Guidance* (Ventura, CA: Regal, 1984). This work has been republished under the title, *Hearing God: Developing a Conversational Relationship with God* (Downers Grove: InterVarsity, 1999).

26. Willard, *In Search*, 26.

27. Willard, *In Search*, 7.

28. Willard, *In Search*, 22-23.

29. Willard, *In Search*, 24-26.

30. Willard, *In Search*, 30-31.

31. Willard, *In Search*, 34-42.

32. Willard, *In Search*, 45-71.

33. Willard, *In Search*, 108-120.

34. Willard, *In Search*, 120.

35. Willard, *In Search*, 138-139.

36. Willard, *In Search*, 170-178.

37. Willard, *In Search*, 194.

38. Willard, *In Search*, 196.

39. Willard, *In Search*, 200.

40. Willard, *In Search*, 210-211. Issler's chapter entitled "Communication: Hearing the God Who Speaks," overlaps and supports Willard's view of divine guidance. See Issler, *Wasting Time with God*, 151-182. For further study on divine guidance see Stephen D. Kovach, "Toward a Theology of Guidance: A Multi-faceted Approach Emphasizing Scripture as both Foundation and Pattern in Discerning the Will of God" (Ph.D. diss., Trinity Divinity School, 1999).

41. See Dallas Willard, *The Spirit of the Disciplines* (San Francisco: Harper, 1988).

42. Willard, *The Spirit of the Disciplines*, ix.

43. Willard, *The Spirit of the Disciplines*, 14-15.

44. Willard, *The Spirit of the Disciplines*, 25.

45. Willard, *The Spirit of the Disciplines*, 26.

46. Willard, *The Spirit of the Disciplines*, xi.

47. Willard, *The Spirit of the Disciplines*, 114.

48. Willard, *The Spirit of the Disciplines*, 114-117.

49. Willard, *The Spirit of the Disciplines*, 119.

50. See Ramesh P. Richard, review of *The Spirit of the Disciplines: Understanding How God Changes Lives*, by Dallas Willard, *Bibliotheca Sacra* 146 (July-Sept 2001): 357-

358.

51. Richard believes Willard should have offered more help to save Christians from the abuses that characterized older ascetics. See Richard, review of *The Spirit of the Disciplines*, 357.

52. Willard, *The Spirit of the Disciplines*, 130-155.

53. Willard, *The Spirit of the Disciplines*, 156.

54. Willard, *The Spirit of the Disciplines*, 158-191.

55. Although Willard properly emphasizes spiritual disciplines he does not balance that emphasis with the corresponding truths of the Spirit's role as well as the role of grace. See Richard, review of *The Spirit of the Disciplines*, 357.

56. Willard, *The Spirit of the Disciplines*, 94.

57. Willard, *The Spirit of the Disciplines*, 202. Also see Richard, review of *The Spirit of the Disciplines*, 357.

58. Willard, *The Spirit of the Disciplines*, 237.

59. See Dallas Willard, *The Divine Conspiracy: Rediscovering Our Hidden Life in God*, (San Francisco, Harper, 1998).

60. Willard, *The Divine Conspiracy*, 138-139.

61. Willard, *The Divine Conspiracy* , 138-139.

62. Willard, *The Divine Conspiracy*, 138-139.

63. See David Larsen, *Biblical Spirituality: Discovering the Real Connection Between the Bible and Life* (Grand Rapids: Kregel, 2001), 273.

64. Willard, *The Divine Conspiracy*, 403.

65. Willard, *The Divine Conspiracy*, 116.

66. See Stephen Kovach, review of *The Divine Conspiracy: Rediscovering Our Hidden Life in God*, by Dallas Willard, *Faith and Mission* 15 (Spring 1998): 101-103.

67. Willard, *The Divine Conspiracy*, 146-182.

68. Willard, *The Divine Conspiracy*, 190-196.

69. Willard, *The Divine Conspiracy*, 217.

70. Willard, *The Divine Conspiracy*, 235.

71. Willard, *The Divine Conspiracy*, 274-275.

72. Willard, *The Divine Conspiracy*, 291-299.

73. Willard, *The Divine Conspiracy*, 299-310.

74. Willard, *The Divine Conspiracy*, 347.

75. Personal information on Demarest may be found in his work *Satisfy Your Soul*, 315.

76. See Bruce A. Demarest and Gordon R. Lewis, *Integrative Theology: Historical, Biblical, Systematic, Apologetics, Practical*, 3 vols. in 1 (Grand Rapids: Zondervan, 1996). Demarest has also written the highly regarded work entitled, *The Cross and Salvation: The Doctrine of Salvation*, Foundations of Evangelical Theology Series (Wheaton: Crossway, 1997). Other works by Demarest include *General Revelation: Historical Views and Contemporary Issues* (Grand Rapids: Zondervan, 1982); *Jesus Christ: The God-Man* (Wheaton: Victor, 1978); and co-authored with Gordon R. Lewis, *Challenges to Inerrancy* (Chicago: Moody, 1984).

77. Demarest, *Satisfy Your Soul*, 27.

78. Demarest, *Satisfy Your Soul*, 29B31. Demarest's emphases.

79. See Bruce A. Demarest, "Spirituality and Christian Living," in *New Dimensions in Evangelical Thought: Essays in Honor of Millard J. Erickson*, ed. David S. Dockery (Downers Grove: InterVarsity, 1998).

80. Demarest, *Satisfy Your Soul*, 376.

81. Demarest, *Satisfy Your Soul*, 384.

82. Demarest, *Satisfy Your Soul*, 66-68.

83. Demarest, *Satisfy Your Soul*, 68-70.

84. Demarest, *Satisfy Your Soul*, 70-74.

85. Demarest, *Satisfy Your Soul*, 38.

86. Demarest, *Satisfy Your Soul*, 37.

87. Demarest, *Satisfy Your Soul*, 292.

88. McGrath, interview by author.

CHAPTER 6

THE CHALLENGE

Contemporary spirituality has been described by George Gallup as "a grab bag of random experiences that does little more than promise to make our eyes mist up or our hearts warm."[1] He adds, "We need perspective to separate the junk food from the wholesome, the faddish from the truly transforming."[2] After surveying Americans concerning their views on spirituality Gallup stated, "Americans seem ready for a fresh approach to universal heart hungers and soul needs that have never really gone away, only been ignored or brushed past. A breeze that feels wildly real and life-changing seems to be blowing. We can only wonder what sparks of renewal it will carry."[3]

Although this desire for renewal has great potential, it also brings great cause for concern: "Americans face constant temptations to pass over the wisdom of the ancients in favor of the guru of the month. In today's postmodern world, 'spirituality' may as easily refer to the cult of the goddess, or to channeling occult spirits, as to the practice of historic Judeo-Christian piety."[4] In view of our present generation's spiritual obsession, Gallup believes the task of defining truth is abundantly strategic.[5]

In surveying evangelical writers of spirituality, varying emphases were found. Some were subjective and experientially oriented while others were more theological in their basis. It is the perspective of this writer that Alister McGrath distinguishes himself by successfully bringing together both the experiential and theological. His own story of his Christian pilgrimage amply illustrates both the struggle and the balance.

> In my first period as a Christian, I found my attention focusing on *understanding* my faith. I continued to regard this as being of utmost importance. There is a marvelous coherence to Christian doctrine, and wrestling with the great truths of our faith provided me with both spiritual encouragement and intellectual challenge. Yet it seemed to me that my 'knowledge' of the Christian faith was rather dry and cerebral.
>
> Part of the difficulty was that I was, like most people of my generation, deeply influenced by the Enlightenment. Christianity was all about *ideas*—and it was important to get those ideas right. As a result, theological correctness had become something of an obsession with me. I had failed to realize that the gospel affects every level of our existence—not just the way

we think, but the way in which we *feel* and *live*. The Enlightenment had championed the role of reason, and vetoed any engagement with emotions or imagination. Yet I knew that writers such as Jonathan Edwards and C. S. Lewis had stressed the importance of precisely these aspects of our lives. I gradually came to the realization that my faith was far too academic.

My realization of the importance of spirituality began about 1989, but really blossomed from about 1992. I was invited to lead a regular summer school course in Oxford on 'medieval and Reformation spirituality.' This allowed me to engage with some of the great texts of Christian spirituality, including many from the period of the Reformation. As my students and I wrestled with these texts, we found ourselves challenged to deepen the quality of our Christian faith through being more open to God. I found that the quality of my Christian life deepened considerably as a result.

As I mentioned earlier, my basic understanding of Christian doctrine has not changed over the last ten years. I remain deeply committed to the fundamentals of Christian orthodoxy. What has happened is that these ideas have taken on a new depth, both as I appreciated more their implications, and as I realized that my grasp of the totality of the Christian gospel had been shallow. Perhaps I could say that I experienced a deepening in the quality of my faith, rather than any change in what I believed.[6]

McGrath's personal pilgrimage uniquely prepared him to address the issues of theology and spirituality. However, his conclusions would not have impacted the Christian community or world to the degree that they have without the presence of his prolific pen. Besides writing a multitude of books and journal articles, he has also authored chapters in other books, and has edited additional works. As previously documented in chapter one, McGrath's books address four different communities: scholarly, educational, evangelical leaders, and the church layperson. In these works, McGrath seeks to combine this balance of good theology and its application. In so doing he fills a void which other evangelical theologians surveyed are failing to completely bring about.

Yet McGrath's influence goes beyond his writings. Serving as the Principal of the Church of England's leading evangelical seminary, Wycliffe Hall, which is part of the world-renowned Oxford University, McGrath participates in training a generation of evangelical Christian leaders. In an effort to exert a transforming influence upon the church, Wycliffe Hall has a commitment to Biblical theology and its outworking in evangelism and missions.

Additionally, McGrath's influence extends from his many lectureships and addresses at major universities, seminaries, and centers of learning. In the 1990s he delivered major academic lecture series as well as single lectures in many of the world's most prestigious schools on four continents. These include schools such as Oxford University, University of Cambridge, Harvard Divinity School, Princeton Theological Seminary, Wheaton College, Dallas Theological Seminary, and University of Geneva.

McGrath defines Christian spirituality as the "reflection on the whole Christian enterprise of achieving and sustaining a relationship with God, which includes both public worship and private devotion, and the results of these in actual Christian life. . . . Christian spirituality concerns the quest for a fulfilled and authentic Christian existence, involving the bringing together of the fundamental ideas of Christianity and the whole experience of living on the basis of and within the scope of the Christian faith."[7] In this definition McGrath includes both the believer's relationship with God as well as his living out that relationship in sanctification.

This close connection between spirituality and theology undergirds McGrath's views as he insists that spirituality must be built on a solid and reliable foundation in the self-revelation of God. He sees the relationship between spirituality and theology as preventing spirituality from degenerating into a human-centered quest for heightened religiosity as well as preventing theology from becoming an abstract speculation about God.

McGrath's evangelical theology is clearly thought out and articulated. His themes support the main and central aspects of the Bible's message. Attempting not to fall into the danger of Enlightenment rationalism or postmodern subjectivism, McGrath lays a solid foundation on which an individual spiritual life can be built.

McGrath's spirituality is clearly evangelical through its foundation and connection to the core tenets of his theology. Although he openly admits being heavily influenced by the rationalism of the Enlightenment, he brings correction to this without swinging the pendulum to the extreme subjectivism of postmodernism. Such balance is vitally needed today. Evident is the fact that McGrath's evangelical theology is thorough and soundly accurate and forms the basis of an evangelical spirituality that is balanced and real.

Spirituality without truth is a dangerous pit into which myriads are falling. As reviewed in chapter four, a spiritual survey of western culture over the last fifty years evidences this disturbing trend. This half-a-century shift away from objective truth initiated an era in which subjective experiences became the defining norm. As a result, spirituality has become little more than the latest fad or the most recent craze.

Coinciding with this spiritual transition in the last half of the twentieth century has been the evolution of society itself. The modern era, initiated by the Enlightenment, delivered a rationalist approach based upon observation and experimentation, giving assent to the certainty of objective knowledge. This era elevated mankind as the final and most complete measure of truth. Such an inaccurate standard was of course incompetent to gratify the cognitive, much less the emotional exigence of that generation.

The inability of the modern era to satisfy mankind's deepest spiritual needs gave way to the views of postmodernism. Postmodernism questions the capacity of discovering truth through reason and instead emphasizes intuition. Truth, when acknowledged at all, is community based. The objectivity of knowledge is denied since absolute fact is uncertain. Subjectivity has become the norm of the day with pluralism, its central hallmark.

An eye opening example of the combination of spirituality and postmodernism, also reviewed in chapter four of this study, is found in looking at The Omega

Institute in Rhinebeck, New York, co-founded by Elizabeth Lesser in 1997. This institute has become America's largest adult-education center on wellness and spirituality. Lesser encourages her readers to walk a spiritual path with or without religious help because all paths are available and none are exclusively right or wrong or required. She highly elevates the ideal of meeting and merging all religious traditions unless one's religious beliefs cause difficulty. In such cases of religious rigor Lessor urges the laying aside of that individual, troublesome religious belief.

How has the subjectivity of postmodernism effected spirituality among evangelicals? In overviewing the works of five evangelical writers of spirituality, two authors heavily emphasized the subjective experience without giving equal emphasis to the corresponding theological foundation. Henry Blackaby, an influential leader among Southern Baptists, wrote the best-selling book *Experiencing God*. In this work he correctly emphasizes the believer's need to personally experience God. Yet he fails to fully encase this teaching within its proper theology.   Similarly, the influential Quaker, Richard J. Foster, author of the widely acclaimed book, *Celebration of Discipline,* has enormously impacted contemporary evangelical spirituality. Most scholars acknowledge his contribution as having more influence than any other contemporary writer. In this work Foster challenges Christians to develop greater depth in their spiritual lives as he argues that the classical disciplines of the spiritual life are the primary catalysts which move Christians from surface living into the depths of the spiritual realm. Yet Foster appears to lack a theological compass to guide him, especially with the many authors he favorably quotes. These various authorities that Foster deems worthy of quotation fall into a wide range over the theological spectrum, with few being of an evangelical persuasion. Although Blackaby and Foster have much to commend, it appears they have been greatly influenced by subjectivism.

Gary Thomas, founder and director of the Center for Evangelical Spirituality, seeks to integrate Scripture, church history and the Christian classics. He believes a great deal can be learned from historic Christian traditions without compromising essential evangelical tenets. Thomas promotes Christian growth and the refinement of authentic Christian spirituality while accepting Scripture as the final word. He undergirds much of his work with a solid theological orientation, notably of a more substantial theological nature than either Blackaby or Foster. Yet Thomas has no written theological statement for his center, and he apparently has no problem with affirming spiritualities of different traditions even though their dogmas are quite divergent.

The final two writers surveyed have sought to consciously build their evangelical spirituality upon a solid theological base. Dallas Willard, a university teacher of philosophy, seeks to bring about a practical theology that answers questions regarding how one grows spiritually. He sees the overall task of practical theology as proclaiming the gospel message and making disciples of all nations. The task of making disciples has largely been omitted according to Willard. He sees the revival of the disciplines for the spiritual life as having great significance and potential for eliminating this omission. His concern lies with a void among evangelicals of understanding the theological basis for the disciplines. Willard believes there is a need for a foundation: a practical, workable theology of spiritual disciplines. Though this writer questions some of Willard's Biblical presentations and emphases, his work solidly stands as a good example of building one's spirituality upon an evangelical theological foundation.

Similarly, Bruce Demarest, long-time seminary professor of theology, seeks to undergird his teaching on spirituality with a sound evangelical theology. When answering what distinguishes Christian spirituality from non-Christian alternatives, Demarest launches into the theological arena. He identifies the distinctives of Biblical and Christian spirituality as Trinitarian, revelational, Christ-centered, creational, salvational, and pneumatic. He also emphasizes the balance of orthodoxy (right beliefs), orthopathy (right affections), and orthopraxy (right actions). Demarest's main weaknesses appear in the application of his thought in such areas as icons, dreams, and the labyrinth walk. However, like Willard, Demarest is to be commended in his work to build spirituality upon an evangelical theological framework.

Conclusion

Just as postmodernism burst upon the scene to influence the thought of society and culture, at least one author is heralding its collapse. Gene Veith, an expert on cultural trends and thought states, "If the fall of a great work of architecture is a milestone for cultural change, then surely the collapse of the World Trade Center—twin towers of 110 stories utterly destroyed by a terrorist attack—marks the end of postmodernism."[8] He continues his assessment by stating,

> Postmodernists rejected the very possibility of objective truth, insisting that reality is only a construction of the culture or of the mind. But the planes that crashed into the buildings and into every American's consciousness were no mental constructions. Objective reality in all of its hard edges asserted itself.
> Postmodernists rejected the very possibility of objective morality. What is right or wrong varies, they said, according to the culture or the individual. If a person *chooses* certain values, that makes them right for that person. The terrorists certainly made a *choice*, and what they did was right for *them*. But somehow their cold-blooded murder of thousands of ordinary men, women, and children was seen as pure, objective evil, something postmodernists had professed not to believe.[9]

If Veith's assessment is correct, what implication will it have for evangelicals and the church?

McGrath, in considering the future of Christianity,[10] offers a compelling idea using the categories of the traditional intellectual and the organic intellectual from Marxist theorist Antonio Gramsci.[11] Paralleling the traditional intellectual with an academic theologian, McGrath says the academic theologian is one who weds himself to the norms and values of modern western academic culture and tends to sneer at popular culture as well as ridicule those who seek to engage it. Because of this, McGrath believes "much of academic theology is incapable of exercising a genuinely prophetic role, precisely because it is so closely dependent upon the support of academic culture."[12]

In contrast to the academic theologian, and paralleling the organic intellectual of Gramsci, McGrath characterizes an organic theologian as "an activist, a popularizer—someone who sees his task as supportive and systematic within the community of faith, and as evangelistic and apologetic outside that community."[13] In further elaborating on that role McGrath states,

> The organic theologian will see himself as working within the great historical Christian tradition, which he gladly makes his own. Even when he feels he must critique the contemporary expressions or applications of that tradition, he will do so from a deep sense of commitment to the community of faith and its distinctive ideas and values. He will not see his task as imposing alien ideas upon his community. . . . His responsibility within the community is to explore and apply its tradition; outside the community, his task is to commend and defend its ideas and communicate them as effectively as possible.[14]

Whether or not the postmodern era has ended is yet to be seen. But without a doubt the attack upon the World Trade Center ushered in a new mindset in the American and even Western way of life and philosophy. At such a pivotal moment when a culture questions itself and its beliefs, a clear and concise message from the Christian community becomes ever more essential.

Now more than ever before our culture needs theologians who can fully relate theology to life, and practitioners who can articulate a credible theology to complement their practical ministry focus. It is the belief of this writer that Alister McGrath offers for evangelicals an excellent model of a theologian who believes the heart and the hands both matter and should compliment the mind. At a strategic moment in history McGrath assures us that the experience of real spirituality based squarely upon a sure foundation of sound theology is both achievable and imperative.

The spiritual aridity and barrenness of modern culture has led many to thirst for a "real spiritual" element in life. Yet too often this has drawn people away from Christianity as individuals seek spirituality in all forms. According to McGrath, this "new interest in spirituality has thus brought dangers, as well as opportunities, for the Christian churches."[15] He believes "there is a real need to adopt a critical perspective towards this development, rather then welcome it uncritically."[16] The emphasis upon spirituality in western society must not be unreservedly embraced by evangelicals as it has very little, if any basis in truth. Spiritual experiences for the sake of spiritual experiences is not enough. One must also evaluate the issue of veracity.

Evangelical writers no longer have the luxury of writing about spiritual experiences unless they first clarify the theological underpinnings of these experiences. It no longer can be taken for granted that a mutual understanding exists as to who God is and how he relates to individuals. Evangelical writers of spirituality such as Blackaby and Foster must make major clarifications concerning their theological foundations. If Thomas is to continue to call his organization "evangelical" he must articulate the beliefs that coincide with that label.

On the same token, if evangelicals are to capture the hearts of a lost and dying world, a dry, cognitive pursuit and proliferation of theological truth is not enough. Writers such as Willard and Demarest must be encouraged to continue their work that brings together evangelical theology and evangelical spirituality. McGrath's vision to build a spirituality which retains a sound theological basis is a clarion call to evangelicals. It is a call that must be heeded. However for now McGrath's example to connect sound theology with real spirituality stands apart in current evangelicalism.

NOTES

1. George Gallup, Jr., and Timothy Jones, *The Next American Spirituality: Finding God in the Twenty-First Century* (Colorado Springs: Cook, 2000), 15.

2. Gallup, Jr., and Jones, *The Next American Spirituality*.

3. Gallup, Jr., and Jones, *The Next American Spirituality*, 36-37.

4. Gallup, Jr., and Jones, *The Next American Spirituality*, 39.

5. Gallup, Jr., and Jones, *The Next American Spirituality*, 127.

6. McGrath, *Loving God with Heart and Mind*. McGrath's emphases.

7. McGrath, *Christian Spirituality*, 2.

8. Gene E. Veith, : Reality in the Rubble: The Fall of the Twin Towers Heralds the Collapse of Postmodernism," *World* 16:39 (October 13, 2001): 16

9. Veith, "Reality in the Rubble," 16. Veith's emphases.

10. See Alister E. McGrath, *The Future of Christianity*. Blackwell Manifestos (Malden, MA: Blackwell, 2002).

11. For further study on Gramsci see Alistair Davidson, *Antonio Gramsci: Towards and Intellectual Biography* (London: Merlin, 1987); David Harris, *From Class Struggle to the Politics of Pleasure: The Effects of Gramscianism on Cultural Studies* (London: Routledge, 1992); and Paul Ransome, *Antonio Gramsci: A New Introduction* (New York: Harvester Wheatsheaf, 1992).

12. McGrath, *The Future of Christianity*, 150.

13. McGrath, *The Future of Christianity*, 151.

14. McGrath, *The Future of Christianity*, 152.

15. McGrath, *Loving God with Heart and Mind*.

16. McGrath, *Loving God with Heart and Mind*.

APPENDIX A

MCGRATH'S CURRICULUM VITAE[1]

Dr. Alister Edgar McGrath, BD, MA, DPhil

Born 23 January 1953

Education

1957-1965	Down High School, Downpatrick, Northern Ireland
1965-1971	Methodist College, Belfast
1971-1975	Wadham College, Oxford
1975-1976	Linacre College, Oxford
1976-1978	Merton College, Oxford
1978-1980	St John's College, Cambridge

Degrees

BA   First Class Honours, Final Honour School of Natural Sciences, Oxford University, 1975.

MA   Oxford University, 1978.

DPhil   Oxford University 1978, for research in molecular biology.

BA   First Class Honours, Final Honour School of Theology, Oxford University, 1978.

BD   Oxford University, 1983, for research in late medieval theology.

Posts Held

1980-1983	Curate, St Leonards Parish Church, Wollaton, Nottingham.
1983-1995	Lecturer in historical and systematic theology, Wycliffe Hall, Oxford;
1983-	Member of the Oxford University Faculty of Theology
1993-1999	University Research Lecturer in Theology, Oxford University
1993-1997	Research Professor of Systematic Theology, Regent College, Vancouver, British Columbia
1995-	Principal, Wycliffe Hall, Oxford

1999- Professor of Historical Theology, Oxford University [Titular Professorship]

Major Academic Lecture Series

1990 Bampton Lectures, Oxford University
1990 Tipple Lectures, Drew University, Madison, New Jersey
1992 Anderson Lectures, McGill University
1993 Inch Lectures, Wheaton College, Illinois
1995 Day-Higginbotham Lectures, Southwestern Baptist Theological Seminary
1995 Keynote Speaker, with George Lindbeck, at "Evangelical-Postliberal Dialogue", Wheaton College, Illinois
1995 Eliza Ferrie Lectures, Presbyterian Theological Institute, New South Wales
1996 Annual Church of Ireland Theological Lectures, Queen's University, Belfast
1996 Keynote addresses, Australian and New Zealand Association for Theological Studies, Perth, Western Australia
1997 Griffith-Thomas Lectures, Dallas Theological Seminary
1997 Henderson Lectures, Pittsburgh Theological Seminary
1999 "Biblical Spirituality" lecture series, C. S. Lewis Institute, Washington, DC
2001 Belote Lectures, Hong Kong Baptist Theological Seminary

Single Lectures and Speeches

1990 Princeton Theological Seminary, "Theories of the Atonement".
1990 Invited paper, Sixteenth Century Studies Conference, St Louis, Missouri: "Transition from Calvin to Calvinism".
1991 University of Melbourne
1992 Invited paper, Sixteenth Century Studies Conference, Atlanta, Georgia: "On Writing a Biography of Calvin".
1993 China Graduate School of Theology, Hong Kong: "A Theology of Ministry"
1993 University of Geneva: "La pensée économique de Calvin".
1993 University of Cambridge, systematic theology seminar: "Legal theories of the Atonement".
1994 Lightfoot Society, University of Durham: "The Renewal of Anglicanism".
1994 Selwyn Lectures, Diocese of Lichfield: "Christian Apologetics".
1995 Oxford University Department for Continuing Education: "Interpreting the Reformation".

1995	University of Utrecht: "Recent Trends in Evangelical Theology".
1995	St John's College, Auckland, New Zealand: "Anglican Theology since 1945".
1996	Ethics and Public Policy Center, Washington, DC: "Apects of the Evangelical-Catholic Dialogue".
1996	Virginia Theological Seminary: Commencement Address
1996	University of Durham: "Martin Luther: A Prophet to the Church"
1997	University of Utrecht: "Christian Theology and the Natural Sciences".
1997	Seattle Pacific University, Washington: "The Purpose of Theological Education".
1998	Finnish Theological Institute, Helsinki: "Trinitarian Theology Today"
1998	Harvard Divinity School: "Evangelicalism and Trinitarian Theology"
1998	International Newman Conference, Oxford: "Newman on Justification".
1999	Alliance Theological Seminary, Hong Kong: "The Purpose and Place of Systematic Theology"
1999	Wheaton College, IL: "Religion, Fulfilment and Tranquility: A Theological Foundation". Wheaton College/John Templeton Foundation Conference on Christian Theology and Mental Health.
1999	University of Helsinki, Finland: "Christian Theology and Postmodern Culture".
2000	Whitefield Institute, Oxford: "Postmodern Apologetics: Rediscovering Paul's Areopagus Speech."

NOTES

1. Alister E. McGrath, email to author, May 24, 2000.

BIBLIOGRAPHY

Works By Alister E. McGrath

Books

McGrath, Alister E. *Beyond the Quiet Time: Practical Evangelical Spirituality.* Grand Rapids: Baker, 1995

———. *A Brief History of Heaven.* Blackwell Brief History of Religion Series. Malden, MA: Blackwell, 2003.

———. *Christian Spirituality: An Introduction.* Malden, MA: Blackwell, 1999.

———. *Christian Theology: An Introduction,* 2d ed. Malden, MA: Blackwell, 1997.

———. *A Cloud of Witnesses: Ten Great Christian Thinkers.* Grand Rapids: Zondervan, 1990.

———. *Evangelicalism and the Future of Christianity.* Downers Grove: InterVarsity, 1995.

———. *Explaining Your Faith*, Revised Edition. Grand Rapids: Baker, 1995.

———. *The Foundations of Dialogue in Science and Religion.* Malden, MA: Blackwell, 1998.

———. *The Future of Christianity.* Blackwell Manifestos. Malden, MA: Blackwell, 2002.

———. *The Genesis of Doctrine: A Study in the Foundations of Doctrinal Criticism.* Grand Rapids: Eerdmans,— 1997.

———. *Glimpsing the Face of God: The Search for Meaning in the Universe.* Grand Rapids: Eerdmans, 2002.

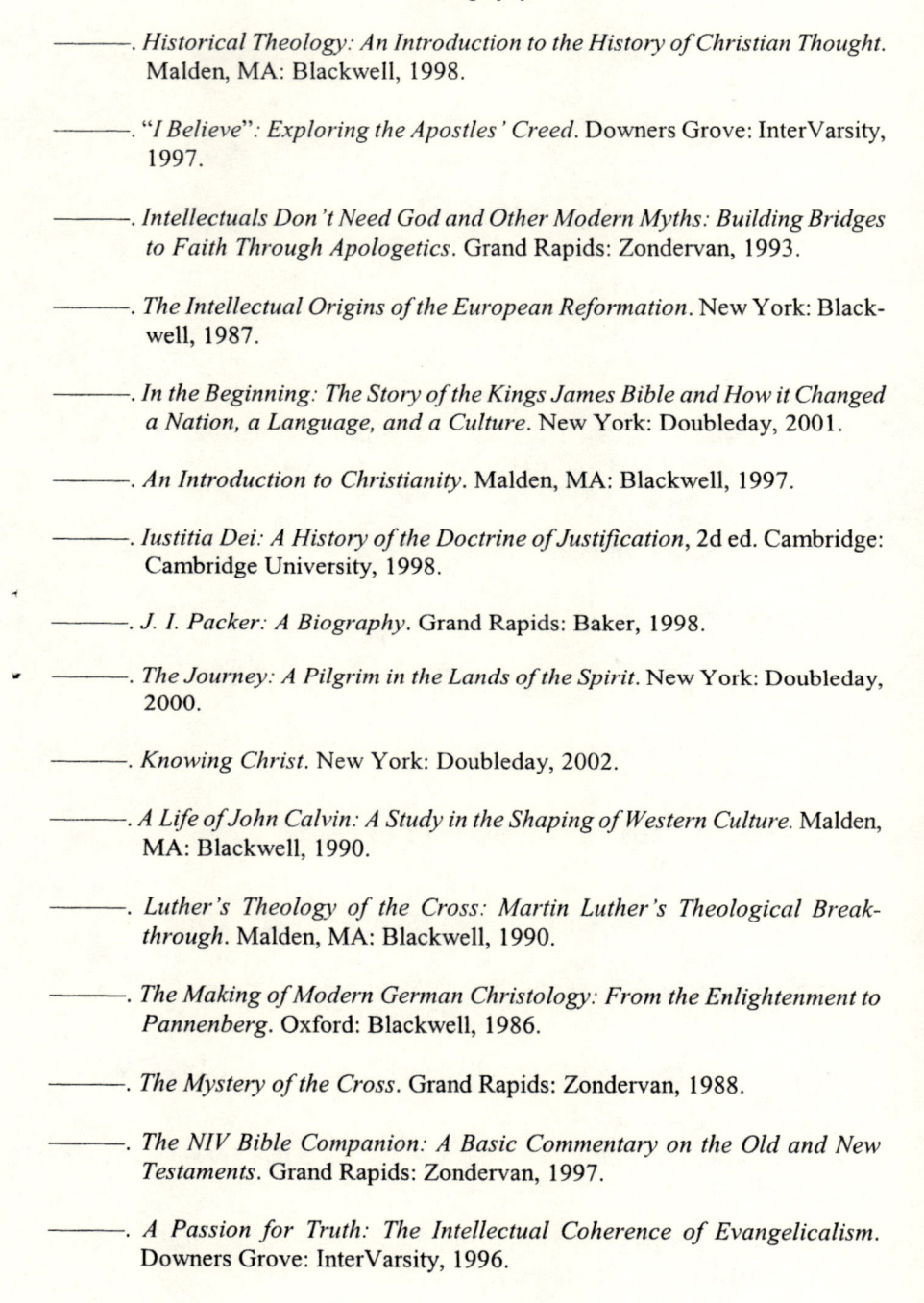

———. *Historical Theology: An Introduction to the History of Christian Thought.* Malden, MA: Blackwell, 1998.

———. *"I Believe": Exploring the Apostles' Creed.* Downers Grove: InterVarsity, 1997.

———. *Intellectuals Don't Need God and Other Modern Myths: Building Bridges to Faith Through Apologetics.* Grand Rapids: Zondervan, 1993.

———. *The Intellectual Origins of the European Reformation.* New York: Blackwell, 1987.

———. *In the Beginning: The Story of the Kings James Bible and How it Changed a Nation, a Language, and a Culture.* New York: Doubleday, 2001.

———. *An Introduction to Christianity.* Malden, MA: Blackwell, 1997.

———. *Iustitia Dei: A History of the Doctrine of Justification*, 2d ed. Cambridge: Cambridge University, 1998.

———. *J. I. Packer: A Biography.* Grand Rapids: Baker, 1998.

———. *The Journey: A Pilgrim in the Lands of the Spirit.* New York: Doubleday, 2000.

———. *Knowing Christ.* New York: Doubleday, 2002.

———. *A Life of John Calvin: A Study in the Shaping of Western Culture.* Malden, MA: Blackwell, 1990.

———. *Luther's Theology of the Cross: Martin Luther's Theological Breakthrough.* Malden, MA: Blackwell, 1990.

———. *The Making of Modern German Christology: From the Enlightenment to Pannenberg.* Oxford: Blackwell, 1986.

———. *The Mystery of the Cross.* Grand Rapids: Zondervan, 1988.

———. *The NIV Bible Companion: A Basic Commentary on the Old and New Testaments.* Grand Rapids: Zondervan, 1997.

———. *A Passion for Truth: The Intellectual Coherence of Evangelicalism.* Downers Grove: InterVarsity, 1996.

———. *Reformation Thought: An Introduction*, 3d ed. Malden, MA: Blackwell, 1999.

———. *Science and Religion: An Introduction*. Malden, MA: Blackwell, 1999.

———. *A Scientific Theology*. Vol. 1, *Nature*. Grand Rapids: Eerdmans, 2001.

———. *A Scientific Theology*. Vol. 2, *Reality*. Grand Rapids: Eerdmans, 2002.

———. *A Scientific Theology*. Vol. 3, *Theory*. Grand Rapids: Eerdmans, 2003.

———. *Spirituality in an Age of Change: Rediscovering the Spirit of the Reformers*. Grand Rapids: Zondervan, 1994.

———. *Studies in Doctrine: Understanding Doctrine, Understanding the Trinity, Understanding Jesus, Justification by Faith*. Grand Rapids: Zondervan, 1997.

———. *Suffering and God*. Grand Rapids: Zondervan, 1995.

———. *The Sunnier Side of Doubt*. Grand Rapids: Zondervan, 1990.

———. *Thomas F. Torrance: An Intellectual Biography*. Edinburgh: T & T Clark, 1999.

———. *The Unknown God: Searching for Spiritual Fulfillment*. Grand Rapids: Eerdmans, 1999.

———. *What was God Doing on the Cross?* Grand Rapids: Zondervan, 1992.

Books by McGrath as Contributor, Co-Author, or Editor

McGrath, Alister E. "Augustine of Hippo." In *Historians of the Christian Tradition: Their Methodologies and Impact*, ed. Michael Bauman and Martin Klauber, 79-93. Nashville: Broadman & Holman, 1995.

———. "A Better Way: The Priesthood of All Believers." In *Power Religion: The Selling Out of the Evangelical Church?*, ed. Michael S. Horton, 301-313. Chicago: Moody, 1992.

———. "Christology: On Learning from History." In *Who do you Say that I Am? Christology and the Church*, ed. Donald Armstrong, 69-90. Grand Rapids: Eerdmans, 1999.

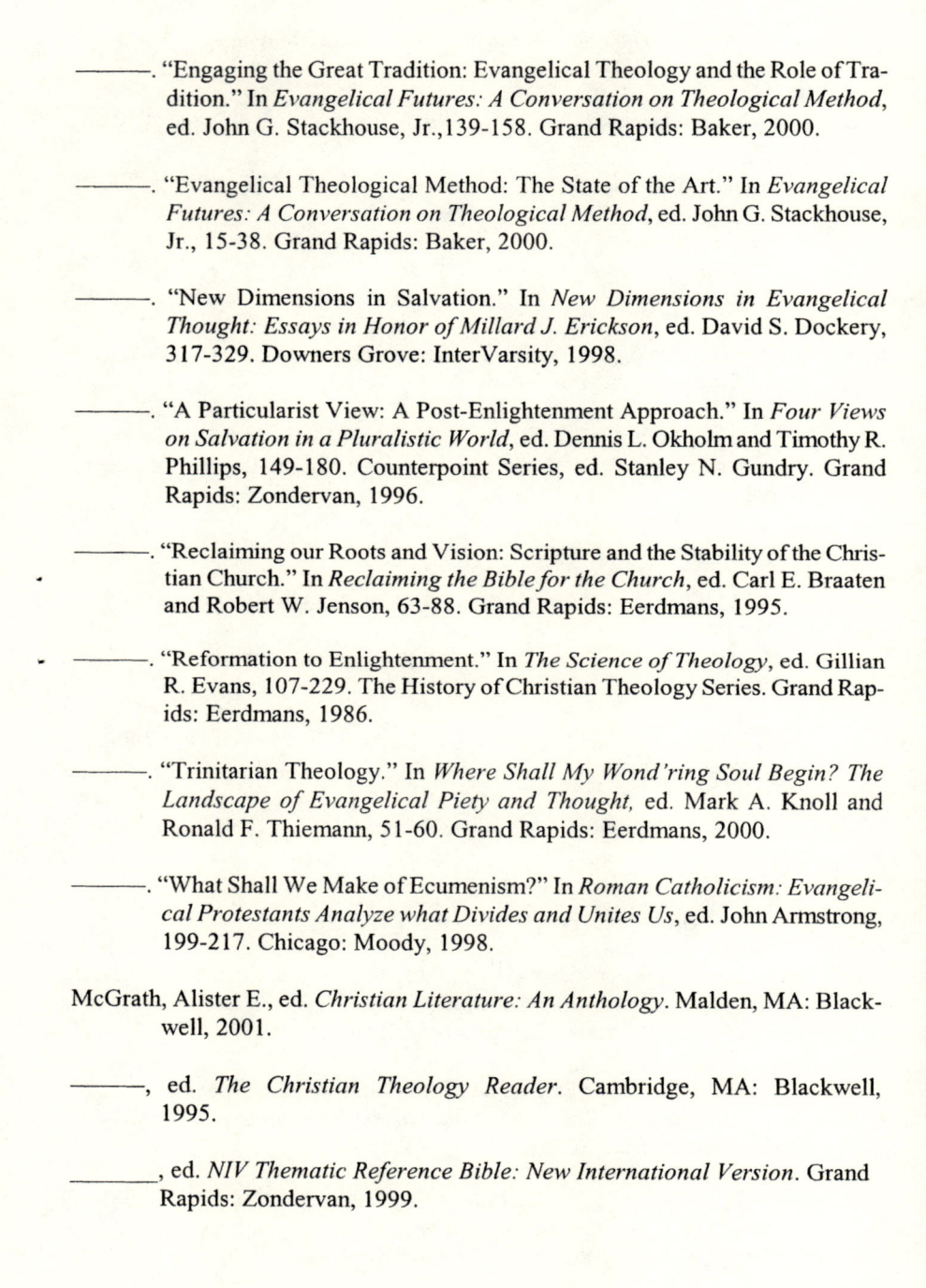

———. "Engaging the Great Tradition: Evangelical Theology and the Role of Tradition." In *Evangelical Futures: A Conversation on Theological Method*, ed. John G. Stackhouse, Jr.,139-158. Grand Rapids: Baker, 2000.

———. "Evangelical Theological Method: The State of the Art." In *Evangelical Futures: A Conversation on Theological Method*, ed. John G. Stackhouse, Jr., 15-38. Grand Rapids: Baker, 2000.

———. "New Dimensions in Salvation." In *New Dimensions in Evangelical Thought: Essays in Honor of Millard J. Erickson*, ed. David S. Dockery, 317-329. Downers Grove: InterVarsity, 1998.

———. "A Particularist View: A Post-Enlightenment Approach." In *Four Views on Salvation in a Pluralistic World*, ed. Dennis L. Okholm and Timothy R. Phillips, 149-180. Counterpoint Series, ed. Stanley N. Gundry. Grand Rapids: Zondervan, 1996.

———. "Reclaiming our Roots and Vision: Scripture and the Stability of the Christian Church." In *Reclaiming the Bible for the Church*, ed. Carl E. Braaten and Robert W. Jenson, 63-88. Grand Rapids: Eerdmans, 1995.

———. "Reformation to Enlightenment." In *The Science of Theology*, ed. Gillian R. Evans, 107-229. The History of Christian Theology Series. Grand Rapids: Eerdmans, 1986.

———. "Trinitarian Theology." In *Where Shall My Wond'ring Soul Begin? The Landscape of Evangelical Piety and Thought,* ed. Mark A. Knoll and Ronald F. Thiemann, 51-60. Grand Rapids: Eerdmans, 2000.

———. "What Shall We Make of Ecumenism?" In *Roman Catholicism: Evangelical Protestants Analyze what Divides and Unites Us*, ed. John Armstrong, 199-217. Chicago: Moody, 1998.

McGrath, Alister E., ed. *Christian Literature: An Anthology*. Malden, MA: Blackwell, 2001.

———, ed. *The Christian Theology Reader*. Cambridge, MA: Blackwell, 1995.

———, ed. *NIV Thematic Reference Bible: New International Version*. Grand Rapids: Zondervan, 1999.

McGrath, Alister E. and Donald M. Lewis, ed. *Doing Theology for the People of God: Studies in Honor of J. I. Packer*. Downers Grove: InterVarsity, 1996.

McGrath, Alister E. and Duncan Forrester, ed. *The Blackwell Encyclopedia of Modern Christian Thought*. Malden, MA: Blackwell, 1993.

McGrath, Alister E. and Martin H. Mansen, ed. *Zondervan Dictionary of Bible Themes: The Accessible and Comprehensive Tool for Topical Studies*. Grand Rapids: Zondervan, 1999.

McGrath, Alister E. and Joanna McGrath. *Self-Esteem: The Cross and Christian Confidence*, Rev. ed. Wheaton: Crossway, 2002.

McGrath, Alister E. and Michael Green. *How Shall We Reach Them? Defending and Communicating the Christian Faith to Nonbelievers*. Nashville: Thomas Nelson, 1995.

Dictionary and Encyclopedia Articles

McGrath, Alister E. "Beil, Gabriel," *Dictionary of Biblical Interpretation*, 1999.

———. "Bucer, Martin," *Dictionary of Biblical Interpretation*, 1999.

———. "Bullinger, J. H.," *Dictionary of Biblical Interpretation*, 1999.

———. "Calvinism," *The Oxford Dictionary of the Christian Church*, 3d ed., 1997.

———. "Calvin, John," *The Oxford Dictionary of the Christian Church*, 3d ed., 1997.

———. "Cross, Theology of the," *A Dictionary of Paul and His Letters*, 1993.

———. "The Fall," *The New Dictionary of Christian Ethics and Pastoral Theology*, 1995.

———. "Justification," *A Dictionary of Paul and His Letters*, 1993.

———. "Justification," *The Oxford Encyclopedia of the Reformation*, 1996.

———. "Justification," *The Oxford Dictionary of the Christian Church*, 3d ed., 1997.

———. "Justification by Faith," *The New Dictionary of Christian Ethics and Pastoral Theology*, 1995.

———. "Lutheranism," *The Oxford Dictionary of the Christian Church*, 3d ed., 1997.

———. "Luther," *Dictionary of Biblical Interpretation*, 1990.

———. "Luther, Martin," *The Oxford Dictionary of the Christian Church*, 3d ed., 1997.

———. "Melanchthon, Philipp," *Dictionary of Biblical Interpretation*, 1999.

———. "Oecolampadius, Johann," *Dictionary of Biblical Interpretation*, 1999.

———. "Reformation," *The Dictionary of Biblical Interpretation*, 1990.

———. "Sanctification," *The Oxford Encyclopedia of the Reformation*, 1996.

———. "Scholasticism," *The Oxford Encyclopedia of the Reformation*, 1996.

———. "Sin and Salvation," *The New Dictionary of Christian Ethics and Pastoral Theology*, 1995.

———. "The Transition to Modernity, 1400-1750," *Encyclopedia of Theology*, 1995.

———. "Vadian," *Dictionary of Biblical Interpretation*, 1999.

———. "Avon Karlstadt, Andreas B.," *Dictionary of Biblical Interpretation*, 1999.

———. "Zwingli," *Dictionary of Biblical Interpretation*, 1999.

Journal Articles, Unpublished Papers, and Interviews

McGrath, Alister E. "The Anti-Pelagian Structure of 'Nominalist' Doctrines of Justification," *Ephemerides Theologicae Lovanienses* 57 (1981): 107-119.

———. "ARCIC II and Justification. Some Difficulties and Obscurities relating to Anglican and Roman Catholic Teaching on Justification," *Anvil* 1 (1984): 27-42.

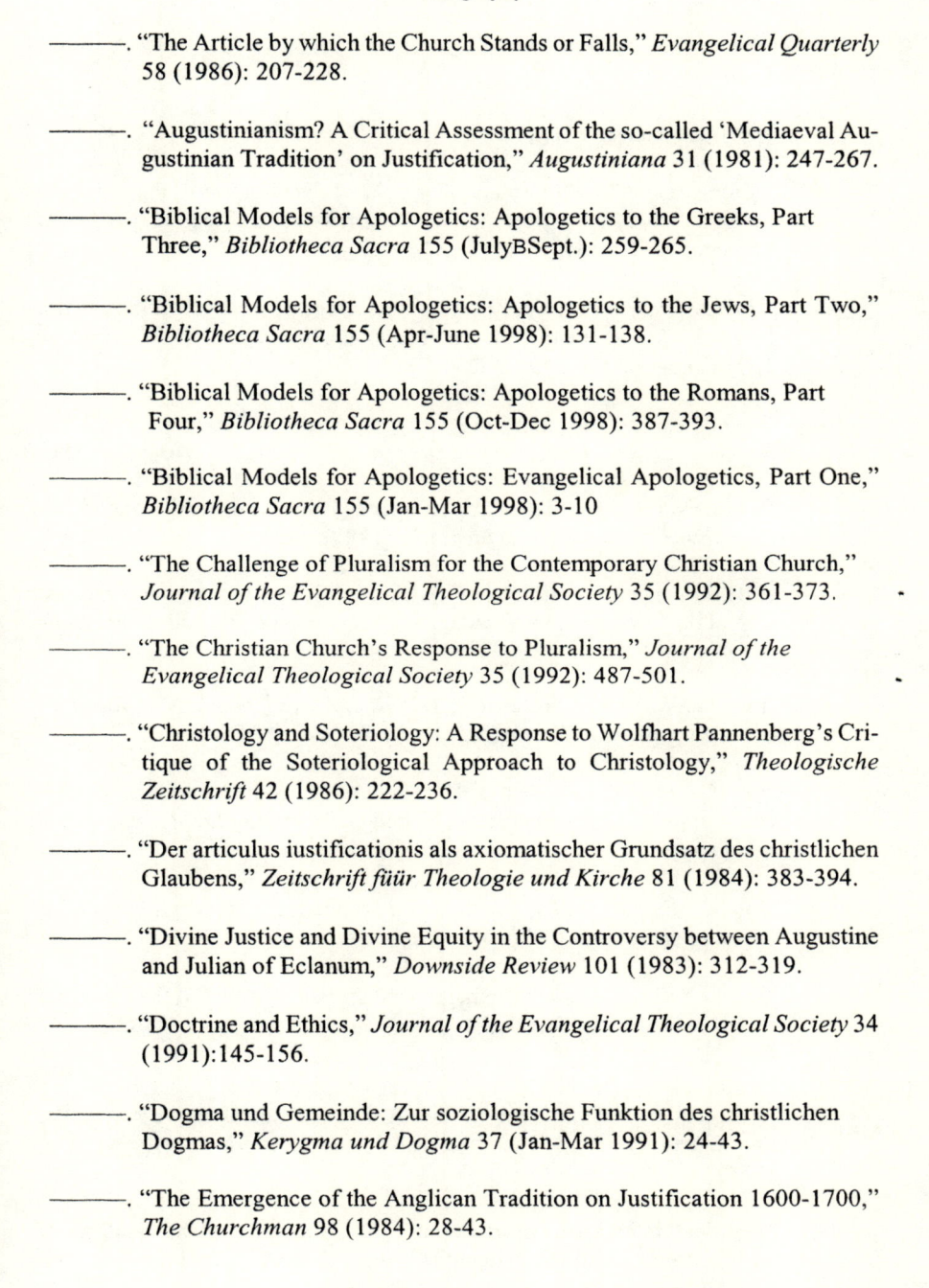

———. "The Article by which the Church Stands or Falls," *Evangelical Quarterly* 58 (1986): 207-228.

———. "Augustinianism? A Critical Assessment of the so-called 'Mediaeval Augustinian Tradition' on Justification," *Augustiniana* 31 (1981): 247-267.

———. "Biblical Models for Apologetics: Apologetics to the Greeks, Part Three," *Bibliotheca Sacra* 155 (JulyBSept.): 259-265.

———. "Biblical Models for Apologetics: Apologetics to the Jews, Part Two," *Bibliotheca Sacra* 155 (Apr-June 1998): 131-138.

———. "Biblical Models for Apologetics: Apologetics to the Romans, Part Four," *Bibliotheca Sacra* 155 (Oct-Dec 1998): 387-393.

———. "Biblical Models for Apologetics: Evangelical Apologetics, Part One," *Bibliotheca Sacra* 155 (Jan-Mar 1998): 3-10

———. "The Challenge of Pluralism for the Contemporary Christian Church," *Journal of the Evangelical Theological Society* 35 (1992): 361-373.

———. "The Christian Church's Response to Pluralism," *Journal of the Evangelical Theological Society* 35 (1992): 487-501.

———. "Christology and Soteriology: A Response to Wolfhart Pannenberg's Critique of the Soteriological Approach to Christology," *Theologische Zeitschrift* 42 (1986): 222-236.

———. "Der articulus iustificationis als axiomatischer Grundsatz des christlichen Glaubens," *Zeitschrift füür Theologie und Kirche* 81 (1984): 383-394.

———. "Divine Justice and Divine Equity in the Controversy between Augustine and Julian of Eclanum," *Downside Review* 101 (1983): 312-319.

———. "Doctrine and Ethics," *Journal of the Evangelical Theological Society* 34 (1991):145-156.

———. "Dogma und Gemeinde: Zur soziologische Funktion des christlichen Dogmas," *Kerygma und Dogma* 37 (Jan-Mar 1991): 24-43.

———. "The Emergence of the Anglican Tradition on Justification 1600-1700," *The Churchman* 98 (1984): 28-43.

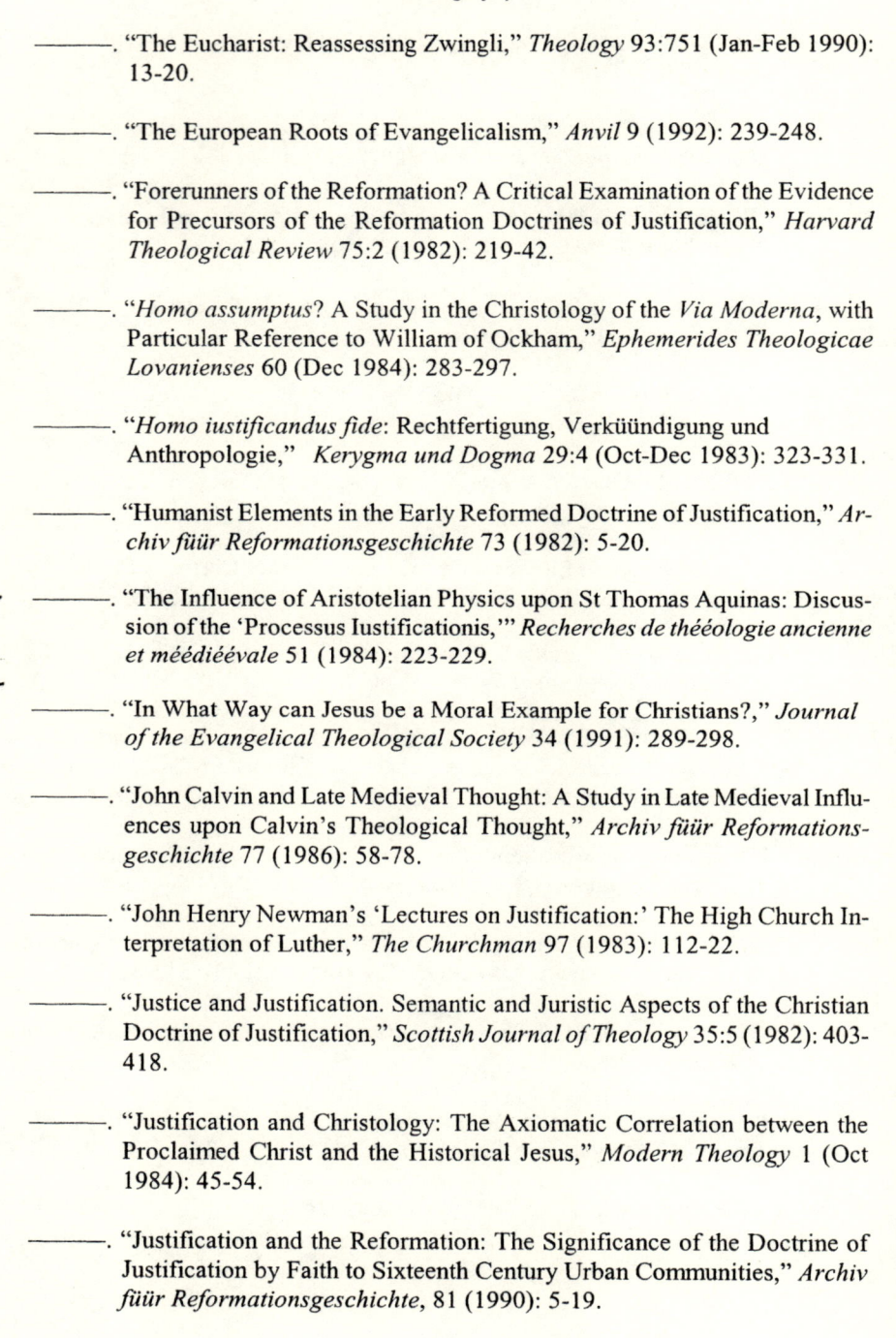

———. "The Eucharist: Reassessing Zwingli," *Theology* 93:751 (Jan-Feb 1990): 13-20.

———. "The European Roots of Evangelicalism," *Anvil* 9 (1992): 239-248.

———. "Forerunners of the Reformation? A Critical Examination of the Evidence for Precursors of the Reformation Doctrines of Justification," *Harvard Theological Review* 75:2 (1982): 219-42.

———. "*Homo assumptus*? A Study in the Christology of the *Via Moderna*, with Particular Reference to William of Ockham," *Ephemerides Theologicae Lovanienses* 60 (Dec 1984): 283-297.

———. "*Homo iustificandus fide*: Rechtfertigung, Verküündigung und Anthropologie," *Kerygma und Dogma* 29:4 (Oct-Dec 1983): 323-331.

———. "Humanist Elements in the Early Reformed Doctrine of Justification," *Archiv füür Reformationsgeschichte* 73 (1982): 5-20.

———. "The Influence of Aristotelian Physics upon St Thomas Aquinas: Discussion of the 'Processus Iustificationis,'" *Recherches de thééologie ancienne et méédiéévale* 51 (1984): 223-229.

———. "In What Way can Jesus be a Moral Example for Christians?," *Journal of the Evangelical Theological Society* 34 (1991): 289-298.

———. "John Calvin and Late Medieval Thought: A Study in Late Medieval Influences upon Calvin's Theological Thought," *Archiv füür Reformationsgeschichte* 77 (1986): 58-78.

———. "John Henry Newman's 'Lectures on Justification:' The High Church Interpretation of Luther," *The Churchman* 97 (1983): 112-22.

———. "Justice and Justification. Semantic and Juristic Aspects of the Christian Doctrine of Justification," *Scottish Journal of Theology* 35:5 (1982): 403-418.

———. "Justification and Christology: The Axiomatic Correlation between the Proclaimed Christ and the Historical Jesus," *Modern Theology* 1 (Oct 1984): 45-54.

———. "Justification and the Reformation: The Significance of the Doctrine of Justification by Faith to Sixteenth Century Urban Communities," *Archiv füür Reformationsgeschichte*, 81 (1990): 5-19.

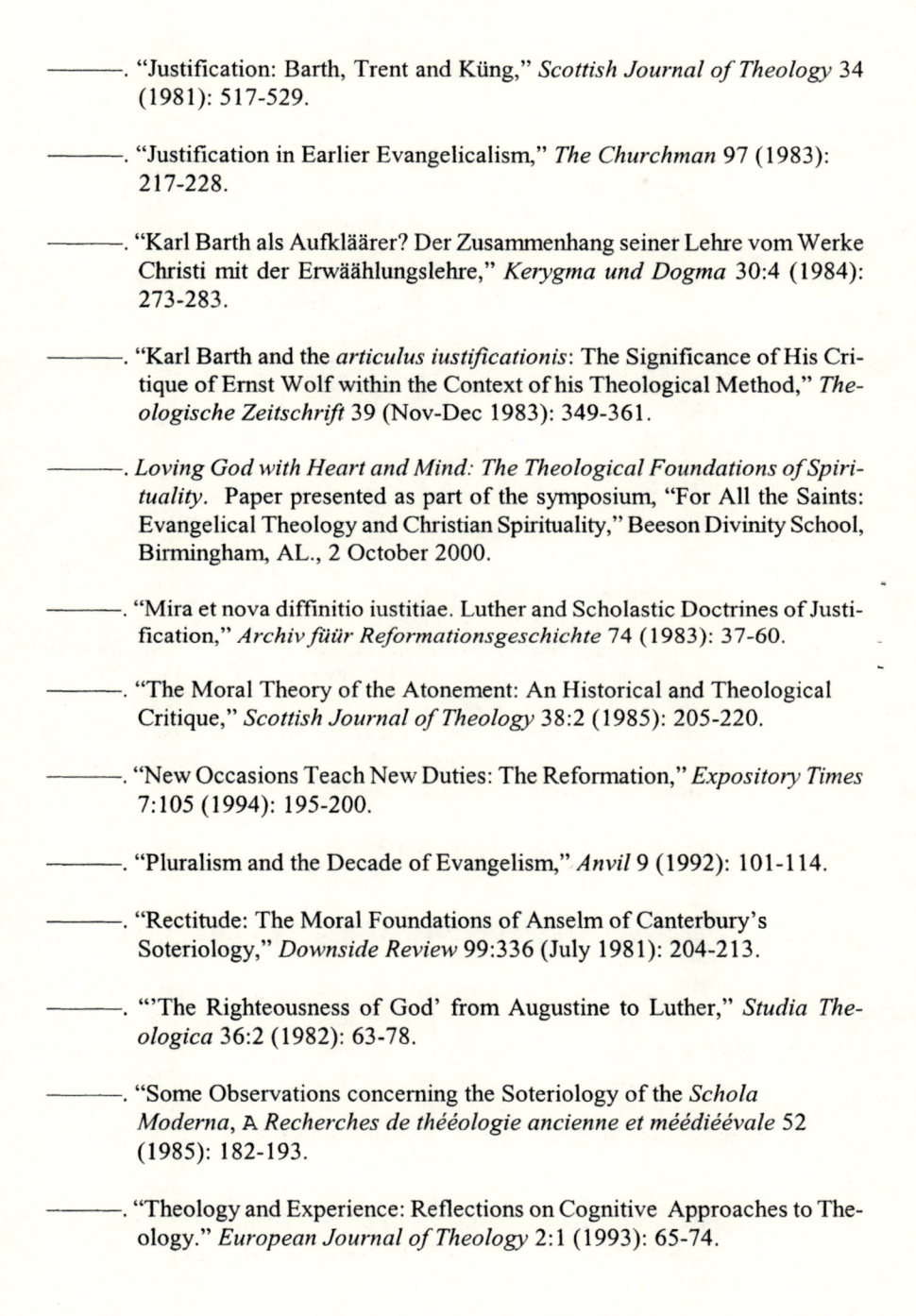

———. "Justification: Barth, Trent and Küng," *Scottish Journal of Theology* 34 (1981): 517-529.

———. "Justification in Earlier Evangelicalism," *The Churchman* 97 (1983): 217-228.

———. "Karl Barth als Aufkläärer? Der Zusammenhang seiner Lehre vom Werke Christi mit der Erwäählungslehre," *Kerygma und Dogma* 30:4 (1984): 273-283.

———. "Karl Barth and the *articulus iustificationis*: The Significance of His Critique of Ernst Wolf within the Context of his Theological Method," *Theologische Zeitschrift* 39 (Nov-Dec 1983): 349-361.

———. *Loving God with Heart and Mind: The Theological Foundations of Spirituality.* Paper presented as part of the symposium, "For All the Saints: Evangelical Theology and Christian Spirituality," Beeson Divinity School, Birmingham, AL., 2 October 2000.

———. "Mira et nova diffinitio iustitiae. Luther and Scholastic Doctrines of Justification," *Archiv füür Reformationsgeschichte* 74 (1983): 37-60.

———. "The Moral Theory of the Atonement: An Historical and Theological Critique," *Scottish Journal of Theology* 38:2 (1985): 205-220.

———. "New Occasions Teach New Duties: The Reformation," *Expository Times* 7:105 (1994): 195-200.

———. "Pluralism and the Decade of Evangelism," *Anvil* 9 (1992): 101-114.

———. "Rectitude: The Moral Foundations of Anselm of Canterbury's Soteriology," *Downside Review* 99:336 (July 1981): 204-213.

———. "'The Righteousness of God' from Augustine to Luther," *Studia Theologica* 36:2 (1982): 63-78.

———. "Some Observations concerning the Soteriology of the *Schola Moderna*, A *Recherches de thééologie ancienne et méédiéévale* 52 (1985): 182-193.

———. "Theology and Experience: Reflections on Cognitive Approaches to Theology." *European Journal of Theology* 2:1 (1993): 65-74.

McGrath, Alister E., C. G. Morgan, and G. K. Radda, "Positron Lifetimes in Phospholipid Dispersions," *Biochimica at Biophysica Acta* 466 (1976): 367-372.

McGrath, Alister E., C. G. Morgan, and G. K. Radda, "Photobleaching: A Novel Fluorescence Method for Diffusion Studies in Lipid Systems," *Biochimica at Biophysica Acta* 426 (1976) 173-185.

McGrath, Alister E., Principal of Wycliffe Hall. Interview by author, 3 October, 2000, Birmingham, AL. Tape recording. Beeson Divinity School, Birmingham, AL.

Works Cited

Books

Alexander, Donald L., ed. *Christian Spirituality: Five Views of Sanctification.* Downers Grove InterVarsity, 1988.

Ammerman, Nancy. *Baptist Battles: Social Change and Religious Conflict in the Southern Baptist Convention.* New Brunswick, NJ: Rutgers, 1990.

Anderson, Walter T. *Reality Isn't What it Used to Be: Theatrical Politics, Ready-to-Wear Religion, Global Myths, Primitive Chic, and Other Wonders of the Postmodern World.* New York: HarperCollins, 1990.

Bainton, Roland H. *Here I Stand: A Life of Martin Luther.* Nashville: Abingdon, 1950.

Barr, James. *Fundamentalism.* Philadelphia: Westminster, 1977.

Barton, John. *People of the Book?* Louisville, KY: Westminster/Knox, 1988.

Bauman, Michael. "Alister E. McGrath." In *Handbook of Evangelical Theologians*, ed. Walter A. Elwell, 445-465. Grand Rapids: Baker, 1993.

Baxter, Richard. *The Practical Works of Richard Baxter.* 4 vols. London: Bohn, 1854.

―――. *The Reformed Pastor: A Pattern for Personal Growth and Ministry*, ed. James Houston. *Classics of Faith and Devotion* Series. Portland: Multnomah, 1982.

———. *The Saint's Everlasting Rest.* New York: American Tract Society, 1758.

Bebbington, David W. "Evangelicalism in its Settings: The British and American Movements since 1940." In *Evangelicalism: Comparative Studies of Popular Protestantism in North America, the British Isles, and Beyond, 1700-1990*, ed. Mark A. Noll, David W. Bebbington, and George A. Rawlyk, 365-388. New York: Oxford, 1994.

———. *Evangelicalism in Modern Britain: A History from the 1730s to the 1980s.* London: Unwin Hyman, 1989.

Blackaby, Henry T. and Claude V. King. *Experiencing God: How to Live the Full Adventure of Knowing and Doing the Will of God.* Nashville: Sunday School Board of the Southern Baptist Convention, 1990.

Blackaby, Henry T. and Claude V. King. *Experiencing God: How to Live the Full Adventure of Knowing and Doing the Will of God.* Nashville: Broadman & Holman, 1994.

Blackaby, Henry T. and Claude V. King. *Fresh Encounter: Experiencing God Through Prayer, Humility and a Heartfelt Desire to Know Him.* Nashville: Broadman & Holman, 1996.

Bloesch, Donald G. *Essentials of Evangelical Theology.* 2 vols. San Francisco: Harper & Row, 1978-1979.

Blumhofer, Edith L. and Joel A. Carpenter, *Twentieth Century Evangelicalism: A Guide to the Sources.* New York: Garland, 1990.

Bouwsma, William J. "The Spirituality of John Calvin." In *Christian Spirituality: High Middle Ages and Reformation*, ed. Jill Raitt, vol. 2, 318-333. New York: Crossroad, 1987.

Bouyer, Louis. *A History of Christian Spirituality.* Vol. 1, *The Spirituality of the New Testament and the Fathers.* Translated by Mary P. Ryan. London: Burns and Oates, 1963.

———. *A History of Christian Spirituality*. Vol. 3, *Orthodox Spirituality and Protestant and Anglican Spirituality*. Translated by Barbara Wall. London: Burns & Oates, 1969.

Bouyer, Louis, Jean Leclercq, and Francois Vandenbroucke. *A History of Christian Spirituality*. Vol 2. *The Spirituality of the Middle Ages*. Translated by the Benedictines of Holme Eden Abbey. London: Burns and Oates, 1968.

Bradshaw, John. *Homecoming: Reclaiming and Championing Your Inner Child*. New York: Bantam, 1990.

Brown, Colin. *Christianity & Western Thought*. Vol. 1, *A History of Philosophies, Ideas & Movements*. Downers Grove: InterVarsity, 1990.

Bush, L. Russ. "Evangelism and Biblical Authority." In *Evangelism in the Twenty-First Century: Twenty-One Contributors in Honor of Lewis A. Drummond*, ed. Thom Rainer, 103-111. Wheaton, IL: Shaw, 1989.

Cahoone, Lawrence, ed. *From Modernism to Postmodernism: An Anthology*. Malden, MA: Blackwell, 1996.

Calvin, John. *Golden Booklet of the True Christian Life*. Translated by Henry J. Van Andel. Grand Rapids: Baker, 1952.

———. *Institutes of the Christian Religion*, ed. John T. McNeill, 2 vols. *The Library of Christian Classics*, vols. 20B21. Philadelphia: Westminster, 1960-1961.

———. *John Calvin: Writings on Pastoral Piety*, ed. and translated by Elsie A. McKee. The Classics of Western Spirituality: A Library of the Great Spiritual Masters. Mahwah, NJ: Paulist, 2001.

———. *The Piety of John Calvin: An Anthology Illustrative of the Spirituality of the Reformer*. Ed. and trans. Ford L. Battles. Grand Rapids: Baker, 1978.

Cantor, Norman. *The American Century: Varieties of Culture in Modern Times*. New York: HarperCollins, 1998.

Carson, D. A. *The Gagging of God: Christianity Confronts Pluralism*. Grand Rapids: Zondervan, 1996.

Carson, D. A., ed. *Telling the Truth: Evangelizing Postmoderns*. Grand Rapids: Zondervan, 2000.

Chafer, Lewis Sperry. *He That Is Spiritual*. Grand Rapids: Zondervan, 1967.

Chan, Simon. *Spiritual Theology: A Systematic Study of the Christian Life*. Downers Grove: InterVarsity, 1998.

Chopra, Deepak. *How to Know God: The Soul's Journey into the Mystery of Mysteries*. Philadelphia: Running Press, 2001.

———. *The Seven Spiritual Laws of Success: A Practical Guide to the Fulfillment of Your Dreams*. San Rafael, CA: Amber-Allen, 1995.

Chung, Sung Wook, ed., *Alister E. McGrath and Evangelical Theology: A Vital Engagement*. Grand Rapids: Baker, 2003.

Dawn, Marva. *Unfettered Hope: A Call to Faithful Living in an Affluent Society*. Louisville: Westminster/Knox, 2003.

Deiter, Melvin E., ed. *Five Views on Sanctification. Counterpoint* Series. Grand Rapids: Zondervan, 1987.

Demarest, Bruce A. *The Cross and Salvation: The Doctrine of Salvation*. Foundations of Evangelical Theology Series. Wheaton: Crossway, 1997.

———. *Jesus Christ: The God-Man*. Wheaton: Victor, 1978.

———. *General Revelation: Historical Views and Contemporary Issues*. Grand Rapids: Zondervan, 1982.

———. *Satisfy Your Soul: Restoring the Heart of Christian Spirituality*. Colorado Springs: NavPress, 1999.

———. "Spirituality and Christian Living." In *New Dimensions in Evangelical Thought: Essays in Honor of Millard J. Erickson*, ed. David S. Dockery, 374-393. Downers Grove: InterVarsity, 1998.

Demarest, Bruce A. and Gordon R. Lewis. *Challenges to Inerrancy*. Chicago: Moody, 1984.

———. *Integrative Theology: Historical, Biblical, Systematic, Apologetics, Practical*, 3 vols. in 1. Grand Rapids: Zondervan, 1996.

Dockery, David S. "Millard J. Erickson." *Baptist Theologians*, ed. Timothy George and David S. Dockery, 640-659. Nashville: Broadman, 1990.

Drummond, Lewis A. *Charles Spurgeon*. Grand Rapids: Kregel, 1990.

Dupre`, Louis and Don E. Saliers, ed. *Christian Spirituality*. Vol. 3, *Post-Reformation and Modern*. New York: Crossroad, 1989.

Duvall, J. Scott and J. Daniel Hays, *Grasping God's Word: A Hands-On Approach to Reading, Interpreting and Applying the Bible*. Grand Rapids: Zondervan, 2001.

Elliott, Ralph. *The 'Genesis Controversy' and Continuity in Southern Baptist Chaos: A Eulogy for a Great Tradition*. Macon, GA: Mercer University Press, 1992.

Elwell, Walter A., ed. *Handbook of Evangelical Theologians*. Grand Rapids: Baker, 1993.

Erickson, Millard J. *Concise Dictionary of Christian Theology*. Grand Rapids: Baker, 1986.

———. *Contemporary Options in Eschatology: A Study of the Millennium*, 2d ed. Grand Rapids: Bake, 1999.

———. *Christian Theology*, 2d ed., Grand Rapids: Baker, 1998.

———. *Does It Matter How I Live: Applying Biblical Beliefs to Your Daily Life*. Grand Rapids: Baker, 1994.

———. *The Evangelical Left: Encountering Postconservative Evangelical Theology*. Grand Rapids: Baker, 1997.

———. *The Evangelical Mind and Heart: Perspectives on Theological and Practical Issues*. Grand Rapids: Baker, 1993.

———. *God in Three Persons: A Contemporary Interpretation of the Trinity.* Grand Rapids: Baker, 1995.

———. *God the Father Almighty: A Contemporary Exploration of the Divine Attributes.* Grand Rapids: Baker, 1998.

———. *How Shall They Be Saved? The Destiny of Those Who do not Hear of Jesus.* Grand Rapids: Baker, 1996.

———. *Introducing Christian Doctrine*, ed. L. Arnold Hustad, 2d ed. Grand Rapids: Baker, 2001.

———. *Postmodernizing the Faith: Evangelical Responses to the Challenge of Postmodernism.* Grand Rapids: Baker, 1998.

———. *The Postmodern World: Discerning the Times and the Spirit of Our Age.* Wheaton: Crossway, 2002.

———. *Responsive Faith.* Arlington Heights, IL: Harvest, 1987.

———. *Truth or Consequences: The Promises and Perils of Postmodernism.* Downers Grove: InterVarsity, 2002.

———. *The Word Became Flesh: A Contemporary Incarnational Christology.* Grand Rapids: Baker, 1991

Farley, Edward. *Theologia: The Fragmentation and Unity of Theological Education.* Philadelphia: Fortress, 1983.

Fee, Gordon and Douglas Stuart. *How To Read the Bible for All Its Worth: A Guide to Understanding the Bible*, 2d ed. Grand Rapids: Zondervan, 1993.

Ferrara, Miranda H., ed., *The Writers Directory 1998-2000*, 13th ed. Detroit: St. James, 1997.

Forbes, Cheryl. *Imagination: Embracing a Theology of Wonder.* Portland: Multnomah, 1986.

Foster, Richard J. *Celebration of Discipline: The Path to Spiritual Growth.* San Francisco: Harper & Row, 1978.

———. *Celebration of Discipline: The Path to Spiritual Growth*. Rev. ed. San Francisco: HarperSanFrancisco, 1988.

———. *The Challenge of the Disciplined Life: Christian Reflections on Money, Sex & Power*. San Francisco: Harper & Row, 1985.

———. *Freedom of Simplicity*. San Francisco: Harper & Row, 1981.

———. *Meditative Prayer*. Downers Grove: InterVarsity Press, 1983.

———. *Prayer: Finding the Heart's True Home*. San Francisco: HarperSanFrancisco, 1992.

———. *Streams of Living Water: Celebrating the Great Traditions of Christian Faith*. San Francisco: HarperSanFrancisco, 1998.

Gallup, Jr., George and Timothy Jones. *The Next American Spirituality: Finding God in the Twenty-First Century*. Colorado Springs: Cook, 2000.

Geisler, Norman L., ed. *Inerrancy*. Grand Rapids: Zondervan, 1980.

Gerard of Zutphen. *The Spiritual Ascent*. Translated by J. P. Arthur. London: Burns & Oates, 1908.

Green, Michael. *But Don't All Religions Lead to God*. Grand Rapids: Baker, 2002.

———. *Evangelism in the Early Church*. Grand Rapids: Eerdmans, 1970.

———. *Evangelism Through the Local Church*. Nashville: Nelson, 1992.

———. *I Believe in the Holy Spirit*. Rev. ed. Grand Rapids: Eerdmans, 1989.

———. *The Second Epistle General of Peter and the General Epistle of Jude: An Introduction and Commentary*, Rev. ed. *The Tyndale New Testament Commentary* Series, vol. 18. Grand Rapids: Eerdmans, 1988.

Grenz, Stanley J. *A Primer on Postmodernism*. Grand Rapids: Eerdmans, 1996.

———. *Revisioning Evangelical Theology: A Fresh Agenda for the 21st Century*. Downers Grove: InterVarsity, 1993.

Grudem, Wayne. *Systematic Theology: An Introduction to Biblical Doctrine.* Grand Rapids: Zondervan, 1994.

———. *Bible Doctrine: Essential Teachings of the Christian Faith*, ed. Jeff Purswell. Grand Rapids: Zondervan, 1999.

———. *The First Epistle to Peter: An Introduction and Commentary.* The *Tyndale New Testament Commentary* Series, vol. 19. Grand Rapids: Eerdmans, 1988.

Grudem, Wayne, ed. *Are Miraculous Gifts for Today? Four Views.* Grand Rapids: Zondervan, 1996.

Grudem, Wayne and John Piper, eds. *Recovering Biblical Manhood and Womanhood: A Response to Evangelical Feminism.* Wheaton: Crossway, 1991.

Grudem, Wayne and Vern S. Poythress. *The Gender-Neutral Bible Controversy: Muting the Masculinity of God's Word.* Nashville: Broadman and Holman, 2000.

Grundler, Otto. "Devotio Moderna." In *Christian Spirituality.* Vol. 2, *High Middle Ages and Reformation.* ed. Jill Raitt, 176-193. New York: Crossroad, 1987.

Guigo II. *The Ladder of Monks and Twelve Meditations.* Translated by Edmund Colledge and James Walsh. Kalamazoo, MI: Cistercian, 1978.

Gunton, Colin E. *The Actuality of Atonement.* Grand Rapids: Eerdmans, 1989.

Heelas, Paul. *The New Age Movement: The Celebration of the Self and the Sacralization of Modernity.* London: Blackwell, 1996.

Henry, Carl F. H. *God, Revelation, and Authority.* 6 vols. Waco, TX: Word, 1976-1983.

Henry, Matthew. *The Complete Works of Matthew Henry: Treatises, Sermons, and Tracts.* Grand Rapids: Baker, 1997.

———. *An Exposition of the Old and New Testament.* 6 vols. New York: Haven, 1833.

———. *The Quest for Communion with God.* Grand Rapids: Eerdmans, 1954.

Hick, John, ed. *The Myth of God Incarnate.* Philadelphia: Westminster, 1977.

Hollenweger, Walter J. *Pentecostalism: Origins and Developments Worldwide.* Peabody, MA: Hendrickson, 1997.

Holt, Bradley. *Thirsty for God: A Brief History of Christian Spirituality.* Minneapolis: Augsburg, 1993.

Holy Bible, New International Version. Grand Rapids: Zondervan, 1978.

Horton, Michael. *In the Face of God: The Dangers and Delights of Spiritual Intimacy.* Dallas: Word, 1996.

———, ed. *Power Religion: The Selling Out of the Evangelical Church?* Chicago: Moody, 1992.

Houston, James. *The Heart's Desire: A Guide to Personal Fulfillment.* Batavia, IL: Lion, 1992.

———. *The Transforming Friendship.* Batavia, IL: Lion, 1989.

Hustad, L. Arnold. "Millard J. Erickson." In *Handbook of Evangelical Theologians,* ed. Walter A. Elwell, 412-426. Grand Rapids: Baker, 1993.

Hutchinson, Mark. "Interview with Alister McGrath." *Lucas: An Evangelical History Review* 16 (December 1993): 72B82.

Issler, Klaus. *Wasting Time with God: A Christian Spirituality of Friendship with God.* Downers Grove: InterVarsity, 2001.

Jencks, Charles. *The Language of Post-Modern Architecture.* London: Academy Editions, 1984.

Kelley, Dean M. *Why Conservative Churches are Growing: A Study in Sociology of Religion.* Rev. ed. Macon, GA: Mercer University Press, 1986.

Lane, Tony. *Exploring Christian Thought.* Nashville: Nelson, 1996.

Larsen, David L. *Biblical Spirituality: Discovering the Real Connection Between the Bible and Life*. Grand Rapids: Kregel, 2001.

Lesser, Elizabeth. *The New American Spirituality: A Seeker's Guide*. New York: Random House, 1999.

Lewis, C. S. *God in the Dock: Essays on Theology and Ethics*. Ed. Walter Hooper. Grand Rapids: Eerdmans, 1970.

Lienhard, Marc. "Luther and Beginnings of the Reformation." In *Christian Spirituality*. Vol. 2, *High Middle Ages and Reformation*, ed. Jill Raitt, 268B299. New York: Crossroad, 1987.

Luther, Martin. "The Freedom of a Christian." In *Luther's Works*. Vol. 31. Translated by W. A. Lambert and rev. by Harold J., 327-377. Grimm. Philadelphia: Concordia, 1957.

———. "Prefaces to the Old Testament." In *Luther's Works*. Vol. 35. Translated by Charles M. Jacobs, 233-253. Philadelphia: Fortress, 1960.

———. "A Simple Way to Pray." In *Luther's Works*. Vol. 43. Translated by Carl J. Schindler, 187-211. Philadelphia: Fortress, 1968.

Marsden, George M., ed. *Evangelicalism and Modern America*. Grand Rapids: Eerdmans, 1984.

———. *Fundamentalism and American Culture: The Shaping of Twentieth Century Evangelicalism, 1870-1925*. New York: Oxford, 1980.

———. *Understanding Fundamentalism and Evangelicalism*. Grand Rapids: Eerdmans, 1991.

May, Gerald G. *Addiction and Grace: Love and Spirituality in the Healing Addictions*. New York: HarperCollins, 1988.

McGinn, Bernard and John Meyendorff, ed. *Christian Spirituality*. Vol. 1, *Origins to the Twelfth Century*. New York: Crossroad, 1985.

McIntosh, Mark A. *Mystical Theology: The Integrity of Spirituality and Theology*. Malden, MA: Blackwell, 1998.

McMinn, Mark R. *Psychology, Theology, and Spirituality in Christian Counseling*. Wheaton: Tyndale, 1996.

Metzger, Linda, ed. *Contemporary Authors*. Vol. 15. Detroit: Gale Research, 1985.

Miller, J. Keith. *A Hunger for Healing: The Twelve Steps as a Classic Model for Christian Spiritual Growth*. San Francisco: HarperSanFrancisco: 1991.

Moltmann, Jurgen. *The Spirit of Life: A Universal Affirmation*. Minneapolis: Fortress Press, 1992.

Moreland, J. P. *Love Your God with All Your Mind: The Role of Reason in the Life of the Soul*. Spiritual Formation Series, gen. ed. Dallas Willard. Colorado Springs, CO: NavPress, 1997.

Morris, Leon. *The Apostolic Preaching of the Cross*. Grand Rapids: Eerdmans, 1955.

Noll, Mark A. and Ronald F. Thiemann, ed. *Where Shall My Wond'ring Soul Begin? The Landscape of Evangelical Piety and Thought*. Grand Rapids: Eerdmans, 2000.

Oden, Thomas C. *Two Worlds: Notes on the Death of Modernity*. Louisville, KY: Westminster/Knox, 1989.

Okholm, Dennis and Timothy R. Phillips, ed. *Four Views on Salvation in a Pluralistic World*. The Counterpoint Series, ed. Stanley N. Gundry. Grand Rapids: Zondervan, 1996.

Osborne, Grant R. *The Hermeneutical Spiral: A Comprehensive Introduction to Biblical Interpretation*. Downers Grove: InterVarsity, 1991.

Owen, John. *Sin and Temptation: The Challenge of Personal Godliness*. Classics of Faith and Devotion Series, ed. James Houston. Minneapolis: Bethany House, 1996.

———. *The Works of John Owen*, ed. William H. Goold, 16 vols. Carlisle, PA: Banner of Truth, 1965-1968.

Packer, J. I. *Knowing God*. Downers Grove: InterVarsity, 1973.

Peck, M. Scott. *The Road Less Traveled: A New Psychology of Love, Traditional Values and Spiritual Growth*. New York: Simon & Schuster, 1978.

Peterson, Eugene H. *A Long Obedience in the Same Direction: Discipleship in an Instant Society*. Downers Grove: InterVarsity, 1980.

———. *Reversed Thunder: The Revelation of John and the Praying Imagination*. San Francisco: Harper & Row, 1988.

Pressler, Paul. *A Hill on which to Die: One Southern Baptist's Journey*. Nashville: Broadman & Holman, 1999.

Raitt, Jill, ed. *Christian Spirituality*. Vol. 2, *High Middle Ages and Reformation*. New York: Crossroad, 1987.

Reid, Alvin L. *Introduction to Evangelism*. Nashville: Broadman & Holman, 1998.

———. *Light the Fire: Raising Up a Generation to Live Radically for Jesus Christ*. Enumclaw, WA: WinePress, 2001.

———. *Radically Unchurched: Who are They? How to Reach Them*. Grand Rapids: Kregel, 2002.

Richard, Lucien J. *The Spirituality of John Calvin*. Atlanta: Knox, 1974.

Richard, Lawrence O. *A Practical Theology of Spirituality*. Grand Rapids: Zondervan, 1987.

Rose, Margaret. "Defining the Post-Modern." In *The Post-Modern Reader*, ed. Charles Jencks. New York: St. Martin, 1992.

Sproul, R. C. "The Internal Testimony of the Holy Spirit." In *Inerrancy*, ed. Norman L. Geisler, 337-356. Grand Rapids: Zondervan, 1980.

Spurgeon, Charles H. *Our Manifesto*. In *The Metropolitan Tabernacle Pulpit: Sermons Preached and Revised by C. H. Spurgeon during the year 1891*. Vol. 37, 37-50. Pasadena, TX: Pilgrim, 1975.

Stackhouse, John G., Jr., ed. *Evangelical Futures: A Conversation on Theological Method*. Grand Rapids: Baker, 2000.

Steer, Roger. *Guarding the Holy Fire: The Evangelicalism of John R.W. Stott, J. I. Packer, and Alister E. McGrath*. Grand Rapids: Baker, 1999.

Stott, John R. W. *The Cross of Christ*. Downers Grove: InterVarsity, 1986.

Sutton, Jerry. *The Baptist Reformation: The Conservative Resurgence in the Southern Baptist Convention*. Nashville: Broadman & Holman, 2000.

Sweet, Leonard I. *SoulTsunami: Sink or Swim in New Millennium Culture*. Grand Rapids: Zondervan, 1999.

Thomas a' Kempis. *The Imitation of Christ*. Ed. and translated by Joseph N. Tylenda. Vintage Spiritual Classics. New York: Random House, 1998.

Thomas, Gary L. *The Glorious Pursuit: Embracing the Virtues of Christ*. Colorado Springs: NavPress, 1998.

――――. *Sacred Marriage: What if God Designed Marriage to Make Us Holy more than to Make us Happy?* Grand Rapids: Zondervan, 2000.

――――. *Sacred Pathways: Discover Your Soul's Path to God*. Grand Rapids: Zondervan, 2000.

――――. *Seeking the Face of God: The Path to a More Intimate Relationship*. Eugene, OR: Harvest House, 1999.

Thomas, Gary L., contrib. *NIV Spiritual Formation Bible*. Grand Rapids: Zondervan, 1999.

Toon, Peter. *The Art of Meditating on Scripture: Understanding Your Faith, Renewing Your Mind, Knowing Your God*. Grand Rapids: Zondervan, 1993.

――――. *Meditating as a Christian: Waiting Upon God*. London: HarperCollins, 1991.

Trosky, Susan M., ed. *Contemporary Authors*, vol. 134. Detroit: Gale Research, 1992.

Vanhoozer, Kevin J. *Is There a Meaning in This Text? The Bible, The Reader, and the Morality of Literary Knowledge.* Grand Rapids: Zondervan, 1998.

Veith, Jr., Gene E. *Postmodern Times: A Christian Guide to Contemporary Thought and Culture.* Turning Point Christian Worldview Series, ed. Marvin Olasky. Wheaton: Crossway, 1994.

Wagner, C. Peter. *The Third Wave of the Holy Spirit.* Ann Arbor, MI: Servant, 1988.

Warfield, Benjamin B. *The Inspiration and Authority of the Bible.* Ed. Samuel G. Craig. Phillipsburg, NJ: Presbyterian & Reformed, 1948.

Whitney, Donald S. *How Can I Be Sure I'm a Christian? What the Bible Says About Assurance of Salvation.* Colorado Springs: NavPress, 1994.

———. *Spiritual Discipline for the Christian Life.* Colorado Springs: NavPress, 1991.

———. *Spiritual Disciplines within the Church: Participating Fully in the Body of Christ.* Chicago: Moody, 1996.

———. *Ten Questions to Diagnose Your Spiritual Health.* Colorado Springs: NavPress, 2001.

———. "Unity of Doctrine and Devotion." In *The Compromised Church*, ed. John Armstrong, 241-262. Wheaton: Crossway, 1998.

Wicks, Jared. *Luther and His Spiritual Legacy.* Theology and Life Series, vol. 7. Wilmington, DE: Glazier, 1983.

Willard, Dallas. *The Divine Conspiracy: Rediscovering Our Hidden Life in God.* San Francisco: HarperSanFrancisco, 1998.

———. *Hearing God: Developing a Conversational Relationship with God.* Downers Grove: InterVarsity, 1999.

———. *Logic and the Objectivity of Knowledge: A Study in Husserl's Early Philosophy*. Athens, OH: Ohio University Press, 1984.

———. *In Search of Guidance*. Ventura, CA: Regal, 1984.

———. *The Spirit of the Disciplines*. San Francisco: Harper, 1988.

Wuthnow, Robert. *After Heaven: Spirituality in America since the 1950s*. Berkeley: University of California Press, 1998.

Journals and Book Reviews

Carson, D. A. "The Difficult Doctrine of the Love of God, Part 1." *Bibliotheca Sacra* 156 (Jan-Mar1999): 7-9.

———. "The Difficult Doctrine of the Love of God, Part 4." *Bibliotheca Sacra* 156 (Oct-Dec 1999): 397-398.

Buschart, David W. Review of *The Genesis of Doctrine: A Study in the Foundations of Doctrinal Criticism*, by Alister E. McGrath. *Journal of the Evangelical Theological Society* 36 (September 1993): 380-382.

Dalberg, Bob. Review of *Experiencing God: Knowing and Doing the Will of God*, by Henry Blackaby and Clyde King. *Reformation and Revival Journal* 6 (Winter 1997): 161-166.

Ford, Gene. Review of *Experiencing God: How to Live the Full Adventure of Knowing and Doing the Will of God*, by Henry T. Blackaby and Claude V. King. *Affirmation and Critique* 1:2 (1996): 58-59.

Hammett, John S. Review of *J. I. Packer: A Biography*, by Alister E. McGrath. *Faith and Mission* 15 (Spring 1998): 104-106.

———. Review of *Renewing the Center: Evangelical Theology in a Post-Theological Era*, by Stanley J. Grenz. *Faith and Mission* 19:1 (2001): 112-114.

Kereszty, Roch. "Theology and Spirituality: The Task of Synthesis." *Communio* 10 (Winter 1983): 316-320.

Kovach, Stephen. Review of *The Divine Conspiracy: Rediscovering Our Hidden Life in God*, by Dallas Willard. *Faith and Mission* 15 (Spring 1998): 101-103.

Kostenberger, Andreas. Review of *The Genesis of Doctrine: A Study in the Foundations of Doctrinal Criticism*, by Alister E. McGrath. *Faith and Mission* 16 (Summer 1999): 117-120.

Lewis, Gordon R. "The Church and the New Spirituality." *Journal of the Evangelical Theological Society* 36 (1993): 433-444.

Musk, Bill. "Dreams and the Ordinary Muslim." *Missionology: An International Review* 16:2 (1988): 163-172.

Packer, J. I. "An Introduction to Systematic Spirituality." *Crux* 26:1 (1990): 2-8.

———. "What did the Cross Achieve? The Logic of Penal Substitution." *Tyndale Bulletin* 25 (1974): 3-45.

Pinnock, Clark. Review of *A Passion for Truth*, by Alister E. McGrath. *Pro Ecclesia* 8:1 (1999): 115.

Plantiga, Richard J. Review of *Christian Theology: An Introduction*, by Alister E. McGrath. *Calvin Theological Journal* 31 (April 1996): 262-264.

Stephen L. Porter, "On the Renewal of Interest in the Doctrine of Sanctification: A Methodological Reminder." *Journal of the Evangelical Theological Society* 45:3 (2002): 415-426.

Pyne, Robert A. Review of *A Passion for Truth*, by Alister E. McGrath. *Bibliotheca Sacra* 154:614 (1997): 227.

Richard, Ramesh P. Review of *The Spirit of the Disciplines: Understanding How God Changes Lives*, by Dallas Willard. *Bibliotheca Sacra* 146 (July-Sept 2001): 357-358.

Sailer, William S. Review of *Justification by Faith: What It Means for Us Today*, by Alister E. McGrath. *Evangelical Journal* 7:1 (1989): 42-44.

Sarles, Ken L. Review of *Justification by Faith: What It Means for Us Today*, by Alister E. McGrath. *Bibliotheca Sacra* 147:586 (1990): 238-239.

Smith, David L. Review of *More Than One Way? Four Views of Salvation in a Pluralistic World.* Dennis L. Okholm and Timothy R. Phillips, eds. *Didaskalia* 7:1 (1996): 65-66.

Solc, Josef. Review of *The Glorious Pursuit: Embracing the Virtues of Christ*, by Gary L. Thomas. *Faith and Mission* 17:1 (1999): 107-108.

Tan, Siang-Yang. "Practicing the Presence of God: The Work of Richard J. Foster and its Applications to Psychotherapeutic Practice." *Journal of Psychology and Christianity* 15:1 (1996): 17-28.

Tiessen, Terrance L. Review of *More Than One Way? Four Views on Salvation in a Pluralistic World.* Dennis L. Okholm and Timothy R. Phillips, eds. *Evangelical Review of Theology* 21:1 (1997): 91-92 .

Trueman, Carl R. Review of *A Passion for Truth*, by Alister E. McGrath. *Westminster Theological Journal* 59:1 (1997): 137.

Van Gelder, Craig. "Postmodernism as an Emerging Worldview.@ *Calvin Theological Journal* 26 (November 1991): 412-420.

Willard, Dallas. "A Realist Analysis of the Relationship Between Logic and Experience." *Topoi* 22:1 (2003): 69-78.

———. "Robin D. Rollinger, Husserl's Position in the School of Brentano." *Husserl Studies* 18:1 (2002): 77-81.

Williams, Michael. Review of *Christian Theology: An Introduction*, by Alister E. McGrath. *Journal of the Evangelical Theological Society* 39 (June 1996): 311-314.

Miscellaneous

"The Amsterdam Declaration." www.billygraham.org, accessed August 25, 2000.

Bruce, F. F. "Interpretation of the Bible." *Evangelical Dictionary of Theology*, 1984.

Center for Evangelical Spirituality. www.garythomas.com, accessed June 23, 2000.

Christianity Today. www.christianitytoday.com. accessed March 31, 2003.

Davids, P. H. "*Devotio Moderna.*" *Evangelical Dictionary of Theology*, 1984.

Dockery, David. "Variations in Inerrancy." *SBC Today* (May 1986): 10-11.

Foster, Richard J. "Under Fire: Two Christian Leaders Respond to Accusations of New Age Mysticism." *Christianity Today* 31 (September 18, 1987): 17-21.

Houston, James. "Spirituality." *Evangelical Dictionary of Theology*, 1984.

Hutchinson, Andrew T. G. "Personal Godliness: Puritan and Contemporary, An Evaluation of the Theology of Personal Godliness in the Writings of Richard Foster in Light of the Practical Writings of Richard Baxter." Master of Christian Studies thesis, Regent College, 1988.

Kelly, Douglas F. "Scottish Realism." *Evangelical Dictionary of Theology*, 1984.

Keylock, Leslie R. "Evangelical Leaders You Should Know: Meet Millard J. Erickson." *Moody Monthly* 87:10 (1987): 71-73.

King, Martin. "Henry Blackaby 'Transitions' to New Ministry Organization." *Baptist Press* Release, May 11, 2000.

Kronk, Richard K. "Non-literary Personal Revelation: The Role of Dreams and Visions in Muslim Conversion." Th.M. thesis, Dallas Theological Seminary; 1993.

Kovach, Stephen D. "Toward a Theology of Guidance: A Multi-faceted Approach Emphasizing Scripture as both Foundation and Pattern in Discerning the Will of God." Ph.D. diss., Trinity Divinity School, 1999.

Packer, J. I., Professor of Theology at Regent's College. Personal conversation with author, 1 August, 2000, Amsterdam. Billy Graham Evangelistic Association's Amsterdam 2000, Amsterdam.

Pitzl, Beth. "Celebration of Discipline в New Age in the Christian Churches." *The Watchman Expositor*, www.watchman.org, accessed July 13, 2000.

Reid, Alvin L. www.alvinreid.com, accessed April 15, 2003.

Robinson, Jeff. "Seminary Dean Calls for Unity of 'Odd Couple' Disciplines." *Baptist Press* Release, October 28, 2002.

Saucy, Robert L. *Spiritual Formation in Theological Controversy*. Paper presented as part of the Evangelical Theological Society Annual Meeting, Toronto, Canada, 21 November 2002.

Steinmetz, David C. "*Devotio Moderna*." *The Westminster Dictionary of Christian Spirituality*, 1983.

Veith, Gene E. "Reality in the Rubble: The Fall of the Twin Towers Heralds the Collapse of Postmodernism." *World* 16:39 (October 13, 2001): 16.

Whitney, Donald S. *Defining the Boundaries of Evangelical Spirituality*. Paper presented as part of the Evangelical Theological Society Annual Meeting, Colorado Springs, CO., 15 November 2001.

Whitney, Donald S. www.spiritualdisciplines.org, accessed September 12, 2002.

Willard, Dallas. "Meaning and Universals in Husserl's *Logische Untersuchungen*." Ph.D. diss., University of Wisconsin at Madison, 1964.

Wycliffe Hall. www.wycliffe.ox.ac.uk, accessed February 12, 2003.

Yow, Joel C. "Interpreting the Spirituality of Henry Thomas Blackaby." Th.M. thesis, Southeastern Baptist Theological Seminary, 1999.

INDEX

ad fontes, 11
Amsterdam Declaration, 19
Anselm, 60, 66, 73
Apostles' Creed, 12, 81
apologetics, 1, 4, 5, 13, 15-18, 27, 30, 63, 79
Aquinas, Thomas, 60, 73
Athanasius, 73
atheist, 3
atonement, 9, 10, 98, 106, 115
Augustine, 10, 16, 60, 73, 98, 119, 122
Barth, Karl, 10, 40-41, 52
Barton, John, 39, 50
Baxter, Richard, 54, 66, 79, 96, 105
Bebbington, David, 47
Bible, 13-15, 33-36, 38-41, 43-45, 57, 61, 70-71, 93, 94, 97-99, 107, 109-112, 116, 119, 131
Billy Graham Evangelistic Association, 19
Blackaby, Henry, 20, 92-95, 103-104, 130, 133
Bloesch, Donald, 40-41, 51
Bunyan, John, 66
Calvin, John, 11, 26, 36, 43, 49, 54, 60, 64-65, 119
Carson, D. A., 30, 32, 45-46, 77, 80, 90, 102
Chafer, Lewis Sperry, 30, 46
Charismatic Movement, 67-68, 98, 118
Chicago Statement of Biblical Inerrancy, 41, 52
Christ, *See* Jesus.
Christianity Today, 5, 105, 107
Christology, 9, 10, 30, 35-36, 38, 48, 57
Chritus victor, 58
church, 7, 16, 57, 67, 69, 70, 72, 93, 95, 98, 110, 128, 133
contemplation, 42
contextualization, 61
cross, 9, 16-18, 27, 59, 60, 74-75, 98, 106, 114
Demarest, Bruce A., 8, 20, 31-32, 46, 92, 95, 103, 117-121, 125-126, 131, 133
devotio moderna, 42, 53
discipleship, 1, 68, 113-114, 116

discipline, 1, 33, 57, 64-66, 70, 88, 95-96, 99, 105, 112-114, 116, 118, 123-124, 130
doubt, 17, 18, 27
Edwards, Jonathan, 66, 108, 128
Enlightenment, 9, 10, 40-41, 63, 88-89, 127-129
Erickson, Millard, 5, 7-8, 23-24, 76, 88-89, 101-102, 118, 125
ethics, 1, 31
Evangelical, 2-10, 12-14, 18-20, 22-24, 26, 29, 33, 63-64, 66-70, 74, 78, 91-92, 98-99, 107, 114, 116-118, 120, 132-133
evangelism, 5-6, 10, 14, 16-18, 35, 57, 62-63, 68, 70, 77-78, 82, 95, 100, 113-114, 116, 118
evangelist, 4, 79
Foster, Richard J., 20, 52, 92, 95-100, 104-105, 130, 133
Geisler, Norman, 40, 52
grace 7, 17
Green, Michael, 4, 21
Grenz, Stanley, 31, 46, 83-84, 90, 102
Grudem, Wayne, 7, 8, 23-24
Gugio II, 42, 53
Gunton, Colin, 58, 75
Henry, Carl F. H., 5, 39-40, 88
Henry, Matthew, 64, 66, 79
hermeneutics, 10
Holt, Bradley, 30, 46
Holy Spirit, 14, 31, 33, 57, 60, 66-69, 80-81, 93-94, 97, 98, 116-119
Homiletics, 30
Horton, Michael, 20, 103
Houston, James, 31, 37, 46, 50, 79
incarnation, 12, 99
inerrancy, 41, 52, 81, 99-100
Issler, Klaus, 20, 31-32, 46-47, 72, 84
Jesus, 12, 13, 33-39, 58-60, 62, 67, 70-72, 74, 90, 94, 97-98, 106, 114, 116, 118-120, 131
justification, 9-10, 16, 25, 60-61, 64-65, 76, 116
Kant, Immanuel, 10
kerygmatic, 35
Lesser, Elizabeth, 20, 90-91, 102, 130
Lewis, C. S., 5, 61, 66, 77, 128
Luther, Martin, 9, 25, 36, 43-44, 49, 53, 55, 64-66, 83, 122
McGinn, Bernard, 31, 46
McGrath, Joanna, 3, 21, 27, 50
Medieval, 9-10
meditation, 37, 41-45, 55, 96, 112, 119
Melanchthon, 43
Middle Ages, 7, 12, 42

missions, 5, 82
Moltman, Jurgen, 30, 46
Montgomery, John Warrick, 40
neo-orthodoxy, 40
Oden, Thomas, 89, 102
Orthodox, 12, 108
orthodoxy, 2, 6, 120, 128
orthopathy, 120
orthopraxy, 2, 120
Owen, John, 64, 66, 79
Oxford University, 3-7, 39, 128
Packer, J. I., 1, 5-6, 15, 18-19, 22, 37, 46, 49, 59, 66, 70, 76, 82, 96, 103, 107
Pannenberg, 9
Patristics, 7, 42
Peterson, Eugene, 41-42, 52, 57, 75
Pietism, 14, 106, 121, 127
Pinnock, Clark, 40, 52
postmodern, 87, 89-92, 101-102, 129, 130-131
prayer, 6, 14, 35-36, 42-44, 67, 93-97, 105, 109, 112-115, 118-119
propositions, 40, 63, 71
Protestant, 9, 10, 12-13, 43-44, 60, 113, 117
psychology, 15, 37
Puritan, 10, 14, 106, 119, 121
Quadriga, 42, 53
redemption, 12, 74, 111
Reformation, 2, 7, 9-16, 18, 25-26, 32, 36-37, 43, 64, 100, 110, 117, 120, 128
Reid, Alvin L., 78
religion and science, 10, 13, 21, 26
Renaissance, 7
resurrection, 12, 16, 34-35, 37, 59, 74, 98
Ritschl, 10
Roman Catholics, 12, 108, 117-118, 120
salvation, 7, 9, 34, 57-58, 61-62, 66-67, 75, 98-99, 106, 120, 131
sanctification, 8, 24, 31-32, 64-65, 72, 103, 107
Schaeffer, Francis, 5, 40
Schleiermaker, 10
schola augustiniana moderna, 9
scientific theology, 10, 25
Scottish Realism, 39, 51
scripture, *See* Bible
self-esteem, 17-18, 21, 27, 50
sin, 7, 17
soteriology, *See* salvation
sola fide, 45
sola scriptura, 14, 43, 45

Spirit, *See* Holy Spirit
Spurgeon, Charles Haddon, 44, 55
Stott, John R. W., 5, 59, 66, 76
substitution, 59, 106
studia humanitatis, 9
suffering, 17-18, 27, 74
theologia crucis, 9
Thomas, Gary L. 20, 92, 107-108, 109-110, 121-122, 130, 133
Trinity, 7, 12, 16, 23, 30-32, 73-74, 82, 84, 119, 122, 131
Veith, Gene, 89, 101-103, 131-133
via moderna, 9
Wagner, C. Peter, 67, 81
Warfield, Benjamin B., 5, 39-40, 51
Whitney, Donald, 29, 45, 64, 66, 79, 99, 106
Willard, Dallas, 20, 92, 103, 110-116, 122-125, 130-131, 133
worship, 35
Wuthnow, Robert, 20, 87-88, 100-101
Wycliffe Hall, 3, 5-8, 22, 106, 128
Zerbolt, Gert, 42, 54
Zwingli, Huldrych, 43

About the Author

Larry S. McDonald is currently serving as Assistant Professor of Christian Studies at Truett-McConnell College (Cleveland, Georgia). He also teaches as an Adjunct Professor with the Southeastern Baptist Theological Seminary and serves as Visiting Professor with the Uganda Baptist Seminary. Holding two doctoral degrees, Dr. McDonald has completed extensive research in the relationship between theology and spirituality.

A native Mississippian, Dr. McDonald was recognized for his leadership abilities by Leadership Jackson of the Metro Jackson Chamber of Commerce and Leadership Mississippi of the Mississippi Economic Council. He has written articles and book reviews for academic journals as well as devotional columns for Baptist and community newspapers. At Amsterdam 2000, sponsored by the Billy Graham Evangelistic Association, Dr. McDonald served on the Theologian Task Force which assisted in writing "The Amsterdam Declaration."

Dr. McDonald is a member of the Evangelical Theological Society, Evangelical Missiological Society, and the International John Bunyan Society. He also serves on the Advisory Board of the Evangelical Missiological Society's Dissertation Series and a Charter Member of the Advisory Board of the Appalachian Study Center at the North Georgia College and State University.

Larry McDonald resides in the Blue Ridge Mountains of Northeast Georgia with his wife and three children.